Negotiating the Louisiana Purchase

Negotiating the Louisiana Purchase

Robert Livingston's Mission to France, 1801–1804

FRANK W. BRECHER

McFarland & Company, Inc., Publishers
Jefferson, North Carolina, and London

Translations from the French are by Frank W. Brecher unless otherwise noted.

LIBRARY OF CONGRESS CATALOGUING-IN-PUBLICATION DATA

Brecher, Frank W.
   Negotiating the Louisiana Purchase : Robert Livingston's mission to France, 1801–1804 / Frank W. Brecher.
      p.   cm.
   Includes bibliographical references and index.

   ISBN-13: 978-0-7864-2395-8
   softcover : 50# alkaline paper ∞

   1. Louisiana Purchase.   2. United States— Territorial expansion. 3. United States— Foreign relations— 1801–1809.   4. Livingston, Robert R., 1746–1813.   5. Napoleon I, Emperor of the French, 1769–1821— Relations with Americans.   I. Title.
   E333.B85   2006
   973.4'6 — dc22   2006000197

British Library cataloguing data are available

©2006 Frank W. Brecher. All rights reserved

No part of this book may be reproduced or transmitted in any form or by any means, electronic or mechanical, including photocopying or recording, or by any information storage and retrieval system, without permission in writing from the publisher.

On the Cover: Engraving from 1804 painting *Chancellor Robert R. Livigston* by John Vanderlyn; map of the Louisiana Purchase *(both images Clipart.com)*

Manufactured in the United States of America

McFarland & Company, Inc., Publishers
   Box 611, Jefferson, North Carolina 28640
      www.mcfarlandpub.com

Table of Contents

Preface: An Overview   1

1. The Political Setting   7
2. The Failed Negotiations of 1802   30
3. The Monroe Mission and a Diplomatic Breakthrough   53
4. Factors Underlying the Breakthrough   67
5. A Nasty Competition for the Credit   80
6. A Balance Sheet   106
7. Consequences and Controversies— An American Historical Perspective   113

Appendix A: Summary of Livingston's Louisiana Memorandum, July 1802   127
Appendix B: Two Talleyrand-Napoleon Memoranda   130
Appendix C: Summary and Analysis of Selected Sections of Barbé-Marbois's Histoire de la Louisiane...   140
Chapter Notes   149
Bibliography   189
Index   193

"The United States have a unique meridian even as it shares latitude with many."
>Livingston to Attorney General Dallas
of Pennsylvania, June 30, 1802

"Today the United States take their place among the powers of the first rank."
>Livingston at the signing ceremony
for the Louisiana Purchase of
April 30, 1803

"I believe that, next to the negotiation that secured our independence, this is the most important the United States have ever entered into."
>Livingston to Secretary of State Madison,
May 12, 1803

Preface:
An Overview

One day after France signed a treaty with the U.S. at Paris on September 30, 1800, ending their undeclared naval war of the past three years, it signed another treaty in Spain looking toward the Spanish retrocession of Louisiana to France.[1] That second treaty was kept secret due in part to the Spanish fear that the U.S. would seize Louisiana "before Napoleon[2] was ready to take over the province and defend it against invasion."[3] But rumors of its existence quickly began to circulate in capitals. The messages Secretary of State James Madison sent to the U.S. minister to Great Britain, the Federalist holdover Rufus King, on July 24, 1801, and to the soon-to-depart minister to France Robert R. Livingston Jr. on September 22, 1801, well describe the state of knowledge in the U.S. at that time regarding the rumored retrocession. The dispatch to King noted the coming cession of Louisiana from Spain to France but added that no one could ascertain whether the arrangement had been put in final form. The U.S. goal was "to prevent a change of our southern and western neighbors, that is to say, [by] means of peace and persuasion. Should Great Britain interpose her projects also in that quarter, the scene will become more interesting, and require still greater circumspection on the part of the U.S." King was to keep a close eye on Britain with respect to this matter "considering the facility with which her extensive navy can present itself in our front, that she already flanks us on the north, and that, if possessed of the Spanish territories contiguous to us, she might soon have a range of settlements in our rear, as well as flank us on the south also.... It is certainly not without reason that she is the last of neighbors that would be agreeable to the U.S."

Madison's message to Livingston mentioned reports that France and Spain had already or might soon agree to give France "the mouth of the Mississippi with certain portions of adjacent territory." That would be of

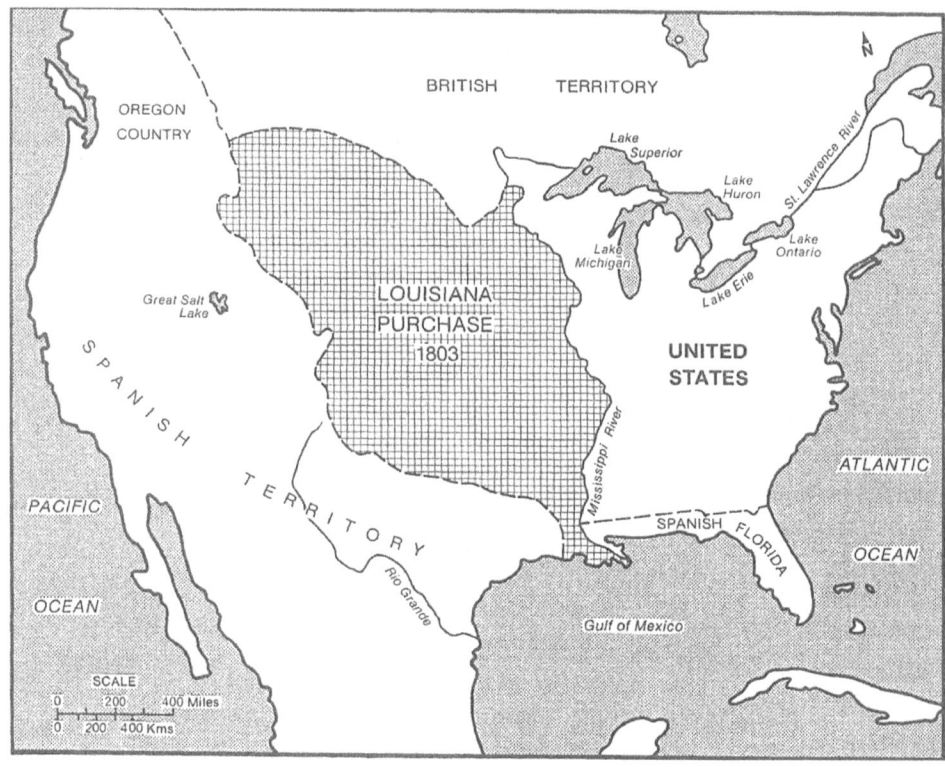

From *Historical Maps on File, Revised Edition.* Copyright © 2001 by Facts on File, Inc. Reprinted by permission of Facts on File, Inc.

"momentous concern" to the U.S. Therefore, instructions had already been sent to Charles Pinckney, Livingston's newly installed counterpart at Madrid, to report on it. The goal was "to dissuade the parties from adhering to their object." Accordingly, Livingston was to emphasize to France that French possession would lead to "collisions" with the U.S., given "a neighborhood under such circumstances." He was also to point out that (a) the predictable wars between France and Britain would lead to "expeditions" between Canada and Louisiana that would be upsetting to America's own "western settlements" and the "southern states, whose numerous slaves have been taught to regard the French as the patrons of their cause"; and (b), the U.S. would closely align itself with France's rival, Britain, which could lead to "crises ... in which a very valuable part of [France's] dominions would be exposed to the joint operations of a naval and territorial power."[4]

A sense of crisis did develop in the U.S. by the following spring, by which time more specific reports had arrived there confirming Louisiana had indeed been retroceded. For example, Livingston on December 30, 1801, sent for Madison's consideration and endorsement a copy of his letter to King of that same date reporting: "The exchange has actually been agreed upon.... A part of the armament destined for Hispaniola, if Toussaint does not give it opposition, is destined for Louisiana...."[5] Spain must have made this cession, which contravenes all her former maxims of policy, ... but she is no longer a free agent." It was his belief that Britain must see this retrocession as giving "an almost unbounded power to her rival.... Our own western territory may be rendered so dependent upon [the French] as to promote their political views." Moreover, the traditional French influence with the Indians, and "the national character of the peasantry of Canada, may render the possession of Britain very precarious. I say nothing of the danger that must threaten their islands in case a respectable establishment should be made by France in Louisiana, which will not fail to be the case as the territory is uncommonly fine and produces sugar and every article now cultivated in the islands."

King was to use these "hints" in urging Britain to join the U.S. in throwing "obstacles" on the Louisiana retrocession plan, "if it is not already too late." But, he was warned, the U.S. could not be seen to be opposing it, since that could be used by Britain "to embroil us with France, and Britain will have sufficient address to endeavor to keep up a mutual jealousy, if possible, between us."[6]

President Jefferson the following 18 April wrote to Livingston: "Perhaps nothing since the Revolutionary War, has produced more uneasy sensations through the body of the nation."[7] A week later, Jefferson wrote a cover letter to his French friend in New York, Pierre S. du Pont de Nemours, who was returning to France as the bearer of that 18 April letter to Livingston (which he was to read and then seal). That cover letter read in part:

> This measure will cost France, and perhaps not very long hence, a war which will annihilate her on the ocean, and place that element under the despotism of two nations, which I am not reconciled to the more because my own would be one of them.... In Europe, nothing but Europe is seen, or supposed to have any right in the affairs of nations. But this little event, of France's possessing herself of Louisiana, which is thrown in as nothing, as a mere make-weight, in the general settlement of accounts, this speck which now appears as an almost invisible point in the horizon, is the embryo of a tornado which will burst on the countries on both sides of the Atlantic and involve in its effects their highest destinies. That it may yet be avoided is my sincere prayer, and if you can be the means of informing the wisdom of Bonaparte

of all its consequences, you [will] have deserved well of both countries.[8]

Americans saw the return of France to the continent of North America as a reversal of the policy they believed had been permanently inscribed by the French in their ceding to Spain all that had remained to them on that mainland after their disastrous war against Great Britain ending in 1762–63. It seemed to the Americans that cession to Spain had been made even more permanent by the terms France agreed to in its treaty of military alliance with the U.S. on February 6, 1778. There, the French promised in Article 6 not to seek to take possession of "any part of the continent of North America which before the Treaty of Paris in 1763 or in virtue of that Treaty [was] acknowledged to belong" to Britain. Secretary of State James Madison, to his distress, would be educated on July 11, 1801, by the French chargé, Louis André Pichon, that "the treaty of 1778 was conceived in a manner to exclude this colony [Louisiana] from renunciation."[9] Pichon's report to foreign minister Talleyrand elaborating on that conversation described Madison as saying:

> It had been understood that the previous government in France considered the possession of a territory bordering on the U.S. to be the same as breaking the peace between the two and that this policy had led France, in the 1778 treaty of alliance, to renounce even the hope of its possessing any colony in North America. Although this treaty no longer existed, the situation undoubtedly was the same.... [Louisiana's] possession by France would cause daily collisions that would jeopardize the peace.

Pichon asked, would the U.S. really "dream of crossing the Mississippi?" Madison answered that he had "no trouble regarding this idea as a phantom.... Mr. Madison ended by repeating to me his refrain that it appeared that, even if there was a Franco-American treaty covering all points of possible contention," and even if France was "more liberal and more enlightened than Spain ... there would still be collisions between the two states."

Given this exchange, it probably was with special satisfaction that Madison, on October 14, 1803, wrote to the U.S. minister in Spain, Charles Pinckney, that France, now having ceded Louisiana to the U.S. by the recent agreement of 30 April, had "return[ed] to her original policy" regarding North America.[10]

But before this happy development arrived for the U.S., it had to confront a series of dangerous events that threatened not only war against France or Spain (or both), but also dissension and disunion domestically.

As newspaper editor William Duane wrote in a letter of November 15, 1802, to Livingston, the fear of a French return to North America was "not from any apprehension of hostilities on the part of France towards our country, but from the use which party spirit may convert this circumstance to."[11] Nevertheless, Duane's view understated the implications for U.S. security of a return of France to North America, because that would have revolutionized the situation at its western border, where France and Britain were bound to fight, drawing in the Americans. While the present arrangement there with Spain was far from satisfactory for the longer term, at least that weak and overextended country did not pose a military problem for the U.S., and ever since Pinckney's Treaty of 1795 there had been a recognized border on the Mississippi River down to the 31st degree north latitude — a line Spain had resisted until then. Moreover, the treaty gave the U.S. the right of navigation down to the Gulf of Mexico and the privilege of deposit at New Orleans or, if that place proved unacceptable after a three-year period, at some other suitable port on that river to be chosen by Spain for the duty-free transshipment of American goods.[12]

It takes little imagination to assess what effect Spain's sudden, unilateral termination of that American privilege at New Orleans — announced there by the local intendant in October 1802 — had on the Americans. It came at a time when France was openly preparing to take possession of that place and all of Louisiana, and, in the American view, it violated Pinckney's Treaty by not including an offer of an alternative port. Were the French, with their powerful influence over Spain, behind the closure? Did it harbor a strangulation of the economy of the western sections of the U.S. as part of a plan to absorb the valuable land east of the Mississippi (no longer protected from French possession now that the 1778 alliance treaty had been abrogated by the U.S. during its quasi-war with France)? At a minimum, would not the western population of the U.S., dependent as it was upon the Mississippi River as an outlet for its trade, find itself drawn into the French orbit and break away from the distant, ineffective Atlantic states, whose political and economic interests seemed alien to theirs? Finally, would not the Federalists seek to make political hay out of the unfriendly behavior of France, the ostensible ally of the Republicans who had displaced them in the elections of 1800?

These are among the matters to be addressed in the pages to come.

An editorial note: This book quotes heavily from the documents of the period. Words in brackets are this author's interpolations or clarifications, unless the bracketed words are in quotes — in which case they are original to the document but located elsewhere in its text — or stricken through, like this: [~~value~~]. The stricken words were written in hand, and discarded, by the authors of the documents.

CHAPTER 1

The Political Setting

Several issues were left unresolved at the signing of the peace treaty between the U.S. and Great Britain on September 3, 1783. They would have a direct bearing on the domestic and international circumstances of the new American republic as it navigated its way through the wars of the French revolutionary and Napoleonic periods.[1] The most important of those wars from the point of view of our subject was the one that began in May 1803, not coincidentally the very period when the U.S. purchased Louisiana from France. Accordingly, it would be worthwhile to examine those issues and circumstances that are so key to an understanding of why a nation as powerful as France, and as determined as it recently had been to regain control of Louisiana from Spain,[2] found it necessary to make that sale — more accurately, that cession — to the U.S., which itself had only recently concluded its own undeclared war against it.

A flavor of just how strongly France under First Consul Napoleon felt regarding securing the retrocession of Louisiana may be gleaned from elements of a memorandum the government in Paris prepared soon after its sale of that self-same territory to the U.S. A copy of that memorandum had been provided to Livingston in Paris as part of a joint effort by the two nations to convince Spain that West Florida properly belonged to historic Louisiana and therefore should be relinquished by it along with New Orleans and the territory west of the Mississippi River.[3] Here is that excerpt:

> Guided by the effective leadership of the First Consul, France requested the restitution of Louisiana under the friendly guise of an exchange of territory, but the inequality of this exchange shows that it was only a pretext.[4] France wanted Louisiana back not at all only in part but complete and in its entirety, just as it had been received [by Spain in 1762–63], because, what had Spain given in exchange? Spain got back in 1783 all it had lost in the Peace of 1763, so why should it

keep what France had given it to give to England in 1762–63? It was for that reason that the October 1780 Treaty of St. Ildefonso stipulated a complete retrocession, i.e., all that France had earlier ceded, whether to Spain, or whether for Spain.[5]

That memorandum, which obviously had been written to serve France's post–Louisiana policy of shoring up American interests on the North American continent vis-à-vis the British, went on in even harsher terms regarding the Spanish position on Florida:

> The St. Ildefonso Treaty necessarily was referring to the entirety of Louisiana and to the reestablishment of France and Spain on the basis of the *status quo* prior to the War of 1755–63. After that cession to Spain of 1762–63, in another war fought by the French and American armies, in which Spain participated only tardily and then hardly doing anything at all except using up its resources against the Rock of Gibraltar, Spain regained its Florida possession.[6] Therefore, it is only fair and just for France to find it necessary to have back Louisiana with the same dimensions it had originally minus any parts Spain may have given up during the period of its possession of that territory. We believe that Spain is too just to question our rights in this regard, or to deny its obligation to return to us Louisiana just as it was, and *just as it is now ceded by France to the United States by the Treaty of Paris of April 30, 1803* [emphasis added].[7]

The U.S. acquisition of Louisiana was the last of three major episodes that characterized early Franco-American relations. The first was the French and Indian War, which ended with France's total evacuation of the North American continent — Canada and the Ohio valley ceded to Britain by virtue of military defeat and Louisiana to Spain by voluntary cession. The second was the American War of Independence, by which France helped defeat Britain as the sole diplomatic and military ally of the rebelling American colonies. The third episode was made possible by France's successful completion in 1802 of a seven-year negotiation with Spain looking toward the retrocession of Louisiana.[8] Clearly, the original thirteen rebelling colonies were the long-term beneficiaries of each of these French activities involving North America, although none of them was designed or executed by France primarily with American interests in mind. In that sense, France willy-nilly and only inadvertently was the most important benefactor of the colonists of British America in their climb to independent nationhood, as follows:

1. The French evacuation of Canada and the Ohio valley relieved those colonists of the need to look to the mother country for protection

from that century-old threat to their safety and barrier to their territorial expansion. In fact, the British Proclamation of 1763 barring the colonists from moving much further westward installed Britain as the new barrier to that expansion. This development, to borrow a thought from John Adams, ushered in a period of revolution and unification starting in 1760 that culminated in their declaration of independence.

2. The decision by Versailles in 1778 to ally militarily with the U.S. was instrumental in securing that independence after a difficult and long conflict whose duration and perhaps even outcome would have been far less favorable to the Americans without that singular alliance. The only other nation to have recognized the U.S. prior to the peace treaties ending the American War of Independence was the Netherlands, and it did so only in 1782 — that is, only after the battle of Yorktown and the change in the leadership of the British government had ended all major fighting in North America. Needless to say, while the Netherlands was a co-belligerent of the U.S. after Britain declared war on it in December 1780, there was no military alliance between the two. As for Spain, beginning in June 1779, it too was a co-belligerent of the U.S., but it never recognized or allied with it during the war, although it did allow an unaccredited U.S. minister, John Jay, to reside there as a "private gentleman."[9]

3. The cession of Louisiana to the U.S. meant that France at once approximately doubled the size of the original American nation; opened the door for its now-certain expansion across the continent, both to the Pacific and the Gulf of Mexico; and eliminated any remaining threat to its borders from the British or the Spanish, whether singly or in cooperation with each other. James Madison wrote Livingston and James Monroe, on October 6, 1803; "The rightful limits of Louisiana are under investigation. It seems undeniable from the present state of the evidence, that it extends eastwardly, as far at least as the River Perdigo [modern-day Perdido, just west of Pensacola], and there is little doubt that we shall make good both a western and a northern extent highly satisfactory to us."[10]

Of these three episodes, only the second may be considered the result of a voluntary move by France rather than one imposed upon it by external circumstances.[11] While the other two manifestly and intrinsically were detrimental to the French national interest, even the victorious Franco-American military alliance of 1778 proved to be but an illusory interlude in the downward spiral of the French monarchy. The resort by the government of Louis XVI to financial expedients in covering the immense costs of the American War contributed importantly to the acceleration of that spiral by leaving it with a debt burden so large that its efforts to manage it led to political developments that grew out of hand even before the end of the 1780s.[12]

The factors that conditioned the French decision to cede Louisiana to the U.S. relate importantly to the near-simultaneous accession to power of that event's two principal actors: Napoleon Bonaparte and Thomas Jefferson. The French general assumed political office in November 1799, following the *coup d'etat* of 18–19 Brumaire, at the head of a Consulate that had displaced the erratic and unwieldy Directory of the previous four years.[13] As first consul, Napoleon's immediate policy was, first, to see France recover militarily from the painful defeats it had suffered in 1799, especially in Italy. He largely succeeded in doing so by achieving a major victory over an Austrian army at Marengo on June 14, 1800, which had the additional beneficial effect of facilitating the exchange of Louisiana for a kingdom in Italy for the Duke of Parma.

Napoleon then progressively sought to create a calm international atmosphere in which he would be able to reestablish a sense of order and stability within France itself—and not incidentally to establish himself as its essential and unquestioned leader. Livingston referred to this policy in connection with his very first meeting with Napoleon on December 6, 1801, which was a few weeks after the signing of a preliminary peace treaty in London between France and England. For that meeting, Livingston had prepared a formal statement, which in fact he did not read out but only handed over to foreign minister Talleyrand, in which he congratulated the first consul for having had "the humanity which stops the progress of war even in the full [flush?] of victory when the interest of his country and the happiness of mankind call for a peace."[14] That Livingston would continue to adhere to this line in his communications to the French authorities for the next year and a half is clear from his letter of March 16, 1803, to Talleyrand, in which he described Napoleon as "an enlightened statesman who, after advancing his country to the highest pinnacle of military glory and national prosperity, had determined to give perpetuity to that prosperity by establishing it upon the firm basis of religion, good faith, justice, and national credit."[15]

In his official and private correspondence to Americans, Livingston naturally revealed a more cynical view of Napoleon's character and policies. His frank conclusions after a full year of studying the situation—even though obviously tinged with personal frustration and a sense of failure in his diplomatic mission—are worth summarizing. The following is from his letter of January 13, 1803, to New York lawyer and politician Ambrose Spencer:

The principles of liberty were never understood here. The philosophers substituted to it wild chimeras drawn from ancient records ill understood, and the knaves took advantage of this by exalting it to madness. In the first assembly [beginning in 1789], scoundrels such as Mirabeau had no other idea but that of making their fortunes out of the hardship of the reigning family, or by changing the dynasty. The Duke d'Orleans used his wealth for personal goals. Subsequent events drove off the men of probity and property, and put the power into the hands of the worst and the weakest of men. Posterity will hardly believe the horrors that this introduced, and none but a man upon the spot can verify them.

The subsequent change was not effected by the people, and so the power that made that change can only limit itself, and, as it is not the nature of power to stop, you must calculate upon its progressing till it falls under its own weight. As a sovereignty exists in the First Consul, a nobility becomes necessary. For example, the Legion d'Honneur gives territorial rights, and now thirty senators are to be given an income arising out of forfeited property at which they occasionally reside in a palace.

Of course, by the time Livingston penned those thoughts, war clouds in Europe were already visible with the rising tension between France and Britain. The two indeed would renew hostilities a few short months later. Livingston was far from loathe to see that development occur, because he, along with most of his American colleagues, believed, and correctly so, that it would open up an opportunity for the U.S. to achieve its goals in regard to Louisiana and the Floridas.

For our purposes, the twin international events at the very start of the new century preparing the way for the U.S. acquisition of Louisiana were (a) the treaty negotiations completed by the Adams Administration with France and signed at Paris on September 30, 1800, and (b) the preliminary peace treaty signed at London between France and England in October 1801 and then definitively negotiated at Amiens by March 27, 1802.[16] Thus, while 1800–02 was still a time of great flux and uncertainty in the world of diplomacy, the general direction seemed toward international peace, allowing Jefferson to state in his message to both houses of Congress on March 4, 1802, that he was pleased to "announce to them on grounds of reasonable certainty, that the wars and troubles, which have for so many years afflicted our sister nations, have at length come to an end."[17]

This trend was reinforced by still another positive development: the convention signed by the U.S. and Britain in London on January 8, 1802, settling the issue of prewar, bona fide American commercial debts to British creditors under the peace treaty of 1783 and confirmed in the Jay

Treaty of November 1794. That the settlement terms were very favorable for the U.S. is clear from a letter King sent Livingston on March 24, 1802, which reported that the affected British creditors, asserting that they were owed ƒ5 million while the convention only called for a U.S. payment of ƒ600,000, were petitioning Parliament for the difference; and those creditors believed the convention to be the result of a British desire for a "political" settlement with the U.S.[18] (The U.S. government advised a receptive and grateful British government that half the claims of the British creditors were baseless.)

The Franco-American treaty of 1800 was designed to reestablish relations following the rupture caused mainly by the large-scale, mutual seizures of merchantmen and their cargoes by French and American privateers and warships during the recent hostilities between those two nations. Those hostilities, in turn, had begun largely in consequence of the turn in relations between the U.S. and France following the rapprochement between the Americans and British as embodied in the Jay Treaty. That treaty, while it created deep tensions within the body politic of the U.S., was finally ratified and proclaimed by February 1796. Its contents were perceived by the French as signifying American subservience to British war policies, notably regarding the severe restrictions London had placed on neutral rights at sea.[19]

The resultant crisis arrived just as John Adams was assuming the presidency. He called Congress in extraordinary session, which, as he explained in an address to it on May 16, 1997, was due to "information that the French government had expressed serious discontent at some proceedings" of the U.S. France in December 1796 had rejected accrediting a new American minister, Charles C. Pinckney, who had been sent to replace the recalled one, James Monroe, in the hope of smoothing relations.[20] Talleyrand had explained to Monroe that no new minister would be received "until after the redress of grievances demanded of the American government." Moreover, that French minister, acting for the Directory, forced Pinckney to leave France in January 1797, when he moved to Amsterdam. Adams informed the Congress that, by all this, France had treated the U.S. "neither as allies nor as friends nor as a sovereign state."

Adams also reported to the Congress that, at a public audience on the occasion of Monroe's taking leave of the Executive Directory, that body's president, Barras, gave a speech that, in Adams's words, disclosed "sentiments ... more dangerous to our independence and union." This therefore required the U.S. to show France "we are not a degraded people ... fitted to be the miserable instruments of foreign influence." Adams concluded with the observation that all this had become public knowledge, so he could not "throw a veil over these transactions." Still, as a hint of that president's future flexibility, he went to say that he did want that "the wound ... be healed."

Considering the future role of Monroe in the negotiation of the Louisiana Purchase, it would be worthwhile here to repeat two reports sent to his government from Paris by minister C. C. Pinckney on this and related developments. On 20 December, Pinckney wrote that, after arriving on 5 December and giving Monroe his recall papers:

> I have seen Mr. Monroe very often since my arrival; his conduct has been open and candid, and I believe he has made me every communication which he thought would be of service to our country. He undoubtedly felt himself hurt at his being superseded, but I am convinced he has not on that account left anything undone which he thought would promote the objects of my mission.[21] The Directory and ministers had for some time before they were informed of his removal treated him with great coolness, but as soon as they heard of his recall, their attentions to him were renewed.

On 6 January, Pinckney sent in the text of Barras's speech with the commentary that "by endeavoring to persuade our countrymen that they can have a different interest from their fellow citizens, who themselves have [been] chosen to manage their joint concerns," Barras's speech, which was pre-prepared and read right after Monroe's "valedictory address," was "not an answer" to it, but "it does make clear the Directory's policy towards the U.S." Following are excerpts from Barras's speech:

> By presenting today your letters of recall to the Executive Directory, you give to Europe a very strange spectacle ['as a consequence of'] the condescension of the American government to the suggestions of her former tyrants ... ['The French hope that'] the successors of Columbus ['Raleigh'] and Penn ... will never forget that they owe ['their liberty'] to France.... The craftiness of certain perfidious persons [is] bringing them back to their former slavery.... The good American people ... will always have our esteem.... You, Mr. Minister Plenipotentiary ... have combated for principles, you have known the true interests of your country — depart with regret.

In the meantime, Secretary of State Pickering was being badgered along similar lines by letters from the French minister, Adet, to the point that that very Anglophile American exasperatedly wrote Pinckney on January 16, 1797:

> Will the ministers of the French Republic never cease to reproach us with "ingratitude"? If indeed "France wrought" as well as "guaranteed the independence of the U.S," as Mr. Adet asserts, ... our obligations are greater than we have hitherto imagined. But it is time these claims to our gratitude were investigated, and their extent ascertained.

Pickering did just that in the next several pages of this document, all designed to minimize to the extent possible France's contribution to the American victory over Britain. Pickering there described Adet's various claims as powerful and emotional demonstrations of how strongly France felt toward the U.S., which it considered an erstwhile ally, now that it had ratified the Jay Treaty. According to Adet, that treaty "deprives France of all the advantages stipulated in a previous treaty." He said that "the Executive Directory regards the Treaty of Commerce concluded with Great Britain as a violation of the treaty made with France in 1778, and equivalent to a treaty of alliance" with it. (By the time Pickering and Pinckney were corresponding, the Directory had suspended Adet's functions, while making clear that it was not more than a suspension, and that it was only "a mark of just contempt" rather than a "rupture between France and the U.S.")

The negative effect of the Jay treaty on Franco-American relations in its turn would soon be exacerbated by the celebrated XYZ affair, which began in 1798 with the publication of diplomatic correspondence reporting that the commissioners Adams had sent to France to negotiate a settlement had been confronted in December 1797 with a demand for money as a prerequisite to proceed.[22] This scandal, which effectively aborted President Adams's initial effort to renew relations with France, involved a request to the three visiting American commissioners (John Marshall, Charles C. Pinckney, and Elbridge Gerry), transmitted through three private persons serving as mediators for members of the French government and Directory, for a payment of $f50,000$ [$222,000]. Especially once reports of this demand became public knowledge, Adams on April 21, 1798, declared to Congress that the negotiations were at an end and that "he will never send another minister to France without assurances that he will be received, respected and honored, as the representative of a great, free, powerful and independent nation."[23] This sense of outrage deepened the chasm between the U.S. and France and culminated in a formal, unilateral American abrogation of "the Franco-American treaties" of February 6, 1778. While such a "unilateral abrogation" qualified as "a *casus belli*, if not tantamount to a declaration of war, that the U.S. did not deny," France wanted peace and so acquiesced.[24]

For their part, the Republicans, in the words of one historian, generally regarded the "frenzy" over this French "bid for a bribe" as having been artificially "drummed up" in the service of "President Adams's naval war with France."[25] In Vice President Jefferson's expressed view, it was a "delusion."[26] This analysis by the opposition party — although it was initially premised on the erroneous notion, at least on Jefferson's part, that there was in fact no such solicitation of a bribe — would soon be vindicated when Adams, overruling the dominant view in his own Federalist Party that a renewed approach to France was not in the national interest, accepted the assurances of the French authorities in 1799 that they would be receptive to such an approach.[27] Accordingly, and to the disadvantage of his own political prospects in the upcoming presidential elections, Adams designated a new set of negotiators (William V. Murray, Oliver Ellsworth and William R. Davie), who succeeded in reaching that agreement of September 1800. As Adams stated to Congress on November 22, 1800, before he knew of the successful conclusion of the negotiations: "The envoys extraordinary and ministers plenipotentiary from the U.S. to France were received by the First Consul with the respect due to their character; and three persons with equal powers were appointed to treat with them."

A word needs to be said here regarding the historical role of Foreign Minister Talleyrand in the events surrounding the Louisiana Purchase. One of the ironies of this period was that Talleyrand, the very government official who was most directly implicated in the payment demand at the heart of the XYZ affair, would nevertheless soon receive the credit in America, first, for having kept the two nations formally at peace, and second, for encouraging the renewal of the negotiations that led to the reestablishment of relations in 1800–01.[28] The basis for this American appreciation was (a) the key role that Talleyrand's correspondence of 1799 had played in giving Adams the assurances he was demanding of France as a precondition for his appointing a new American negotiating team (the president, as just mentioned, accordingly sent to France a new set of negotiators), and (b) Talleyrand in 1800, now as Napoleon's foreign minister in a reorganized French government, helped to see the subsequent negotiations through to their successful conclusion.[29]

There would remain an ambiguity in the American attitude toward Talleyrand, who continued to be seen by many in America as a *bête noire* in efforts to reestablish smooth U.S.-French relations. This was certainly Livingston's view at times throughout his tenure, as for example in his letter of March 14, 1802, to Madison: "The fact is Talleyrand is decidedly unfriendly to the U.S."[30] On the other hand, that American readily would acknowledge Talleyrand's helpful role in February 1803, when he arranged — and advised on — an unusual, direct correspondence with the first consul that, as will be discussed, contained some ideas incorporated in the 30 April agreement.[31]

Given Talleyrand's notorious reputation for exceptional guile and corruptibility, this ambiguity was to be expected, and it would be reflected down to the present in the writing of the history of the period. In the matter specifically of the Louisiana Purchase, it seems that in March and April of 1803 he had been considering accepting a British bribe designed to convince Napoleon to keep the peace by acquiescing in Britain's retaining Malta.[32] This had a bearing on Louisiana, because one incentive for Napoleon's keeping the peace would be the prospect of thereby allowing him to proceed with his plan to take possession of Louisiana. Napoleon, when he got wind of this bribery plan through reports in British newspapers, apparently decided at least partly for that reason to entrust the negotiations entirely to the honest (and pro-sale of Louisiana) Marbois, cutting his foreign minister out of the picture. Some historians claim that the British bid had undermined Livingston's own alleged effort to bribe Talleyrand through a Florida land-sale scheme in which Livingston and his friends also would have benefited (see the following for a refutation of this claim).

On balance, Talleyrand surely meant what he wrote to Pichon for Murray's eye in 1799 — that it was not in France's national interest to see a weak and divided U.S. in North America, but rather the reverse, because only a strong U.S. could counter British efforts to dominate in the Americas, and because a thriving America could help France curb British attempts at hegemony on the high seas. Whether Talleyrand always acted on this fundamental view in the same way Americans would have wished, and whether he veered from it at times strictly for reasons of personal monetary gain, is a complex question that must be left open and is beyond the scope of this study. But, given the evidence of history, it is clear that Talleyrand — who was *not*, as some historians have written, the minister who had countered Marbois's pro-cession position in the famous, if doubtful, April 1803 two-man debate before Napoleon[33] — had either tried to and failed, or more likely did not even try, to block the sale of all of Louisiana to the Americans. Recall that the Louisiana issue fell under the bureaucratic responsibility of the minister of navy/colonies and that the financial issue of French responsibility for the payment of debts under the Convention of September 30, 1800, also fell outside the direct purview of the foreign ministry. A day before Livingston learned from Marbois of Napoleon's decision to cede all of Louisiana to the U.S., Talleyrand had mentioned this prospect to him at a meeting of 11 April. That Tallyrand shortly thereafter backed off from that line with Livingston has been interpreted by some as due to his having been bought off by the British; a much more likely explanation is that Talleyrand learned only after that 11 April meeting that it was to be Marbois, and only Marbois, who would be the negotiator of that cession. (The British bribe was already a month old by that time, reportedly having been first offered to French officials in early March of 1803.)

The two memoranda from Talleyrand to Napoleon of 1804 and 1806 (see Appendix B) strongly reinforce the point of view just outlined. Also reinforcing it is an account of the advice Talleyrand was giving to Napoleon in the period leading up to the events of April 1803, in which the minister was urging the first consul to recognize that (a) France was already over-extended regarding colonies to administer; (b) while France needed colonies, it did not need those that were far away and of large size, but rather those which were capable of being peopled, cultivated and well-governed; and (c) France's industrial level barely matched the market size created by its existing colonial possessions, whose own overall commercial demands, moreover, exceeded France's ability to satisfy them. Renaut's summary assessment of this advice was that "never has a counsel of moderation been more opportune."[34]

To return to the political climate deriving from the rapprochement of September 1800, that event, coupled with the loss of power soon thereafter by the Federalists and John Adams, helped sustain a political climate in Paris that, while certainly not determinative, would be conducive to the success of the treaty negotiations of 1803. The advent of the Republican Administration under Thomas Jefferson was perceived in France, in keeping with the language of the time, as nothing less than a "diplomatic revolution." For example, Napoleon, at the accreditation ceremony for negotiator Murray on June 9, 1801, "expressed a great regard for the new administration of the U.S."[35] The French were fully appreciative of the Republican Party's having sought to prevent the American abrogation in 1798 of the 1778 treaties.[36] Also helpful from the French view was the equally strong opposition the Republicans had earlier presented to the Jay Treaty when, during the ratification process of 1795, they more or less publicly labeled that treaty as an "infamous act, which is really nothing more than a treaty of alliance between England and the Anglomen of this country" (Jefferson), and as having been due to "the exertions of Aristocracy, Anglicism, and Mercantilism" (Madison).[37] James Monroe's above-mentioned stance in Paris as U.S. minister during the ratification process of the Jay Treaty, when he failed to support the policy of his own government, also contributed to the French perception of the Republican Party as strongly in favor of close Franco-American relations. Still one more factor from this earlier period that would prove helpful to the outcome of 1803 was that a private channel used by Livingston to reach Napoleon's desk in the months leading up to the cession of Louisiana was Joseph Bonaparte, who had been Napoleon's key negotiator for the rapprochement convention of September 1800 — and who would spend his post–Napoleonic years as a resident of New Jersey.[38]

As regards that treaty of 1800, one of its central provisions was a rather loose commitment by the two parties to discharge their respective "debts" to citizens of the other country whose goods had been seized as a result of the taking of prizes at sea or of embargoes. By far, the larger liability rested with the French; while American seizures of French prizes were valued at $300,000, French seizures were put at over $4,000,000. Much to Livingston's regret, the U.S. not only promptly appropriated the necessary funds but also began to pay its debt to French claimants even before France had made any move to meet its own treaty obligations; he saw that as having unnecessarily given up leverage needed for his negotiations in Paris. As he put it in a note to Talleyrand, while the U.S. had, for its part, "paid the debt contracted under Louis XVI" and also that regarding the damages caused by the U.S. during the Directory, the government of France seemed now to be saying that it would be responsible under the 1800 treaty only for the "present" government's debts and not for the Directory's. For his part, Secretary Madison rebutted Livingston's criticism by arguing that the U.S. expected France fully to reciprocate America's own way of having paid off French citizens' claims under the 1800 treaty — i.e., "so readily and so liberally."[39]

The ratification of the treaty between the two republics remained incomplete well into 1801, forcing newly installed President Jefferson to delay Livingston's departure for France. Madison wrote Monroe on 6 May that Livingston "will not embark on his foreign mission till the ratification of the treaty in France arrives here."[40] Livingston himself felt uncertain enough about the ratification process as to have delayed formally resigning from his post as chancellor until July.[41] The situation at the time of Jefferson's inaugural on March 4, 1801,[42] was well described by Acting Secretary of State Levi Lincoln in his dispatch of 1 March to the two of the three signatories of the September 1800 treaty who were still in Europe — Ellsworth and Murray (in fact, only Murray remained in Paris). As he described, the treaty had been presented to the Senate on 16 December, and ratified on 3 February, but only with the "suppression of the second article … and the addition of an article limiting its duration." Due to the change in administration, no "exchange of ratifications" had as yet taken place, and so it was late according to the treaty schedule. The two Senate changes were, as Lincoln told the signatories, "chiefly of your own soliciting," therefore, no difficulties were anticipated with France.

Their original instructions were to require "a limited duration. This is a necessity for a nation such as ours, which cannot be bound forever to a treaty unless the other power agrees to end it.... [U.S.] circumstances [and] relations change so rapidly.... Our increasing strength is daily facilitating the command of just dispositions on the part of others.... [The U.S. always has insisted upon "short terms" in treaty durations.] Therefore the duration limit of eight years was non-negotiable. We now look forward ... to the moment when we shall be free from compact with every nation, and have a right to govern ourselves."

In the meanwhile, the U.S. was implementing the Convention: "All hostilities on the sea have been forbidden, our vessels are returning into port, the prisoners in our possession [are to be returned].... Commercial intercourse is resumed ... orders given for the restitution of vessels.... So soon as [the French ratification document] is received here, a minister plenipotentiary will be sent on our part to reside with that nation."[43]

As regards the U.S rejection of the second article of the treaty, its text read in part as follows: "Not being able to agree at present, respecting the treaty of alliance [of 1778] ... the treaty of amity [also 1778] ... and the convention of November 14, 1788, nor upon the indemnities mutually due, or claimed, the parties will negotiate ... at a convenient time, and until they may have agreed ... the said treaties ... shall have no operation."

This excision left only "debts" to be paid by the two parties, but not "indemnities claimed on account of captures, or confiscations" (Article 5).[44] The import of the U.S. action expunging Article 2 has been succinctly described by one historian, Albert Bowman, who declared that retention would have allowed the parties to reserve for renewed negotiation "at a convenient time" the question of "indemnities for ... spoliations" as provided in the treaties of 1778 and, as such, it would have represented not only an "agreement to disagree on the indemnities" but also on "old treaties." In other words, retention of Article 2 would have implied that the 1778 treaties, after all, were still possibly valid.[45]

This, of course, would have been contrary to the postwar trend in U.S. policy as just described by Lincoln's dispatch of March 1801 and therefore had to be rejected. That Livingston in Paris was not entirely happy with these treaty-related actions by the U.S. government and the Congress is clear from his letter to Rufus King of January 28, 1802: "The striking out of the second article of the treaty, and consequent delay of the ratification, has hurt us in many views, but the refusal to renew the treaty of 1778 still more."[46]

Predictably, in the eyes of legal historian Miller, France "flatly refused" to approve without conditions the American excision,

> fearing that it would mean an agreement on their part that the earlier treaties ... were at an end (as had been contended by the U.S.), but at the same time leaving the American claims against France under those treaties still existing. The French insisted that the claims in question should not be advanced in the future. Accordingly ... a clause was written into the French instrument of ratification [of July 31, 1801] to the effect that the "respective pretensions which are the object" of Article 2, were renounced on each side.[47]

Miller also observes that Murray, the American negotiator in Paris, was "without instructions on the point" [but] "assumed the responsibility and agreed to the exchange; he believed, rightly, that the matter should and would go again to the Senate."

Jefferson did, in fact, on 11 December, ask the Senate for its advice and consent, explaining to it that the first consul's "ratification not being pure and simple, in the ordinary form, I have thought it my duty, in order to avoid all misconception, to ask a second advice and consent of the Senate." The Senate resolved on 19 December that it considered "the convention between the United States and the French Republic as fully ratified," and the president duly promulgated it on 23 December.[48] When informed of this action, a relieved but seriously mistaken Livingston wrote a note to Talleyrand on March 13, 1802, observing that the expeditious promulgation demonstrated the friendly policy of the U.S. government—which, he said, did not return the convention to the Senate despite the points contained in the French declaration regarding the changes made by the U.S. in the ratification process.[49]

Madison, even prior to the arrival of the French document itself, wrote Livingston at Clermont, the chancellor's estate south of Albany, on September 22, 1801, that with advance news of the French ratification of "the Convention as altered by the Senate," the U.S. government was pleased at the "termination of the late painful differences" and, accordingly, was now authorizing Livingston to depart for France.[50] Madison was acting on negotiator Murray's report of 9 June that Napoleon, at the accreditation ceremony, "did not appear much pleased with the provisional ratification; but intimated that the exchange of ratifications would not meet with insurmountable difficulties."[51] Even prior to Madison's letter, Jefferson had written Livingston on 28 August that " the convention with France probably ratified."[52]

By 2 October, the Department of State had not only issued the new minister his "commission and instructions,"[53] but added the advice that Thomas Sumter Jr. would "live with you and perform the duties of your private secretary" and would be "cloathed with the character of secretary of the legation" so as to assure "continuance of the diplomatic functions in any event that might otherwise interrupt them."[54] As will be shown, the unilateral manner in which the government had recruited Sumter, who was totally unknown to Livingston, and the terms of reference it established for his relationship with the minister as both his private and legation secretary, would the very next year have disastrous results for those two incompatible diplomats—with attendant complications for American negotiations with France as well as for the personal reputation of Livingston.

The choice of Livingston as minister to France was predictable. President Washington also had offered that same post to him in 1794, when he was seeking a successor to his then-minister to France, the indiscreetly pro–Bourbon Gouverneur Morris, who had made himself unwelcome to a revolutionary France that was in the midst of its terror phase.[55] Livingston, for various reasons, not excluding personal disappointment in the general for having failed to offer him a suitable cabinet post early in his first administration, turned down the offer, which he realized would have put him in the service of a government whose French policy was not consistent with that of his own. As Livingston put it in a letter to Jefferson on March 12, 1801, he had rejected President Washington's "reiterated" offers of "a similar position" for fear "no Republican representative would be safe with the then-administration."[56] The end result was that Washington managed to recruit the even more rabidly pro–French James Monroe, whose tenure at Paris, as described previously, predictably ended very unhappily for all concerned with his recall by Washington in 1796 for having failed to act in support of the government's policy regarding the Jay Treaty.

Livingston in 1801 naturally was much more receptive to the offer of the Paris post from his fellow Gallican President Jefferson, who had at first tried to recruit him as secretary of the navy, an unattractive position that the administration was having difficulty filling. Livingston had been hoping for a more rewarding cabinet post, such as a return to his foreign secretaryship. The two men had long maintained a friendly relationship, beginning with their having served together as members of the Continental Congress's drafting committee for a declaration of independence. (As his N.Y. delegation lacked authority from its legislature to approve a declaration of independence, Livingston "sat in silence" on that committee and in his later writings never referred to this committee role.)[57] In the postwar period, Livingston and Jefferson corresponded irregularly and mostly not about politics but about their common interests in agricultural matters. An insight into their relationship may also be gleaned from President Jefferson's extra-curricular appeal to Livingston, while he was in Washington in late May 1801 for pre-departure consultations, for legal advice on a matter Jefferson had to resolve regarding the imprisonment of the above-mentioned William Duane by the Adams administration under the Alien and Sedition Act. At that time, the president wrote Livingston that, given the absence of

> our attorney general ... and none of the other members of the administration being professional lawyers ... I am obliged to decide for myself in a case of law [Duane was "in jail 30 days for contempt for printing matters, not pretended to be untrue"], which, in whatever way I decide, will make a great deal of noise in this situation. I ask the favor of you as a friend, and as a lawyer still in the habits of law reading, which I have not been for 30 yrs.... My affectionate esteem....[58]

Livingston's letters, from Washington on 31 May, and from his New York home, on 15 June, included references to "common law jurisprudence of the courts of the U.S.," the power of "pardon" by the "Executive," and "the easiest way of taking this business down."

On 15 October, Livingston — along with his wife, Mary ("Polly"); his two daughters, Elizabeth and Margaret; and their husbands, among other invited passengers, notably Sumter, John Graham (Sumter's counterpart in Madrid), and "Mlle. Delarge," an "adopted daughter" of Aaron Burr and bride the next year of Sumter — was finally able to leave New York for Europe, too late for the "summer's sea" that he had originally in mind for his family's, as well as his own "first voyage."[59] Around the time the president nominated Livingston to the Senate on 5 March, that New Yorker rather naively had thought this would entail holding off government pressure for him to leave for France prior to the arrival of summer. By 6 April, he realized the opposite problem was true: "I am somewhat fearful that if my departure is delayed until Mr. Dawson's [he was the courier to France of the ratification instruments] return, that we shall make the voyage later in the season than ... July."[60]

In any event, the trip proved to be a relatively short and pleasant one of three weeks. Nevertheless, it was with a great sense of relief that the family arrived in France on November 12, because it had suffered a last-minute scare just off the stormy coast that had forced it into a port, L'Orient, which wasn't its original destination. At Livingston's request, the Navy had changed the frigate *Boston*'s destination to that of any safe and convenient port of France, although Nantes had remained as the ship's target port.⁶¹ Going from L'Orient to Paris via Nantes, some 200 miles from Paris, Livingston and entourage arrived at the capital the evening of 3 December, where the family moved into rooms procured for it by Lafayette. By 6 December, the new minister was received by Napoleon at a public audience. That first consul's opening comment was an implied, perhaps sarcastic reference to the XYZ affair: "You have come to a very corrupt world."⁶²

Jefferson's choice of Livingston for the Paris post was in keeping with his need for political allies in the more northern sections of the country who also shared his pronounced sympathies for the French. After all, from revolutionary days onward, Livingston was closely associated with the so-called Gallican party in the American leadership — some said too closely associated in that his candidacy as foreign secretary had been pressed on the Continental Congress by the French legation at Philadelphia. For example: "We now know that the Secretary of Foreign Affairs in the continental congress owed his office to the French Minister at Philadelphia."⁶³ In contrast to this charge, Livingston's biographer reached the conclusion that he could never have been bought by the French or anyone else; and that his cooperation with the French derived from his own prior convictions.⁶⁴ One might add in favor of the very pro–Gallican Livingston that the Continental Congress, in electing him, was being consistent with its own long-standing view that it was in U.S. national interest to marry its policies to those of its one ally, France.⁶⁵ Moreover, Livingston's major opponent in the election for that office, Arthur Lee, was known to have deeply antagonized Versailles during his diplomatic stay in France, 1777–79, and therefore could hardly have been an effective foreign secretary for the congress.⁶⁶

As noted above, Livingston by 1792 had turned from the Federalists and had become, along with Governor George Clinton and Aaron Burr, a leading member in New York of the party supporting Jefferson's Republicans. The correspondence between Livingston and Gouverneur Morris offers an insight into the domestic political climate of the period. (Morris was a Federalist but also one of Livingston's closest friends since college days, along with John Jay, from whom Livingston had been painfully estranged following their disagreement over the separate peace with Britain of 1782.)⁶⁷ For example, Morris to Livingston, January 23, 1801: "Had you run with Jefferson, the House of Representatives by now would have made you President.... How much I lament that this is not the case I need not say, but I feel equal, and trust that you will feel greater, regret that you should still be bound in the chains of opposition to your oldest and best friends." Livingston on 5 February, after indulging in sentimentalities regarding lost friendships, answered: "But enough of this, which can now lead merely to excite unpleasant sensations."[68]

Morris, a great landowner like Livingston,[69] would deepen his analysis of the political issues now separating former revolutionaries-in-arms when he wrote his friend on October 10, 1802: "I fully accord with you in your ideas of men and things on your side of the water. I wish you at the same time to remember that those who dwell on this side of the water are men also.... The French government cannot I think respect either the government or the people of the U.S." To Morris, power, not wisdom, "is what counts for Europeans." The U.S. having, for example, "an habeas corpus act, a trial by jury," was irrelevant to them. It was "above all the talents of those who are at the head of affairs" that they looked at. Said Morris:

> Much will depend on the union of talents and property ... [in determining how long] "our government" [will last].... There is a considerable mass of genius and courage, with much industrious cunning, now at work to overturn our constitution [and render the U.S. subject to] ... a course of revolutions to military despotism.... Universal suffrage ... takes from men of moderate fortune their proper weight and will in the press of time give undue influence to those of great wealth.... [These last must be countered] by a phalanx of property under the guidance of our ablest men.... [But the prospect is for] the property in this country to continue to be divided on political questions, and if so we may expect mischief.... Many large estates will be put into the melting pot ... [as part of the] scuffle ... [for power where the] hatred of the rich ... [by] a giddy populace ... [will be manipulated by those who think they] can climb into power by civil commotion ... the Clintonites ... [will win over] the Burrhites.... You will all I believe discover at some time or other that, in leaving the mother church of federalism ... [you have brought yourselves] into a state of reprobation.

Morris finished with a quote from Virgil: "The way to Avernus is easy; night and day lie open the gates of death's dark kingdom. But to retrace your steps to find the way back to daylight — that is the task, the hard thing."

The overlap between this analysis and that of aspects of Republicanism is obvious, and it is therefore not surprising that it struck a responsive chord in Livingston's own thinking, as shown in the minister's correspondence from France. Even as it bemoaned the deepening conservative political and social character of that formerly revolutionary country, it reflected an increasing concern over trends in America that favored the growth of cities, the growing power of the national government at the expense of the states, and the empowerment of social and economic classes unworthy of the values for which Livingston and his class had fought a revolution.[70] These sentiments were not new to Livingston, whose liabilities as a politician had always included a pronounced patrician philosophy that encompassed a strong skepticism as to the worthiness of the average American for the great political liberties and economic opportunities afforded him by the successful struggle against the former mother country. During the Revolutionary War, he tended to use these doubts about the worthiness of the American people to justify his periodic bouts of aloofness from political and governmental activity.[71]

That both Livingston and the Jefferson administration as a whole were seen by the French as friendly to their interests surely facilitated France's decision in 1803 to cede Louisiana to the Americans. For example, Livingston and Monroe wrote Madison on June 7, 1803: "It is possible that this government is fearful that the British may take the territory, and we, in consequence, delay the payment.... A belief they stand well with the U.S. ... is their political motive in the transaction."[72] Also note that the cession might not have been so readily made had John Adams, whose recent moves toward rapprochement could not outbalance either his political party's bias toward Great Britain or his long personal history of abrasive relations with France, won a second term. Furthermore, Pichon was reporting from Washington that the Federalists were not to be trusted by France.

Still, Livingston, upon arrival at Paris, felt he had to work hard to demonstrate to the new French leadership that he had not endorsed the violence associated with the events of the earlier part of the 1790s. His efforts had to contend with two personal limitations: he was very hard of hearing, and — as he would confess to the first consul even a full year later, in his letter of February 27, 1803 — he had an "imperfect knowledge of the French language [that] does not allow me to express my ideas as clearly as I'd desire."[73] Nevertheless, by early 1802 he was already pridefully writing home that he, his wife, and younger daughter Margaret were being accepted socially and politically by the new, conservative social and political order in Paris.

Livingston's reference to Margaret brings to mind a letter the then French secretary of legation at Philadelphia, François Barbé-Marbois, had uncannily sent to him twenty years earlier, on May 9, 1780, when the Livingstons were expecting their first child (Elizabeth would be born in July). Marbois wrote that if they had a daughter, "she will resemble her mother, and you will bring her to France where, I guarantee you, she will be well received."[74] In point of fact, Livingston's wife and daughter were well liked and frequently received by the French establishment, and this undoubtedly helped in his diplomatic activities.

Prior to coming to France, the minister clearly had failed to appreciate the scope and especially the political consequences of that earlier period of terror and violence, and he was now witnessing with little surprise but great disappointment the steps being taken by Napoleon in his steady progress toward assuming personal control over the government. For example, Livingston wrote Monroe on April 24, 1802:

> Everything, my dear sir, has totally changed since you were here. That simplicity which approached to burlesque effected by the then people in power has given place to pomp and every species of luxury.... I am very doubtful whether the sound principles of liberty were ever known here.... I am very doubtful ... whether the whole revolutionary business, though it originated in reason and philosophy, was not carried on by interested men with a view to their private emolument rather than to the general good....[75] If liberty can ever be purchased too dear, it will be so here.... The distinctions that separated [the people] from the higher orders of society are in appearance removed.[76] They are happy and personally free.... The reestablishment of religion ... will add a new support to the government and contribute to stop the torrent of corruption, [which] pervades the lower classes of people here.... Everything here is going back to the old order of things.[77]

Another example may be found in Livingston's letter to Horatio Gates of May 12, 1802: "Since I have acquired a more intimate acquaintance with this people, I have satisfied myself that they never had the smallest idea of liberty, at least in our sense of the word.[78] I am also convinced that there never was a people better formed to do without it.... I see your friend Kosciusko frequently; he is much respected but keeps himself aloof from the court."[79] Livingston also said much the same thing about Lafayette, whom he was aiding financially while, along with Dupont and others, encouraging the U.S. government to reward that Frenchman for his past services. (Indeed, Lafayette soon after the Louisiana Purchase would be given a parcel of land in present-day Louisiana that he quickly sold for badly needed cash.) As regards Thomas Paine, that long-time resident of Paris corresponded with Livingston, but the latter studiously kept his distance from him. Thus, Livingston's letter to Morgan Lewis of December 7, 1802, protested that, contrary to reports circulating in America, he never wrote to Paine, "certainly never here in France," never carried to him a message from Jefferson, and never "encourage[d] anything which loosens the bonds of society or the precepts of Christianity." (According to William Duane's letter to Livingston of November 15, 1802, "Mr. Paine arrived at Baltimore last week and is now at Georgetown Potomac.")[80]

A final example of Livingston's sharply changed view of France is from his letter to his sister, Janet Montgomery, of June 14, 1802: "I begin ... to have much less faith in the philosophy of government.... I see mankind more nearly.... We will find ourselves only so far safe as we have the means and the inclination to resist ['the old world's machinations'].... Jefferson, I fear, is running a wonderful government, but one which misses this point." This letter also includes a familiar theme of the American revolutionary leadership: "[The old world] lacks the extent we Americans have of private virtues ... and a government upon the basis of public good."[81]

Livingston expanded on his view of the limitations of Jefferson's understanding of the true situation in France when he wrote his brother-in-law and future successor at Paris, John Armstrong, on May 25, 1802, of his disappointment at the lack of interest in Washington regarding his proposals for stern measures (such as instituting an embargo) to protest against French mistreatment of American cargo ships trading at Hispaniola, where the French forces were in fact heavily dependent — as were the opposing black forces— on supplies from the U.S. Livingston there wrote Armstrong that, to his "great surprise," his letters from Washington mentioned the French mistreatment "without the smallest mark of reprobation." He was in "fear" that he would be

> left in the lurch.... Nothing will be more hurtful than ... timidity. Louisiana will doubtless pass into the possession of France very shortly.... This will produce intrigues with our own western people.... Britain will court us and prudence will require us not to slight her advances.... The true policy of our administration is boldly to meet [the 'unpleasant effect' of French possession] and so to show that [America] fears no enemy and will yield no rights.... [Jefferson] relies upon the good will of this nation towards us, when in fact no such good will exists.... They must necessarily look on us with a [jaundiced?] eye.

By that year 1802, France would be completely dominated by the first consul and bearing all the earmarks of the old court life under the Bourbons.[82] As Livingston wrote in his 25 May letter to Armstrong: Napoleon was to be made first consul for life and,[83] this meant that his family would be successors. All measures here, taken together, "leaves the government at least as strong as the Revolution found it." A day earlier, he had written Morris: "Your prediction with respect to my change of sentiments before my return so far as it relates to France is fully verified.... [Their] delirium [led to] horrors of which I had no conception till I arrived here." This left him "no longer any room to doubt" that the current course reversal allowed only changes from the departure point that would assure no return of the "old rulers" and assured preserving the "spoils" which the "present leaders have acquired." Upon his arrival, he saw that "a respected royalist [read: an Adams nominee] would have been more acceptable" as the U.S. minister. "I know that [my present] sentiments will not be such as are agreeable in America." He was "thankful for our having squeezed perhaps the only moment in which our habits and measures qualified us for freedom.... You see the confidence with which I write you, and you will take care that confidence should not work me injury."[84]

In an earlier letter on 21 April, Livingston wrote to his brother-in-law, Morgan Lewis, that there was no prospect of democracy in France given "the nature and disposition of the inhabitants" and the fact that any premature attempt to install such a government "will replunge them into all those horrors from which they have but just escaped, horrors of which you can have no conception from anything which you have heard or read."

In keeping with his revised opinion of France and the French, Livingston, much more so than the ever-optimistic and forgiving Jefferson when it came to matters French, saw that nation as highly suited to Napoleon's style — one which was giving it strong direction but with a light touch, leaving it free to enjoy life's pleasures, its only real interest. Livingston was ready to return home at the first decent opportunity, as shown in his overreaching suggestion to Aaron Burr as early as December 16, 1801: "[Paris], in point of pleasure or society [is great] ... I say this because I have marked you out as my successor as soon as you manage to call me home with honor."

One motive for Livingston's itchiness to return to New York was his increasing perception that the political situation in that state was ripe for his becoming governor. George Clinton was bowing out of that office in 1803 in favor of becoming Jefferson's running mate in the 1804 election, and reports from the minister's political associates were encouraging. For example, he wrote to Virginia governor Monroe on July 3, 1802: "I intend not to suffer my stay here to be so long as to render me indifferent to your politics — tho I like the climate and my situation, yet I like better what I left behind."[85] And, on January 18, 1803, he wrote Armstrong that he was pleasantly surprised at the declarations from his "friends" that they continued "to have the same intentions with respect to me that they had when I left you." In line with this ambition, Livingston a few weeks later was not bashful in urging Jefferson to have now-minister extraordinary Monroe replace him that very year, allowing him to return to America as early as September![86]

By that early period of 1803, Livingston had been regularly trumpeting his own horn in correspondence back home as to how well he was being received in France. He was doing so in large part because, by spring 1802, he had realized that his earlier habit of candidly reporting on his difficulties in attracting the attention of the French authorities to American concerns was damaging to his personal image and playing into the hands of British propaganda designed to stir up friction between the U.S. and France. Accordingly, we now see Livingston writing to King in London on May 10, 1802: "I hear from America that great pain has been taken to represent me as not acceptable to this court.... [While this was the case earlier, when it was believed] that I was the agent of a violent democracy ... I [now] share a portion of the Consul's esteem." Earlier, on April 26, 1802, he had written to Tillotson in New York:

> The politics of Mr. Jefferson were not thought to square with the present state of things here. I have, however, removed the suspicions they appeared to entertain on my arrival by carefully avoiding any sort of interference in the parties of the nation, and by speaking freely my sentiments on the present establishment, who I do sincerely believe, on a nearer view of things, to be best adapted to the situation of this country, in which every man and woman seeks pleasure, and money as a means of procuring it. I see little to prevent the First Consul from obtaining any degree of power that he may wish.[87]

Also that month, Livingston wrote to Morgan Lewis (who would actually be the Republican who succeeded Clinton as governor of New York) claiming that, "In the line of business, I am treated with much more ['polite attention'] than falls to the share of the representatives of any of those sovereigns who have demands to make without power to enforce them."[88]

CHAPTER 2

The Failed Negotiations of 1802

The new American minister's plenipotentiary's principal tasks were twofold, but interconnected. Of course, most visible was the need to fulfill the now-ratified treaty's provisions for compensation to American citizens who had financial claims against France. As noted, those claims amounted to a guesstimate of 20 million livres (nearly $4 million). Livingston's unavailing approach to this task up to the very month of the Louisiana Purchase may be perceived in the following communications:

1. Livingston to Marbois, December 29, 1801: "[Enclosed is a] plan for discharge of American debts.... [It is] not as a minister but as your old friend [that I] submit the enclosed ... [and look forward to a] free conversation ... [conducted in] utmost secrecy." (The gist of Marbois's answer of 9 February was that he had read Livingston's ideas, as had Consul Lebrun, that both backed his commercial goals, and that now was the time "for a solid and equally beneficial connection between us," as he would continue to so state to his colleagues.)[1]

2. Livingston to King, January 25, 1802: "I have hinted at an inclination to purchase West Florida by a payment to their American creditors, but they show no inclination to catch at the idea.... I am inclined to adhere to my instructions, which enjoin me not to remonstrate if the business is finally concluded, but to put the best face upon what we cannot prevent."

3. Livingston to Madison, January 26, 1802: [Six million dollars would just] about cover the liquidated debt. (He was working on a plan involving both the U.S. and France opening up loans as a way to liquidate it, and asked for authorization "to attempt it.")

4. Livingston to Governor Monroe, April 24, 1802: Livingston explained that the negotiators of the U.S.–French treaty of September 30, 1800,

had taken away all their papers, so that he didn't know "the points of difference" at that time: "The business of most interest to us, that of Louisiana, still remains in the state it was.... Very extraordinary ... [is Pinckney's still believing] that the Floridas are not included in the cession, and he writes me that he has made a proposition to purchase them.... You may, however, be fully assured that the Floridas are given to France." Even the Spanish ambassador told him "he was sorry" for Spain's having ceded the lands making Americans their neighbors. "I wish our government had been explicit in their instructions to me [and that I had been] empowered to employ some millions ... to ward off [France's obtaining New Orleans and the Floridas].... [Only money offers even] the smallest prospect of success." To Livingston's mind, the U.S. needed to develop Natchez to rival New Orleans; Natchez must be made a "free port" by Congress. If St. Domingue was a problem, France would be desperate for gold, and the U.S. could offer not just financing of American claims against France, but additional funds for "supplies to aid their armaments in the islands."[2]

5. Livingston to Madison, that same 24 April: Pinckney wrote that "he has made a proposition to purchase" the Floridas from Spain, and that he

> still supposes that they are not included in the cession.... You may, however, be fully assured that they are given to France.... You may act upon this information with absolute certainty.... if Congress makes Natchez a free port, and if the state of affairs in St. Domingue should employ the troops designed for Louisiana, time will still be left for gold to operate here. But it must be plentifully and liberally bestowed, not barely in the assumption of debts, but in active capital, offered in supplies, to aid their armaments in the islands.... Tell me [your] utmost amount.

6. Livingston to Madison, May 10, 1802: "[Lacking] a line from you since last December ... [will] necessarily suspend any farther applications to the government on the subject of debts or Louisiana."[3]

This message crossed with one from Madison to Livingston of 1 May in which he stated "[The French] reserve as to Louisiana ... tacitly contradicts the language first held to you ... [by Talleyrand and which had given us] hopes.... [However,] since the receipt of your last communication, [in which Talleyrand made a "virtual denial of the cession"], no hope remained except possibly as a result of problems of French implementation and the effect of Livingston's arguments, such as that, with French control of New Orleans, "the worst events are to be apprehended." Therefore, he said, it was important to "spare no efforts" in making that case. The U.S. needed to learn how much France would take for New Orleans and the Floridas, "if both of these are included in the cession." The U.S. would be especially "liberal" if debt payments and "restitutions would also be included in the price. The President is personally looking forward to frequent reports."

7. Livingston to Madison, February 18, 1803: "The only basis on which I think it possible to do anything here is to connect our claims with our offer to purchase the Floridas."[4]

8. Livingston to Napoleon, Feb 27, 1803: "If the plan which I have proposed regarding Louisiana is adopted ... the debt of the U.S. to France would be larger than the totality of the claims of the Americans."

But Livingston's second task, although initially based only on rumors and unsubstantiated diplomatic reporting, was even more nettlesome, because it was increasingly perceived by the U.S. government as touching upon — indeed threatening to— the most basic of America's national interests: blocking the retrocession itself of Louisiana, including New Orleans and even possibly both Floridas, east and west. An illustration of just how unclear the situation was— not just for the Americans but also for the French and Spanish signatories themselves— is contained in Livingston's follow up letter to Monroe of July 3, 1802, amending his earlier assertion that Florida certainly had been handed over to France: "A mystery still hangs over the affairs of Louisiana.... Some little difference [exists] between the parties to that treaty as to its extent, for though I was at first assured it comprehended the Floridas, yet I have reason at present to think otherwise, at least so far as regards West Florida.... I am in hopes that it may still be kept out of their hands— but everything on this subject is uncertain, because there is little that France can not effect with Spain if they wish it."

That Secretary Madison was receiving and repeating ever-changing and contradictory reports regarding Florida's status is suggested by his dispatch to Pinckney on the 26th of that same month of July: On the basis of "information from Paris," the Floridas, "including New Orleans," were made part of the retrocession; therefore, there was no need for Pinckney to set a price for Spain to sell them to the U.S.— negotiations had to be between the U.S. and France. One can easily imagine Madison's later surprise upon receiving Livingston's dispatch of 30 July, which, aside from confirming receipt of the 18 April presidential message hand-carried to him by Dupont, reported that the Spanish ambassador had now told him "that the Floridas are not included" in the treaty France and Spain signed on March 21, 1801.

The prospect of a change in sovereignty over Louisiana immediately raised a number of issues for the U.S.: Would France respect American rights won under their 1795 treaty with Spain regarding free navigation down the Mississippi into the Gulf of Mexico, including the right of deposit of goods, initially at New Orleans or (after 3 years) at an equivalent, suitably located port?[5] Could the substitution by ambitious France of a weak Spain as the sovereign power in Louisiana and possibly the Floridas be tolerated by a U.S. fearful of being dragged into a predictable future war between France and Britain? And, could the western population of the U.S. resist equally predictable French pressure to cooperate in their political, and perhaps even military, plans in a North America that France had seemingly promised in Article 6 of its 1778 alliance treaty with the U.S. never to return to?

This problem of retaining the political loyalty of the American west would later prompt Madison to include the following in his instructions to Livingston and Monroe of March 2, 1803: "Feel the pulse of the French government with respect to a stipulation that each of the parties may, without the consent of the other, admit whomsoever it pleases to navigate the river and trade with their respective shores, on the same terms as in other parts of France and the U.S." While France was unlikely to concur, the U.S. would look good in Great Britain, and it would show "a just attention to interests of our own western citizens, whose commerce will not otherwise be on an equal footing with that of the Atlantic states."[6]

Similarly, the U.S. legation at Madrid had been urging Livingston to press the French to assure American rights on the Mississippi, lest the western population gain the impression that "any advantages they may enjoy on the Mississippi are more indebted to the good intentions of the French government than to the exertion of their own."[7]

It was in regard to the danger of having France as the neighbor of the U.S. on the Mississippi that Livingston rued Washington's decision not to reaffirm the 1778 Franco-American alliance treaty, as had been proposed by the French negotiators in preparing the 1800 treaty. He wrote to Madison on January 15, 1802:

> The reluctance we have shown to a renewal of the treaty of 1778 has created many suspicions, [and the French] say expressly that they would have had no pretence, so far as related to the Floridas, to make this exchange had the treaty been renewed, since by the sixth article they are expressly prohibited from touching the Floridas. I own I have always considered this article and the guarantee of our independence as more important to us than the [U.S.] guarantee of the islands is to France.[8]

Continuing on this theme, Livingston on March 10, 1802, asserted in a letter to his London counterpart and fellow New Yorker Rufus King, who thought his position overstated, that Britain had a "right" to introduce "this business at Amiens." Livingston justified his view with the argument that many Indians in Louisiana preferred the French due

> both from the disposition and manners of the people and from the whole body ... [of traders with Indians] being native Canadians and much the greater part of them mongrel French. It is impossible to say what their influence may be upon our western country in case of a controversy with Great Britain.... Nor is the right of Britain to interfere ['in this business' of the retrocession of Louisiana] unfounded. By the 6th article of the treaty with the U.S. of 1778, [the French] absolutely renounce all right to take under any circumstances any part of the country possessed then or before by Britain on that continent ... [While we] have relinquished all advantages deducible from the treaty, yet, in so far as other nations were interested in it at the close of the last war, they have a right to enforce it, and surely it was a very important guarantee to Britain of her colonies, and it might have had great influence upon the terms of the ... peace.[9]

In their interesting and friendly correspondence,[10] which led to a relatively lengthy visit by King to Livingston at Paris in fall 1802, King correctly noted that, while respect for that article might have blocked France from taking any part of Florida, that consideration alone could not have prevented the Spanish retrocession to it of Louisiana, including New Orleans. King also argued that post–Bourbon France, in any event, would not have been restrained by a provision of a 1778 treaty, and he concluded by characterizing Livingston's point as merely raising a "fun" issue. An excerpt from King's letter to Livingston of April 25, 1802, is worth repeating here:

> Louisiana, including New Orleans and consequently both banks of the Mississippi with its mouth, might have been ceded to France without affecting, or being restrained by, the treaty to which you refer.... The renunciation of France, whatever may be the territorial limits to which it applies, took effect and was complete as soon as the treaty was concluded, and, being an executed and not an executory stipulation, cannot be defeated by the abolition of the treaty.... Lastly (supposing that neither of these remarks are well-founded) does the conduct of France in other instances, and towards other states, authorize the belief that she would have desisted from her long meditated project respecting Louisiana had the treaties remained in force?[11]

King's last point is reinforced by the vehemence with which France, as shown earlier in this study, had pressed Spain to the end to relinquish at least West Florida to it as part of the retrocession of Louisiana; West

Florida, under Article 6, would have been precluded from returning to French sovereignty after having been ceded to the British in the peace of 1763. Still, it is true that he did raise the relevancy of the Franco-American alliance treaty to present circumstances in his correspondence with the British government. Thus, he wrote foreign minister Hawkesbury on April 21, 1802, that, by the treaty of 1778, France had "renounced forever the possession of every part of the continent of America lying to the east of the course of the River Mississippi. This renunciation [confirmed] that which had been previously made in the treaty of 1763 between Great Britain and France." King continued that reports held Spain had ceded "Louisiana and the Floridas" to France. Since the Anglo-American treaty of 1783 gave both countries "free and open" navigation of the Mississippi, he would appreciate learning whether Britain had received "any communication ... from the government of France or the government of Spain respecting the said cession," or whether Britain had "acquiesced in or sanctioned the same, so as to impair or affect the stipulation" in the Anglo-American treaty of 1783.

Hawkesbury's answer of 5 May was to the effect that, were France to take Louisiana, that would have to come "subject to all the engagements which appertained to it at the time of the cession" by Spain to Britain. Therefore, there was no way France could exclude British or American citizens "from the navigation" of the Mississippi. Moreover, "No communication whatever" had been received from France or Spain regarding a cession "of Louisiana or the Floridas," and, in any event, Britain would never, "in any manner, directly or indirectly, acquiesce in or sanction this cession."[12]

Livingston, despite King's arguments, seems never to have changed his mind on the issue of whether the U.S. erred in terminating the 1778 treaty. For example, he wrote his friend from the days of the American Revolution, Du Ponceau, who now had returned to his native France, on June 30, 1802: "I say nothing to you of Louisiana. It is a delicate subject, but what are we to do? Had our old treaty not been given up, the Floridas at least could never [have passed] pass into the hands of France, and, as to the rest, it is of less importance."[13] Similarly, on 24 April, Livingston wrote the following to Governor Monroe:

> Not renewing the treaty of 1778 had been the most unwise thing we ever did. By the 6th article of it, we were secured against France ever possessing the Floridas. These are now in their hands. The evils that this exchange with Spain may occasion are incalculable. They have the most exalted ideas of their importance, and they will compel us to keep up an expensive confrontation on their frontier. Something should instantly be done to give the trade to the Natchez or some other port

within our territory. When they find their visionary plans are not realized, they may perhaps change this favorite system.

Regarding the point that the U.S. in this period lacked interest in obtaining land west of the Mississippi River, Livingston confirmed it directly to the French when, at a meeting with Joseph Bonaparte on 26 October of that year, having been asked "whether we should prefer the Floridas to Louisiana, I told him there was no comparison in their value, but that we had no wish to extend our boundary across the Mississippi, or give color to the doubts that had been entertained of the moderation of our view, that all we sought was security and not an extension of territory." Joseph responded that Spain would not make "any new cession."[14]

Here we see early evidence of a French interest in ceding Louisiana west of the Mississippi to the U.S. Also worth noting is that Livingston's disinterest in procuring land west of the Mississippi was fully shared by the U.S. government as reflected in the instructions Madison gave him and Monroe on March 2, 1803 (see following). A final observation regarding this important conversation: it hinted at Livingston's skepticism, which he would maintain right up to the start of the negotiations of April 1803, that Spain was also adamantly against ceding at least the western part of Florida back to France.

For the entire first half of Livingston's three-year tour, he experienced total frustration regarding both his tasks. France was nearly bankrupt; and it was unwilling even to acknowledge officially to the world that it had reached an agreement with Spain for the retrocession of Louisiana. The financial obstacle was self-evident, although not all that insurmountable in Livingston's skeptical eyes. Livingston wrote to Morris on January 14, 1802 that the government of France had already "consumed three months of their next year's revenue." But, more skeptically, he wrote to Brockholst Livingston on September 23, 1802 that "expensive" projects were being undertaken in France even as it pleaded poverty regarding its foreign debts. By February 1803, the minister was so increasingly frank with the French authorities regarding his views of French financial policy that he elicited some equally frank comments from Talleyrand in a letter of March 11, 1803. Tallyrand stated the first consul had seriously considered his "memoire" [of 27 February]; he had also had a report made on all relevant documents cited in that document and had authorized Talleyrand to state to Livingston that all French treaty commitments to the U.S. would be "punctually and scrupulously implemented"; none of the "difficulties" in doing so that Livingston referred to were related to any kind of "disposition" or "financial situation" of the French government. According to Tallyrand,

"The First Consul is persuaded that the assumptions which have misled you on this point are without foundation and are due to your concerns over our goodwill [*inquietude de bienveillance*], but these assumptions do not at all accord with the facts. There are no financial problems whatever in France." The French government could and would meet all "legitimate claims," but it did not see how those claims could amount to 20 million livres; the first consul asked Livingston for an exact accounting: "His full confidence in you precludes any doubt that your account will be based on your discernment and candor of character.... Be sure, M., that, once your account is presented, all will be paid promptly and precisely."[15]

Livingston treated this letter as a breakthrough and trumpeted it throughout the American commercial community. To the extent this public move added pressure on the French authorities to live up to its 1800 treaty with the U.S., if only to avoid seeing the first consul lose credibility, it can be considered as a distinct contribution to Napoleon's decision shortly thereafter to sell Louisiana to the Americans.[16] Although the financial authorities in the French government failed to provide Livingston with the cooperation that was necessary to his presenting the "exact accounting" requested by the first consul, he managed to develop sufficient data to enable the negotiations of the very next month to produce the last of the three conventions that comprised the agreement of 30 April (i.e., the assumption by the U.S. government of the responsibility for the estimated 20 million livres owed by France to American claimants). The pay-out process of 1803–04 was to cause Livingston endless personal anguish in his final year as minister at Paris, because it was fraught with conflict and accusations of favoritism, all of which besmirched that minister's reputation. As one historian noted: "Sharp differences of opinion arose between Livingston and the American commissioners" charged with adjudicating the American claims in consultation with the French government.[17] (Once a claim was endorsed, Livingston's role was to authorize payment on the U.S. Treasury.) Even before the agreement of 30 April, Livingston had been the target of personal criticisms for his allegedly inept handling of the debt problem; for example, he wrote to Ambrose Spencer on January 13, 1803, that that problem was the source of "lies" about him in the U.S. newspapers due to reports from American claimants in France who were "nine out of ten ... Tories."[18]

It did not help matters for Livingston's brother, John, to have been an interested party in the debt issue. For example, John wrote Robert on March 3, 1803, that war between the U.S. and France could not be long as the U.S. was much agitated with respect to the Mississippi "business," and, that he had his "power of attorney to enable you to settle my French concerns" as soon as possible given the "prospect of war."

But the reasons for French (along with Spanish) reticence on Louisiana and the Floridas were even more bewildering and upsetting in Livingston's mind than was the problem of the American claimants. He believed that it was his country's perceived military weakness that best explained French disregard of his demands for information and formal reassurances with respect to American legal rights in the lower Mississippi as well as in West Florida, where other rivers originating in the U.S. also flowed into the Gulf of Mexico. Livingston expressed his views perhaps most strongly and uninhibitedly in a letter to Spanish ambassador D'Azara at Paris on May 28, 1802. That letter throws interesting light not only on the issues underlying the negotiation of the Louisiana Purchase, but also on the related ones between the U.S. and Spain that would continue after that purchase and end with America's forceful seizures of both Floridas.[19]

According to Livingston, Spain should have informed the U.S., its neighbor and friend, of the cession that it was generally understood Spain had made of Louisiana to France. As regards the 1795 treaty, how far had Spain, in its arrangements with France, provided for the stipulations secured therein to the U.S.? Undoubtedly, Spain had respected the boundary between their respective governments, but, in accordance with the fourth Article, the mid-channel of the Mississippi was the dividing line, and navigation there was to be confined to the subjects of Spain and the citizens of the U.S. unless extended to others by special convention. He was solicitous to know in what manner the rights of the citizens of the U.S. in this river were preserved by the terms of the cession. In the Spanish-controlled two banks, the U.S. by treaty had a qualified right of navigation of which they could not be divested, and also the assurance of Spain that no other nation should share this right unless by convention. He saw that provision as requiring a prior U.S.–Spanish understanding.

He presumed that, in the cession Spain had made, the Floridas were not included because of the evident interest it had in retaining them as a security for its territories in South America, if unfortunate events were thereafter to produce a rupture between France and Spain. In such a situation, the Floridas would be at the rear of the French colonies and so could serve as an effectual check to them as well as to those turbulent spirits in the adjoining U.S. who might, in spite of the efforts of their government have been inclined to associate in the intrigues of France. The U.S.-Spanish treaty mutually gave each of them the right to expect some security regarding this subject; therefore, the U.S. required explicit information on the cession to France. D'Azara should recall that under Article 5 Spain was to restrain by force all hostilities on the part of the Indian nations living within its boundary either on the citizens of the U.S. or on the Indians residing within U.S. territory. Spain could not without the consent of the U.S. place itself in a situation to render this national obligation of no effect. According to Article 22, Spain stipulated to permit the citizens of the U.S. to deposit their goods at New Orleans. If the Floridas were part of the cession, what stipulations were in it insuring to the U.S. this important privilege? If the cession was a naked one without attention to these articles, the U.S. would have reason to complain of the measure. Therefore, there would be propriety for the U.S. to be one of the parties to any treaty in which its rights could be so materially affected.

The letter continued, such an observation would be made by the U.S. officially at Madrid, but in the meantime, as it was his intention to address himself upon this subject to the government of France, Livingston wished to receive from the ambassador every information that might throw light on the subject. D'Azara was asked to treat this letter as an unofficial note and as a mark of his confidence in him. The ambassador thereby had an opportunity to help Livingston give efficacy to a treaty that had served as the basis of friendship between their two countries.

Livingston followed up this letter with one to his counterpart in Madrid, Charles Pinckney, on 2 June that merely summarized the points he made in it, but that did enclose D'Azara's answer, which Livingston highlighted as follows: The Floridas were not included, and D'Azara "is not entrusted with the negotiations." Livingston therefore underlined to Pinckney that "it is important that you should know these facts which I now have ascertained," and that, given the key role being played by France "in this business," he should keep him informed so that "I may aid your measures as far as lays in my power." In the event, Madrid would make clear to Pinckney that it was in France, not Spain, that the U.S. should seek to satisfy its goals regarding Louisiana. Graham's 12 July dispatch to Livingston reported that Pinckney had been orally informed by the Spanish foreign minister that, "if the King does think proper to part with Louisiana, he will do nothing to the prejudice of the U.S." (It would only be on March 31, 1803, that the Spanish government would make an "acknowledgment in writing ... [that Louisiana] was ceded subject to the subsequent treaties of Spain with other powers"—as Pinckney put it on April 3, transmitting the text of that acknowledgment from Cevallos, here was "the declaration in writing which you and I have been long trying to get.")[20]

To return to the message of 12 July from Graham, who had spent private time with an impressed Madison prior to leaving for Spain, and who developed a warm relationship with Livingston during their trans–Atlantic voyage and onward trip to Paris, it included the advice that the question of Louisiana regarded

> a great national affair which will now be under your management.... This is not, in my opinion, the candid answer [by the government of Spain] which ought to have been given to questions so direct.... We have but little to expect from the friendship or even justice of this nation, particularly if to aid us they are obliged to move in opposition to the wishes of France.... You will receive but little aid from them in your negotiations to obtain from the French government a [confirmation?] of our rights on the Mississippi.[21]

Meanwhile, on June 30, 1802, Livingston had written to King in London reporting that D'Azara had "answered with great frankness that he was a stranger to this transaction ... but that he had reason to believe that the Floridas were not included." Livingston there opined that the U.S., failing to buy West Florida, should work to keep it under Spain "under the mutual guarantee of France and the U.S." while pressuring France to give "a renunciation of it similar to that contained in our former treaty" (that is, Article 6 of the 1778 treaty of alliance). Livingston continued that if France did indeed obtain West Florida under the cession from Spain, "it should be restored to Madrid or sold to the U.S ... and New Orleans should become a free port and, if possible, a free state."

King's response of 12 July was that, once Louisiana was ceded, he saw Spain as having also to cede all the Floridas, because they were only useful to it if Louisiana was a Spanish possession. He observed that even if the Floridas were not ceded to France, the latter could seize them any time it wished, and this was a fact the U.S. had to recognize in its policy toward Florida. (King might have added more germanely that the reverse was also true: without the Floridas, a French Louisiana would always be militarily insecure as regarded the British and Americans. This strategic fact helps explain France's persistent, if unsuccessful, effort, even after its 30 April agreement with the U.S., to have the Floridas west of Pensacola included in the Spanish cession of Louisiana; and it probably contributed to Napoleon's decision to cede a Louisiana that lacked the Floridas to the U.S.) King, taking exception to Livingston's idea of a joint Franco-American guarantee of Spanish Florida, observed that, given the importance of navigation, the U.S. must sooner or later, one way or another, have both New Orleans and the Floridas. Therefore, it must avoid giving any guarantee to France regarding the Spanish possession of the Floridas. He justified this by underlining that any new war between France and Britain would then require the U.S. to fight against Britain, because the latter would surely try to "take possession of New Orleans and the Floridas"; moreover, such a guarantee could be a block to their seizure by the U.S. King further recalled that Spain, fearful of a U.S.-style revolt by its American colonies, had pressed Thomas Pinckney in 1795 to guarantee those colonies, and that Pinckney declined to do so. King concluded by arguing against the U.S. giving "explicit sanction to the transfer of [the Floridas] from Spain to any other power," and against the U.S. giving "money in order that they may be left in this situation," even though "we may at present be content they should remain the possession of Spain."

Interestingly, the Jefferson Administration, in its anxiety to obtain New Orleans and the Floridas, authorized Pinckney to offer Spain a U.S. guarantee of its remaining possessions in North America (i.e., the territory west of the Mississippi). Pinckney did so in March 1803, further complicating the question of Spain's role in the negotiations over the Floridas and drawing the following reprimand of 20 April from Livingston:

> I am fearful that you have in some sort mistaken the intentions of government in the offer you made.... Spain has no possessions on the west of the Mississippi but Mexico since the cession of Louisiana, and it certainly cannot have been the intention of our government to guarantee Mexico, to which length the generality of your expressions would go. But as Monroe ... will, if necessary, be with you, you will of course suspend any further offer on the ground you have taken.[22]

Livingston summarized his views on the question of Louisiana and the Floridas along the following lines in a dispatch to Madison on July 30, 1802: "I am now preparing a lengthy memoir on the subject of the mutual interest of France and the U.S. relative to Louisiana, by which I hope to convince that, both in a commercial and political view, the possession of it would be disadvantageous to France." The Floridas were most surely not in the cession, and he had "been applied to by one of the ministers here to know what we understood in America by Louisiana — you can easily conceive my answer." He had also underlined to the French that, according to Article 5 of the French-Spanish treaty of March 26, 1802, the cession of Louisiana was "of Louisiana generally." France "always extended the term to South Carolina," and this naturally would be unacceptable to the U.S.[23]

Livingston finished with: "In the meantime, all that can be done here [pending the departure of the French expedition to Louisiana][24] will be to endeavor to obtain a cession of New Orleans, either by purchase or by offering to make it a port of entry to France on such terms as shall promise advantages to her commerce and give her hopes of introducing her manufactures and wines into our western country.... [This could] only be hurtful to Britain."

Were the U.S. to have the Floridas and New Orleans, any French colonies west of the Mississippi "would be too feeble to injure us. I find them very anxious to have the ports of Pensacola and Augustine, as they dread our having the command of the Gulf. I confess this appears to me no very important object, and, if they would be content with this, and give us West Florida and New Orleans, even at a large price, we should not hesitate." He still needed an upper amount the U.S. could offer France.[25]

On 2 August, Livingston wrote King that he would send him a copy of his Louisiana memoir, copies of which had been "struck off" in French "with a view to place them in such hands as have influence to serve us. I think with you on the subject of the guarantee." On arrival, Livingston's letter continued, he was told the Floridas were part of the cession, but Talleyrand's reticence, which forced him to "sound" the Spanish ambassador — coupled with the fact that "Louisiana" in the French-Spanish treaty of March 1802 always was a "generality" and that France "always extended that term to the territory on both sides of the Mississippi" — probably meant that France "supposed" the Floridas were part of the cession: "I believe the first doubt they had on the subject arose from my note."

In early August, Livingston circulated his "Louisiana memoir" under a third-person cover note (for example, to Consuls Cambeceres and Lebrun). That note included the point that an earlier memoir of his on the subject of Louisiana "unhappily [did] not lead to the measures Mr. Livingston wished." The note then advised that Livingston was seeking "to avert a measure which he considers as having a dangerous effect upon that harmony which he wishes to promote," and that he had no view of "publication ... several reasons inducing Mr. Livingston to wish that it may not pass into many hands."[26]

However, a mere one day later, Livingston would send a copy of the memoir to his brother, Edward: "You may share this [copy] where you think it will be of use to me, but not suffer for it to be printed." Livingston went on to explain that he was running "a personal risk, since ... I am left without any precise information as to the wishes of the government as would serve to justify anything I may do or leave undone." As to be discussed later, within a year it was, of course, published in newspapers with attendant diplomatic and personal complications for an apologetic Livingston.

By 19 August, Livingston, frustrated that he hadn't received any reaction from Talleyrand to his memoir, wrote that minister that he had hoped France would sell New Orleans and West Florida to the U.S. so that it and France would be left with a "natural boundary." Now, Livingston continued, he heard that

2. The Failed Negotiations of 1802   43

> measures are in agitation for carrying the cession into [~~immediate~~] effect.... It becomes my duty to state that both by treaty with Great Britain and with Spain, the U.S. are entitled [by the treaty with Britain] to a property in a considerable part of the River Mississippi, together with the free navigation of it in its utmost extent. They are also entitled by their treaty with Spain to an entry into the port of New Orleans with the privilege of depositing their goods and exporting from thence subject to no duty whatsoever.

Moreover, the letter continued, the U.S. and Spain had agreed by treaty on "stipulations" regarding the Indians that "are equally important to the U.S. and the nation that may possess the Floridas." The letter concluded:

> These circumstances entitled the U.S. to have been so far parties to the treaty of cession as to have enabled them to make such steps as circumstances might require for the security of their rights. Not however having been called upon to concur in this measure, they have a claim to such information ... and such explanations of the intentions of France as shall leave them no doubts upon the subject.... It was not in the power of Spain to make any cession except such as should be subordinate to their treaties with the U.S.[27].... The military force of France and the change of circumstances may render farther assurances and explanations necessary as well to serve as a director to her own officers.

The very final lines of this letter contained an ominous warning that the government of France's "silence" could well lead to America's taking "such contingency measures as may lay the foundation for future jealousies between the two republics."

This exercise brought Livingston into official contact with Joseph Bonaparte, whose 3 September note was a brief acknowledgment of having received the memoir. That it produced no results is clear from Livingston's plaintive, but significant letter of 24 December to Joseph, asking how Napoleon had reacted to "my project ... [now that] a few weeks" had passed.[28] The situation was particularly worrisome, because Britain was pushing the U.S. to settle "her south western line" with it, and "is anxious to come down to a navigable part of the Mississippi so as to communicate with Canada by that channel."[29] Obviously, Britain's true goal was

> the future possession of the mouth [of that river,] ... a project which would naturally form the moment she saw Louisiana pass into the hands of her rival, and I am sorry to say that it is one she will find no difficulty in executing unless prevented by the U.S., for France is too far to protect a young colony from an established one [i.e., Canada],

aided by numerous savage nations, by provincial troops, and by other troops that Canada may afford.... While the conduct of France speaks a language so harmful to the American government, there is too much reason to believe that [the U.S.] will be little solicitous in so forming their limits as to cover [France's] possessions.[Livingston] would much have preferred to urge Mr. King not to conclude such a boundary agreement as Britain was seeking; and that, if the first consul approved his project for the purchase of New Orleans and West Florida, it will be essential to the security of the possessions of France and the peace of this country, to remove the British boundary as high up the river as possible so as to prevent any communications with Canada by the rivers that fall on the side into the Lakes and on the other into the Mississippi....[30] If my project is obstructed only by the non-conclusion of the treaty with Spain regarding the Floridas ... [negotiations could still go on between France and the U.S.] for New Orleans and the territory above the River Arkansas. [The treaty with the U.S.] could also solve the problem of the French "debt to our citizens" by "advantageous arrangements" for France. [Joseph] should be sure that what I have hitherto written has passed into no hands but those of the First Consul or some other members of your own family, as I fear my communications out of the ordinary channel might be ill-taken where I am solicitous to stand well [read: Talleyrand].

To complete here this aspect of the story, although King in May 1803 did sign an agreement with Britain for establishing a boundary between Canada and the U.S., only in 1842 would a final boundary line be agreed to, and that line fell short of reaching the source of the Mississippi River.[31] Jefferson erred in his letter of August 12, 1803, to Breckenridge when, regarding the extent of the land he had just learned that the U.S. had purchased, he stated that, "The boundaries, which I deem not admitting question, are the highlands on the western side of the Mississippi enclosing all its waters, the Missouri, of course, and *terminating in the line drawn from the northwestern point of the Lake of the Woods to the nearest source of the Mississippi, as lately settled between Great Britain and the U.S.* [emphasis added]." Earlier that year, Jefferson, according to a letter from King to Livingston on 25 April, had told the British minister to the U.S., Thornton, that the retrocession to France "will unavoidably produce jealousies, irritation and hostilities, and, with regard to ['the settlement of our northwestern boundary'], the president suggested the expediency of a diplomatic settlement, by its being agreed to run a line from the western bay of Lake Superior to such part of the Mississippi as is nearest to Lake Superior." This reported presidential suggestion was consistent with Gallatin's note to Jefferson of March 14, 1803, advising that he "has requested Mr. King to project a blank map, giving the whole course of the Mississippi and the Pacific coast from 30 degrees to 55 degrees north latitude, etc." Also note

2. The Failed Negotiations of 1802   45

Livingston's rather boastful post-purchase letter to Madison of June 25, 1803, complaining that Madison had never "noticed or encouraged" his effort to use the "negotiation with Britain for ascertaining your northwestern boundary " as leverage with France in an effort to get to "put us in possession of the country above the Arkansas.... You may attribute the success of our negotiations ... [to my having] carefully concealed my want of powers ... [as I pressured France, and] the firm attitude that our government took."[32]

Returning now to the period immediately following Livingston's distribution of his Louisiana memoir in August 1802, France, of course, had its own reasons, unrelated to its bilateral relations with the U.S., for its policy of "silence" toward the Americans. In point, while the retrocession, thanks to Napoleon's hard line with Madrid, had indeed been agreed to in more or less final form as early as March 1802, it nevertheless still was tied to certain European territorial compensations for the Spanish Bourbons that, along with the related issue of West Florida, delayed the start of its formal implementation until later that year. As Livingston over confidently wrote Madison on November 10, 1802: "France has cut the Gordian Knot. The difficulties relative to Parma and Pleasance ... have ended."[33] (Livingston's personal investment in having the negotiations for the sale of the Floridas to the U.S. take place in Paris rather than in Madrid is one likely explanation for his periodic assurances that Spain indeed had ceded, or certainly would cede, that territory to France; consistent with this personal interest in seeing such a negotiation transpire was his dispatch to Madison of May 28, 1802, where he took undue credit for having "started" the French "doubt" that Spain intended to cede Florida to them as part of the retrocession.)

Livingston again assured Madison, this time on 20 December, that France was very likely to obtain the Floridas, because "Parma is a favorite object of Spain. Pray be specific in the amount I may offer." The minister then urged that the offer be a high one, because Napoleon was stubborn on having Louisiana. Therefore, Madison shouldn't get his hopes up — Talleyrand having told Livingston just the previous day that the first consul was "*entêté* [stubborn] with this project."

However, Livingston, as we have seen in his letter of 24 December to Joseph, soon was having second thoughts on this assurance to Madison that a deal for Florida had been cut. Accordingly, he wrote Graham at Madrid on February 28, 1803, that the French proposed to receive Florida up to Pensacola "in exchange for Parma," and that he should try to block this, if it had not yet been accepted. (It hadn't.) A final example of the connection between the Floridas and European arrangements is from Madison's letter to Livingston, dated October 6, 1803, reporting that recent Spanish notes advised that the Louisiana cession to France was conditioned on France's getting Russia and Great Britain to recognize the Spanish Bourbon "King of Etruria [Etruscan Italy]," and that the French had failed to do so.[34] (Spain in this period was fruitlessly protesting to the U.S. the illegality of the French cession of Louisiana to the U.S.[35])

An even more serious obstacle to the prompt transfer of Louisiana to France was with regard to the military situation. First, there was the uncertain outcome of its struggle to keep control of St. Domingue, for which purpose the first consul, early in 1802, had sent a fresh army there under his brother-in-law, General Leclerc.[36] The evolution of this activity may briefly be traced as follows: (a) Livingston to King, December 30, 1801: "A part of the armament destined for Hispaniola, if Toussaint does not give it opposition, is destined for Louisiana"; (b) King to Livingston, June 18, 1802: "Toussaint's submission will not relieve France from the maintenance of a large military force in Hispaniola, which must be fed from the U.S., but it will enable her to detach a considerable body of troops to the Mississippi"; and (c), Livingston to Jefferson, October 28, 1802: "The Mississippi business ... has met with a check.... Events may possibly arise of which we may avail ourselves." (Napoleon would place the blame for that "check" on General Leclerc for having misplayed his plan, which was not to oppose Toussaint but rather to win his loyalty and then to send "an army of from 25,000 to 30,000 blacks" on expeditions "against Jamaica, the Antilles, Canada, the United States themselves, or the Spanish colonies."[37])

A second reason for the French posture of silence toward Livingston regarding Louisiana concerned the implications of the rekindling of war with Britain, a development that was coming increasingly into view despite the above-noted signing at Amiens of the definitive peace treaty on March 27, 1802. For example, Livingston wrote Madison on August 12 and 16 of 1802 and noted that war seemed to be coming closer between France and England: "Good may arise out of this evil, if it should happen." A key issue, as subsequently explained in King's letter of April 8, 1803, to Livingston, was over British hesitation to withdraw from Malta as required by the Amiens treaty. King wrote that since England, not trusting Napoleon's future military intentions, will not "evacuate Malta, ... all must therefore depend on the First Consul, who must abandon the Treaty of Amiens so far as respects Malta, or take war." On 29 March, King had noted that each side "would prefer to receive, rather than to give, the assault."[38] As more specifically regards the Louisiana question, Napoleon's problem was that, were that war to start with France already in formal possession of New Orleans, Britain would quickly and easily seize it.

On this particular matter, Madison, well before learning of the April breakthrough with Napoleon, penned a dispatch on May 28, 1803, to Livingston and Monroe addressing the question of whether a belligerent could sell a territory to a neutral in order to avoid its capture by an enemy, especially if the latter was known to have actually projected its capture.[39] His answer: (a) Negotiations between the U.S. and France had begun "prior to the war"; (b) a neutral had the right to purchase; (c) there was no "collusion" with France to return the territory to it after the war; and (d), neutrals had a positive right to purchase in the interest of peace over belligerents' right to occupy a territory as a reward of war.[40] Madison also noted that the U.S. had already protected itself against all contingencies consequent to a sale. It did so by having obtained Britain's assurance that, were France in fact to have sold New Orleans to the U.S. even after the renewal of armed conflict between France and Britain, the latter would respect that purchase whatever the outcome of the war. King referred to that assurance in a letter he wrote to Livingston on March 11, 1803: "If you are authorized to negotiate a purchase, would not the occupation [of New Orleans] by the English benefit your bargain, *it being well previously understood that, if we obtain the title, they would give us the possession?* [emphasis added]." King ended this letter as follows: "You see, I write in confidence and without the least nuance; I need not say that it is merely between you and me."[41]

As a matter of fact, King, of course, had already advised Washington of this understanding with Britain and followed this up with a report to Madison on April 2, 1803, regarding his conversation with the British foreign minister. When Addington said, "if the war happens, it would perhaps, be one of the first steps to occupy New Orleans," King answered that,

> True it was, we could not see with indifference that country in the hands of France; but it was equally true, that it would be contrary to our views, and with much concern, that we should see it in the possession of England; we had no objection to Spain continuing to possess it; they were quiet neighbors, and we looked forward without impatience to events which, in the ordinary course of things, must, at no distant day, annex this country to the U.S. [Addington] assured that England would not accept the country, were all agreed to give it to her; ... would not ... keep it, but to prevent another power from obtaining it.... This end would be best effected by its belonging to the U.S.[42]

As for France's take on this matter, Talleyrand in April 1803 rebutted to Livingston that this alleged arrangement between the U.S. and Britain "proceeded upon a supposition of [Britain] making so successful a war as to be enabled to retain her conquests."[43]

Madison, too, had his own position on this, as was made evident in that same 28 May message from the secretary to Livingston and Monroe mentioned earlier. In it, he stated that the British had assured King that, if war came, they would seize New Orleans—but for the U.S. and not for themselves. Then, "If the councils of France should be guided by half the wisdom [of Britain on this matter,] ... your negotiation will be made very easy."

However, the British would try to bring America into the war as the price for New Orleans. In view of these factors, Madison stated, the U.S. government wanted to move forward on reaching an understanding with France, which, given the new situation, should accept a lesser offer from it. Therefore, the original instructions to them were now changed. First, they should request "jurisdiction of a reasonable district on some convenient part of the banks of the Mississippi"; France shouldn't control there either of the river's shores unless there was no other way for "the attainment of the great object we have in view." Second, the U.S. needed to avoid an arrangement with France upsetting to Britain, given what King had been told by that government, whose goal was to preclude French control over New Orleans. Third, the two were to avoid, if possible, granting a "guarantee of the country beyond the Mississippi," especially given that, in line with what Britain was telling the U.S., it was "improbable ... that Great Britain is meditating plans for the emancipation and independence of the whole of the American continent south of the U.S."; any guarantee should only apply "to the state of things as it may be fixed by a peace." Finally, in view of Britain's plan to occupy New Orleans, "the preliminary sum of $2 million or any part of it [should not be paid] ... till possession shall be given to the U.S. ... [unless France agreed to give the U.S.] security against eventual loss."

In effect, while Livingston's approach favored an immediate *American* occupation of New Orleans, if France were to continue blocking it from them after taking possession of it from Spain, and Rufus King's approach would seem to have favored facilitating an *English* occupation, Madison's, as will be further discussed, was neither of these two but rather to limit American efforts entirely to peaceful persuasion unless the French not only declined to offer the U.S. a right of deposit at the mouth of the Mississippi but also closed that river's outlet to American navigation.

A concise picture of Livingston's views on the particular role of Britain regarding Louisiana may be gleaned from his letters of March 8 and 11 to King, sent just prior to his learning from Pinckney of Madrid's cancellation of the intendant's October 1802 action against the U.S.[44] Key points in the first letter are as follows: All at court except, so far, Napoleon, now saw the subject of Louisiana "as I do." He has sent the first consul "a very strong letter" and was laboring to "pave the way" for Monroe: "I have not hesitated to declare that if they kept the port shut after the island [New Orleans] is delivered up, the U.S. will not wait the effects of a negotiation."

Livingston's follow up letter of 11 March included that he was "now sending in a note couched in very plain terms" declaring that there was no way the U.S. would "admit ... [the validity of any] treaty as to our right of deposit or to what we hold ... [under the Pinckney Treaty, unless it contains] an explicit recognition of our rights.... I have no specific powers as to anything.... Mr. Madison informs me that I am to receive them with a new commission by Mr. Monroe. Nothing will be listened to in the way of purchase."

As regards King's worthwhile idea to begin negotiations with Britain, that would guard against the U.S. placing

> ourselves in the situation of the horse in the stable, [but] on the other [hand], we must ... consider well whether we shall not make ourselves parties to the war by the interest the British will have in betraying the secret [that] such a negotiation is made. On the whole, I think it would be more dignified and more safe to act on our [own], and, if we must enter into it, reserve to ourselves all the advantages that may result from it.... Will the British think themselves, as you seem to suppose, authorized to stop the sailing of the armaments in the French and Dutch ports?

The candid "note" Livingston told King he was planning to send Talleyrand was dated 16 March, by which time he had learned of the Madrid court's cancellation of the intendant's action. To Livingston's mind, if the idea of assigning Bernadotte to the U.S. as minister was that of obtaining information "related to the formation of a new treaty, I should find no objection.... But, Sir, it is not a new treaty upon which we press (though one mutually advantageous might certainly be made), but the recognition of an old one." The U.S. would never "relinquish" its rights of "navigation" and "deposit," except "with their political existence." By Spain's now deciding to continue New Orleans beyond the first three years as the site of America's depot, "the U.S. have by this continuance acquired a permanent and irrevocable right to a depot at New Orleans.... Even the assignment of another equivalent establishment cannot at this day be forced [on the U.S.] ... without their consent." France more than Spain should see the importance of New Orleans as America's depot, because she would be able to "exchange [her] produce of ... agriculture and manufactures ... for the raw materials of the U.S.... Under these circumstances, at the very moment that Spain is about to relinquish the possession of the country to France,

[Spain] violates her treaty and leaves the country with a stain upon her character.... [The French will arrive with] an armament ... [and will find] the port has been shut by the order of Spain."[45] Would the French commander "think himself authorized to open it?" If not, Bernadotte would have to arrive at Washington and send information back to his government before the port could be opened. Livingston noted, "There is only one season in which the navigation of the Mississippi is practicable," and therefore the American products would "rot."

Also under these circumstances, there was no way the U.S. government would be able to prevent the American "people" from doing "themselves justice." That would be less likely for the U.S. government to be able to avoid than preventing "the Mississippi from rolling its waters into the ocean." Were the Ottoman Empire to give the Dardanelles to Austria, or were a fleet to block the Chesapeake, that would have less impact than in comparison with the situation at New Orleans. It was hard enough, said Livingston, for the U.S. to keep "from breaking out ... into acts of immediate hostility against Spain," hence the important role of "the mission of a minister" to convince France to give "immediate and express recognition of their rights by France in whose justice and good faith they hope to find a resource against the break of faith by the officers of Spain."

Surely, felt Livingston, the first consul (whose answer to him through Talleyrand on 11 March referenced "such new treaties as it may be for the mutual interest") saw justice and interest as arguing in favor of giving immediate recognition to existing U.S. rights; otherwise, he'd "force them to connect their interests with those of a rival power." Louisiana would never be worth that outcome for any "European power." For all these reasons, and for his "pain" at foreseeing "future enmities," Livingston hoped "they will serve as an apology for anything that appears harsh in this note."

While in the event all three approaches—Livingston's, Madison's and King's—undoubtedly came into play as possible scenarios as Napoleon weighed a decision whether to cede Louisiana to the U.S., it surely was Madison's that was the key to success, because any demonstration of U.S., or U.S.-encouraged, aggression against Bourbon territory prior to that cession would surely have precluded the happy outcome of April 1803. One indication in support of this conclusion — and in clarification of why Livingston on 10 April sent a despairing and personally fateful note to Monroe upon news of his arrival in France — is contained in his plaintive-cum-threatening letter to Talleyrand of 22 March.

"I feel some mortification," he said, "[that the foreign minister's note of the previous day] contained nothing more decisive upon the interesting subject that I have submitted to your consideration [on 16 March] and still more that you should think the sensibility that the inhabitants of the U.S. have manifested upon the change in the situation of Louisiana repugnant to the sentiments of friendship which the former conduct of France ought to inspire." French power and enterprise could, as a neighbor of the U.S., lead, by "a variety of circumstances in the common course of events, to painful [conflict] discussions." France's policy of "secrecy" and exclusion of the U.S. from "the treaty to which they [claim a right] might have expected to be parties," did not help to calm it. Moreover, the treaty itself is "concealed from them." Furthermore, French "armaments prepared for North America remain unexplained to the U.S. minister," who, moreover, was not "informed except through [his colleague at] the medium of another court of the present arrangements with respect to that armament."[46]

Livingston made plain his ultimate fear: "I fear France plans only at the last moment to inform us of what arrangements it proposes as successor" to Louisiana — [leaving us no choice but to acquire] arrangements which its authorities "conceive need only to have been mentioned to have been taken."

Ironically, it was back in the very period when Livingston was most spinning his wheels diplomatically that he initiated — by experiments on the Seine River — his historic partnership with Robert Fulton.[47] His own words, dated November 12, 1802, in a postscript to a brother-in-law, Thomas Tillston, best captures this point:

> I must charge you with a commission that may be of considerable importance to me, and yet I fear that you will laugh at me when I mention it, but I give you leave so to do, provided you by no means neglect to execute it this session of the [New York] legislature through some of my friends. You know my passion for steam boats and the money I have expended on that object. I am not yet discouraged. [Although all] my old partners have given up the pursuit, I have found a new one in Robert Fulton, a most ingenious young man ... who has made so much noise in Europe. We are now actually making experiments on a large scale upon the Seine.... [Please] present to the legislature ... a short petition for a franchise on the Hudson....[48]

Events would prove this new partnership successful and have a tremendous bearing on the year-round commercial exploitation of the Mississippi River in neat complement to Livingston's diplomatic efforts.[49] This aspect of his life would cement his reputation as "a scientist," one whose activities included, during his tenure in Europe as well as at his Clermont home, other widely appreciated achievements, such as developing a better type of wool-producing sheep (the Merino), "revoluciniz[ing] the working of mills by eliminating friction between the millstones," and introducing new varieties of plants and new methods of cultivation.[50] If any of the more famous Founding Fathers exceeded Livingston in contemporary world reputation as a creative scientist, in the loose sense of that term it could only have been Franklin.

CHAPTER 3

The Monroe Mission and a Diplomatic Breakthrough

Livingston's diplomatic breakthrough at Paris came in April 1803. Its total unexpectedness is clear from that minister's correspondence in the weeks leading up to it. Thus, (a) to Madison on January 24, 1803: "I confess to you that I see very little use for a minister here," where the first consul's will governs and he is only concerned with his "personal security and personal ambitions"; (b) to De Witt Clinton on February 5, 1803: There is "very little prospect of succeeding in either" the debt or the Louisiana matter, "and indeed I begin to think that a minister here will never be of any use here till we have fleets and power to enforce our demands, unless it be merely to acquire a knowledge of what is going on in Europe and as a parade officer"; (c) to Jefferson on March 12: "[One reason Monroe's] coming will be extremely pleasing to me [is that] I trust he will be empowered to take my place.... I am sick of courts and the round of ceremony.... The three Consuls occasion three courts."[1]

In a breathtaking example of the unilateral power Napoleon was now wielding, that first consul, following a brief private debate he reportedly conducted on Easter Sunday, 10 April, with two of his ministers (Barbé-Marbois of the Treasury and Denis Decrès of the Navy and Colonies) announced to Marbois, who had taken the pro-cession position in the debate, that he and he alone was to negotiate with Livingston and the soon-to-arrive James Monroe. His goal was a treaty for the sale by France of all that Spain had just ceded to it—that is, Louisiana, including New Orleans, but not any part of the Floridas, which Spain had successfully insisted on retaining, contrary to earlier rumors.[2] (That such a momentous decision could be taken in this manner would not have surprised Livingston, who had written Madison on September 1, 1802: "There never was a government in which less could be done by negotiation than here.... One man is everything.... His ministers are mere clerks."[3]) Napoleon also gave Marbois a sale figure to aim for; according to Marbois's later writings, that figure was below the 80 million livres (about $16 million) he managed to obtain from the U.S., including 20 million livres that was set aside specifically to satisfy American private claims against France for commercial spoliations.[4]

Marbois's ploy was to tell Livingston and Monroe that Napoleon was insisting on at least 100 million livres plus U.S. assumption of all French responsibility for claims upon them by American citizens; these two demands were inserted by Marbois in his 23 April draft of the proposed treaty.[5] One argument Marbois employed was to tell the Americans that Napoleon, "having given the Kingdom of Etruria, whose revenues were 25 million Livres, in exchange for this country, it was natural that the First Consul should estimate it beyond its real value."[6] (One of the Americans' counter-arguments was that, in some 100 years, Louisiana would still only have "50,000 inhabitants, and these scattered over a space of 1,000 miles.") Astonishingly, even if stated only as a negotiating tactic, they went further by arguing that the U.S. "never" sought the west bank and, "were it in their power, after having made the acquisition, to sink the territory into the ocean, they would see the conversion of land into water with pleasure." But they also acknowledged the good reasons the U.S. had for making the purchase, just as France had in offering Louisiana to the U.S. In fact, France should give it, "like the blessing of the Gospel, without money and without price."[7]

That the amounts involved in the purchase were not minor ones for the Americans is evident from the budgetary figures Secretary of the Treasury Gallatin reported to President Jefferson on October 17, 1803: "Balance in the Treasury, $5,850,000. The receipts over $11,300,000 for the year ended September 30 last." Jefferson's message to Congress of the same date as Gallatin's note to him incorporates Gallatin's figures in round numbers. For orders of magnitude, note that Jefferson's message made the following additional points: (a) revenue exceeded "current expenses"; (b) the "debt paid" the previous year totaled $3.1 million, excluding interest payments; (c) the cash balance in the Treasury would be used in part to cover the first installment ($800,000) called for in the agreement with Britain (January 1802) regarding the payment of America's prewar commercial debt to British creditors, and in part to cover the $2 million appropriated in early 1803 for use in connection with the negotiations at Paris and Madrid; and (d) the purchase price of Louisiana was mainly "payable after

15 years," giving the U.S. time in the meanwhile to pay off its "existing debt." (Dupont de Nemours, back in May 12, 1802, had advised Jefferson in a letter from N.Y., regarding the then-existing U.S. schedule of 15 years for paying off its debt burden, that, if he could "acquire New Orleans and the Floridas ... without war," he should do so, even if that meant having to "extend this period by three or four years."[8])

Marbois also was instructed by Napoleon on that 10 April to open the negotiations immediately with Livingston, even prior to Monroe's arrival at Paris.[9] Many possible factors may explain Napoleon's instruction: (a) the urgent need felt by the French to prepare for war with Great Britain — a war that in fact, as noted, would begin the following month[10]; (b) an attendant interest in forestalling any alliance between the British and the Americans; (c) the need to curb his ambitions in America, where, as he had learned by the end of 1802, his army in St. Domingue had been both defeated and decimated by disease, which also had carried off Leclerc[11]; (d) the resistance of Spain to French demands that it include the Floridas in the retrocession — without it, France would lack the Gulf ports needed to help protect New Orleans from enemy attack; and, perhaps most germanely, (e) the desire to avoid even the appearance of having begun the negotiations under the threat Monroe reportedly was carrying from Jefferson for the French either to meet American demands for the sale of New Orleans and the Floridas or face the prospect of a U.S.-British military alliance against them.[12]

One likely basis for the French impression that Monroe would be the bearer of a stark ultimatum was a memorandum presented shortly before April 1803 to Consul Lebrun by the president's unofficial emissary, Dupont de Nemours. For that reason, and because it sheds interesting light on the circumstances prevailing just prior to the cession of Louisiana to the U.S., it would be worthwhile to excerpt much of that memorandum:

> The Mississippi is the sole outlet for five of the American states ... and of other new states whose first seeds have been planted to the west of the Ohio.... This people cannot agree to be deprived of the use of that River.... Far from obstructing this trade, our sole interest is to profit from it and even, if we can, exclusively to profit from it; the U.S. has 70,000 sailors who can satisfy the needs of our colonies and carry out our trade during wartime, were we to show new proofs of our goodwill to its government, which owes its birth to us; [the U.S.] can provide 40–50,000 sailors to England, if we treated it as an enemy.... The interdiction of the entrepot announced by the Spanish Intendant at New Orleans in violation of the existing treaty between Spain and the U.S. has exasperated the Americans, who suspect that France had suggested this step, which they see as part of a French plan to take pos-

session of the territory in a state of commercial exclusions instead of receiving it in a state of reciprocal liberty, friendship and communication, and of having to sustain past treaties; all parties in the U.S., including those traditionally pro–French, are criticizing the President for not having declared and begun a war by taking possession of the colony — which would not have required much time or effort to do; in two months, he could have brought 20,000 men there, and he could ultimately bring there 40,000 and all the necessary artillery.... But Mr. Jefferson is a gentle [*douce*] person, notwithstanding being a proud one, and he is disposed to adopt all peaceful means which wouldn't compromise the honor or security of his country. He still well remembers what we have done for the independence of the U.S. Rather than starting hostilities, as his people are demanding, he has limited himself to nominating Mr. Monroe as envoy extraordinary and minister plenipotentiary in France and in Spain as a way to handling the issue by way of negotiations; our government would do well, if it is agreeable to a negotiation, to advance on its own some reasonable propositions prior to the arrival of this new ambassador, because *he certainly will be bringing the alternative of peace or war* (emphasis added).[13] It clearly wouldn't be good for us to act, even with justice, once a threat is made; and it would be more disagreeable than I could say to have a fight with a nation six times weaker than us, a war where the distance in miles would result in an inequality favorable to it; therefore, I urge the First Consul to listen right now to the proposals of Mr. Livingston, and to agree starting now regarding whatever can be agreed to; I propose we: declare New Orleans a free port for Spain and France, and, for the U.S., entry from above and exit from below by the river: navigation would remain free to the three nations throughout the river's course, under the express condition that the U.S. would exempt from all duties Spanish and French goods entering its territory via the Mississippi or Ohio; this would leave England able to trade only by land and charged with 12 or 15% duties, a prohibitive condition.... The U.S. wants to purchase the Floridas while leaving us the Bay d'Esprits [Tampa] and the neighboring region we'd like to keep;[14] a new treaty could be negotiated on this in the same spirit as regards New Orleans; the Americans, for this, have in mind to offer a considerable sum ... to destroy British influence in the U.S.; as I see it, French interests in this matter are: to deprive the English of American naval help in case of war; to expand our commerce into the interior of the U.S.; and to bring that degree of wealth and prosperity to New Orleans which is achievable in its role as port of call and entrepot for the altar [*d'autel*] of commerce — these are the goals of this little memorandum.[15]

In fact, Jefferson's established policy and the instructions to Monroe and Livingston were somewhat more temperate than that, because the "threat" was to be couched only in the most theoretical and nuanced of terms.[16] For example, as late as April 18, 1803, Secretary Madison wrote Livingston and Monroe along the following lines:

3. The Monroe Mission and a Diplomatic Breakthrough 57

>   [The United States] may find, on the part of France, a temper adverse to harmony.... The President conceives that a common interest may recommend a candid understanding and a closer connection with Great Britain; and he presumes that the occasion may present itself to the British Government in the same light. He accordingly authorizes you, or either of you, in case the prospect of your discussions with the French government should make it expedient, to open a confidential communication with the ministers [of the British government regarding] ... precautions and provisions best adopted to the crisis.... [It would be best, barring] the pressure of a crisis ... [if you would work with Britain's] public minister ... [in Paris rather than going to London, because that might be] viewed by both as a signal of a rupture....[17]
>   The anxiety which Great Britain has shown to extend her dominions to the Mississippi, the uncertain extent of her claims from north to south beyond the western limits of the U.S., and the attention which she has paid to the north coast of America, make it probable that she will connect with a war on this occasion a pretence to the acquisition of the country on the western side of the Mississippi understood to be ceded by Spain to France, or at least of that portion of it lying between that river and the Missouri.... [Also, France and Spain would be upset if England went west of the Mississippi and so threatened South America.]
>   [England should like to know, however,] that France shall not be allowed to retain or acquire any part of the territory from which she herself would be precluded....[18] It will only be allowed to you, that if France should avow or evince a determination to deny to the U.S. the free navigation of the Mississippi, your consultations with Great Britain may be held on the ground, that war is inevitable. *Should the navigation be undisputed and the deposit alone be denied, it will be prudent* ... [to distinguish between the two cases and determine] *how far the latter right may call for an instant resort to arms* [emphasis added].[19]

This belated message to the American negotiators was clearly an elaboration and hardening of the U.S. negotiating posture as described in the original instructions to Livingston and Monroe of 2 March. Here is a summary of those instructions[20]:

>   You will herewith receive a commission and letters of credence, one of you as minister plenipotentiary, the other as minister extraordinary and plenipotentiary ... [regarding] the Mississippi and the territories eastward thereof and without the limits of the U.S.... [The U.S. goal is to] procure ... a cession of New Orleans and of West and East Florida, or as much thereof as the actual proprietor can be prevailed on to part with.... [Talleyrand's] declaration ... [having finally been made] that it was meant to take possession before any overtures from the U.S. would be discussed ... [is one of the factors that] show

the importance which is attached to the territories in question.... [U.S. policy is] to seek by just means, the establishment of the Mississippi down to its mouth, as their boundary.... [France cannot but see that any] manifest tendency of hostile measures against the U.S. ... [would] connect their councils, and their colossal growth, with the great and formidable naval rival of France.... [France presumably] does not mean to force or to court war with the U.S. ... [but there are] dangers [of this happening. They ... lurk under a neighborhood modified as is that of Spain, at present ... [and this situation] must have great weight in recommending the change which you will have to propose.... [France must be made to see in the U.S. reaction] that friendship and peace with the U.S. must be precarious until the Mississippi shall be made the boundary between the U.S. and Louisiana.... [This and other factors in Europe, the West Indies, and French finances, make] the present moment favorable to the object with which you are charged.... It is to be added, that the overtures committed to you coincide in great measure with the ideas of the person [read: Dupont] through whom the letter from the President of April 30 [18?], 1802, was conveyed to Mr. Livingston, and who is presumed to have gained some insight into the present sentiments of the French cabinet....

[Among likely French] considerations ... [in seeking Louisiana is their assumption that the] Atlantic states ... [greatly favor aligning with Great Britain and that France consequently needs to hold] the key to the commerce of the Mississippi ... [so as to] command the interests and attachments of the western portion of the U.S.; and thereby either control the Atlantic portion also, or if that cannot be done, to seduce the former into a separate government and a close alliance with herself.... [In point of fact, the Atlantic states are full of] amity and impartiality ... [to France and Britain, and] our western fellow-citizens are bound to the Union.... [As regards] the advancement of the commerce of France by an establishment on the Mississippi ... [the U.S. will] now and for the ages continue the principal commerce ... [and will offer France commercial advantages] superior to its establishing its own presence [on that river.]²¹

Moreover, U.S. interests do not go to the west of the Mississippi,²² whose production could be transported to the shore opposite New Orleans—which, in any event would be used by the U.S. and other competitors of France. According to the best information, that opposite shore possesses the same facilities for such establishments as are found on the island of New Orleans. Without the latter's cession to the U.S., its commerce would suffer by comparison to France's, because the U.S. right of deposit is so much more circumscribed, and their territory on the Mississippi not reaching low enough for a commercial establishment on the shore, within their present limits.²³

Madison's letter continued:

Regarding Florida ports, the U.S. would give France advantages superior to those France would have by virtue of having them for itself and keeping the U.S. out or restricted in its use of them. Moreover, the U.S.

3. The Monroe Mission and a Diplomatic Breakthrough 59

had a "just claim to the use of the rivers" on the same basis as regards the Mississippi, where, unlike the Florida rivers, it did not have possession at any point over both banks. The Mobile River was reportedly navigable for at least 400 miles north of 31 degrees. France perhaps sought "a colonial establishment having a convenient relation to her West India islands and forming an independent source of supplies for them." The U.S. answer to that was: (a) France would still have Louisiana west of the Mississippi for this purpose; (b) the U.S. in a general period of peace would be able to supply the French West Indies; (c) if there was a French-British war, a neutral U.S. would still be able to supply those islands, even by way of the Mississippi, unlike the French there; and (d) "because in case of war with the U.S., which is not likely to happen without a concurrent war with Great Britain (the only case in which she could need a distinct fund of supplies), the entire command of the sea, and of the trade through the Mississippi, would be against her and would cut off the source in question; she would consequently never need the aid of her new colony, but when she could make little or no use of it."

The letter further outlined "the principles and outline" of "the plan of adjustment" the U.S. favored: (a) France would "[reserve] to herself all her territory on the west side of the Mississippi"; (b) the U.S. would have "the territory east of the Mississippi," including "the islands" known as the "south pass"—that is, those situated north and east of New Orleans island; (c) the boundary would be the mid-channel of the Mississippi from 31° northward; (d) navigation of the entire course of that river "shall be equally free" for U.S. and French citizens; (e) below 31°, only France and the U.S. would be able "to exercise commerce"; (f) for 10 years, each of the two would have the same "duties on their respective shores" as their respective citizens, after which French and U.S. exports would be free of duties, if both did so for each other's ships; (g) the U.S. would "pay to France [30] million of livres tournois" (the 30 million figure was written in code)[24]; (h) payment would be made on claims that "have been or may be acknowledged by the French Republic to be due to American citizens"; (i) the exchange rate could be $1.10 for every 6 livres.

"Observations on the plan" of a treaty that was enclosed were as follows:

1. Do not "insist" on a Spanish role "unless there be ground to suppose that Spain will contest the validity of the transaction."
2. The south pass "is the most navigable of the several channels, as well as the most direct course to the sea"; be certain that the cession includes "the islands north and east of that channel," because "several islands will be thereby acquired, one of which is said to command this channel, and to be already fortified."

3. England, after 1763, proclaimed all the islands up to six leagues of the Florida shore as its own, and no one objected.

4. France will likely have the most difficulty with regard to the navigation article, which "ought and probably will be satisfactory" to it, even as it gives "the least of discontent to Great Britain," because "it secures to [France] all the commercial advantages in the river, which she can well desire"; secondly, because it leaves her free to contest the more "the navigation of the river by Great Britain, without the consent of France.... The article also ... violates no right of Great Britain, nor can she reasonably expect of the U.S., that they will contend beyond their obligation for her interest at the expense of their own"; the article's "silence" on Britain's rights under the 1783 treaty, "or by virtue of contiguous territory ... leaves the claim unaffected"; the 1794 [Jay's] treaty gives Britain the right "to the use of our bank of the Mississippi above" 31°, and this "title will be equally entire"; only regarding commerce "below our present limits" is Britain excluded by the article, which is fully justified for the U.S.; still, "feel the pulse of the French government with respect to a stipulation that each of the parties may without the consent of the other, admit whomsoever it pleases to navigate the river and trade with their respective shores, on the same terms as in other parts of France and the U.S., and as far as the disposition of that government will concur to vary the proposition accordingly"; the French likely will not concur, but the U.S. would look good in Britain, and it also would be "a just attention to the interests of our own western citizens, whose commerce will not otherwise be on an equal footing with that of the Atlantic states"; France might insist on excluding all third parties from "navigating the Mississippi"; "silence" on our part would be sufficient, because that is "merely" a French-English issue; England "never asserted a claim on this subject against Spain," and therefore "it is not to be presumed that she will assert it against France on her taking the place of Spain"; if she does so assert it, we are uninvolved, because our treaties give our "separate consent only to the use of the river by Great Britain, leaving her to seek whatever other consent may be necessary"; if France insists, "it will be better to acquiesce," but do so without being "inconsistent with our treaties with Great Britain"; "In truth," France would have the right to "exclude" third parties from a "use of the river"; England is "understood" not to be adequately "connected with it by territory,"[25] and it "has never asserted against Spain a right of entering and navigating the Mississippi," which was not opened even to the U.S. until the 1795 [Pinckney or San Lorenzo] treaty with Spain.

5. If France insists, agree to an arrangement by which France is granted "the same commercial use" for its citizens on "the shores ... ceded to the

3. The Monroe Mission and a Diplomatic Breakthrough 61

U.S.," even as American citizens are refused that use on France's "shores"; if France insists, also agree either to extend the privilege beyond 10 years, or to omit the proviso entirely, regarding French citizens, vessels, and merchandise having "equality ... with those of the U.S."; the same point holds regarding (a) the 10-year limit on a French right of deposit at New Orleans and (b) the 10-year limit on "the commerce of France in the ports of west and east Florida ... on the same footing with that of the U.S."

6. Regarding "the pecuniary considerations to be offered for the territories in question ... there is some reason to believe that the gross sum, expressed in the above, has occurred to the French government, and is as much as will be finally insisted on"[26]; if a "greater sum be made an ultimatum on the part of France, the President has made up his mind to go as far as [50 in code] millions of livres rather than lose the main object"; France's "urgency ... for money may be such as to overcome their repugnance to part with what we want, and to induce them to part with it on lower terms, in case a payment can be made before the exchange of ratifications," although "it will be essential that the convention be ratified by the French government before any second advance be made."[27]

7. "It is hoped that the idea of a guarantee of the country reserved to France may not be brought into the negotiation"; if France insisted, "it will be better to accede to it," but "mitigating the evil as much as possible, by requiring for the *casus faederis* a great and manifest danger threatened to the territory guaranteed, and by [stipulating] a fixed sum of money payable at the Treasury of the U.S." annually[28]; if exact numbers are unavoidable, be as precise as possible, "that there may be no room for controversy either with France or with her enemy on the fulfillment of the stipulation."

8. Since France may only agree to give part of the territory the U.S. was seeking, use the following pricing formula: "One-fourth of the value of the whole island of New Orleans" is equal to the value of "the Floridas together ... East Florida at one-half that of West Florida.... In case of a partial cession," take any part of New Orleans island that you can get so that the U.S. has "a jurisdiction over space enough for a large commercial town and its appurtenances on the bank of the river, and as little remote from the mouth of the river as may be possible"; try to avoid having the treaty itself identify the location.

9. Short of the above, "it will only remain to explain and improve the present right of deposit" by an express propriety to hold real estate for commercial purposes, to provide hospitals, to have consuls residing there and also other agents who may be authorized to authenticate and deliver all documents "for ships regarding right of deposit traffic; "the United States cannot be kept patient, including America's "western people," under

the restrictions which the existing treaty with Spain authorizes; failing the cession to the U.S. of the Floridas, try to obtain rights of deposit there and also free navigation; recent problems with the Spanish intendant show the "necessity of placing a power somewhere nearer to the U.S. capable of correcting and controlling the mischievous proceedings of such officers towards our citizens"[29]; otherwise, the "good understanding of the two nations" would be threatened; there is a "possibility of some intermediate violence between" U.S. citizens and "the French or Spaniards in consequence of the interruption of our right of deposit"; therefore, they were to seek "indemnification" for "damages" to American citizens and, regarding any "violence," assure that it would "not be taken on either side as a ground or pretext for hostilities."

The non-belligerent nature of these 2 March instructions is further substantiated in a cover note that Madison wrote Monroe on that same day, transmitting the instructions he was carrying to France: "Although the U.S. are deeply interested in the complete success of your mission, the Floridas, or even either of them, without the island of New Orleans, on proportionate terms, will be a valuable acquisition."[30]

To highlight the evolving nature of U.S. government policy toward Louisiana, and to illustrate that Jefferson, although he personally reviewed and approved these March 2 instructions, often had taken a harder, more military-oriented line, than had Madison, one must also compare the above two messages with Jefferson's policy statement of April 18, 1802, which was in the form of a "private" dispatch to Livingston. The letter was carried to that minister by Dupont de Nemours, who, as noted earlier, was authorized by Jefferson to read it before sealing it in order to understand what the U.S. policy was that Dupont hopefully would be able to sell to the first consul. Here are excerpts from that important presidential message, which, as the reader will recall, was cited in the official instructions of March 2:

> The cession of Louisiana and the Floridas by Spain to France, works most sorely on the United States.... There is on the globe a single spot, the possessor of which is our natural and political enemy. It is New Orleans.... France, placing herself in that door, assumes to us the attitude of defiance. Spain might have retained it quietly for years.... The day that France takes possession of New Orleans ... we must marry ourselves to the British fleet and nation. We must turn all our attention to a maritime force, for which our resources place on us very high ground; and having formed and connected together with a power which may render reinforcement of her settlements here impossible to France, make the first cannon which shall be fired in Europe the signal for the tearing up any settlements she may have made, and for

holding the two continents of America in sequestration for the common purposes of the united British and American nations.... However greater her force is than ours, compared in the abstract, it is nothing in comparison to ours, when to be exerted on our soil.... [31]

If France considers Louisiana, however, as indispensable for her views, she might perhaps be willing to look about for arrangements which might reconcile to our interests. If anything could do this, it would be the ceding to us the island of New Orleans and the Floridas.... It would ... relieve us from the necessity of taking immediate measures.... But still we should consider New Orleans and the Floridas as no equivalent for the risk of a quarrel with France [that would be] produced by her vicinage.... Every eye in the United States is now fixed on the affairs of Louisiana. Perhaps nothing since the Revolutionary War, has produced more uneasy sensations through the body of the nation.... I have thought it not amiss by way of supplement to the letters of the Secretary of State, to write you this private one, to impress you with the importance we affix to this transaction. I pray you to cherish Dupont. He has the best disposition for the continuance of friendship between the two nations, and perhaps you may be able to make a good use of him.[32]

While there is room for debate as to whether one should accept at face value Jefferson's threats of possible Anglo-American military cooperation against the French, several points may safely be made: (a) Jefferson was quite serious that he would have to use military force were the French to occupy New Orleans and the Floridas; (b) however, the timing for such use, even under the unacceptable circumstances of a French presence east of the Mississippi, should be delayed to the extent practicable; and, (c) even if war was to come between the U.S. and France, the U.S. would not necessarily act in formal alliance with any other power which may also be at war with France but instead would assure for itself maximum military and diplomatic advantage and flexibility from having cobelligerents.

Jefferson clearly was far from anxious to initiate military operations at that particular period (1802–03). Excerpts from his previously cited letter of October 10, 1802, to Livingston reflected this hesitation and are worth summarizing here:

> We stand completely corrected of the error, that either the government or the nation of France has any remains of friendship for us.... An unfriendly spirit prevails in the most important individuals of the government towards us.... [Therefore, we will sit back and join France or England, depending on which] enemy ... [can best serve us, and only then, if we have to, choose].... Our present system [should be kept as long as possible].... We wish, therefore, to remain well with France ... [and so] we had better give to all our communications with

> [the French] a very mild, complaisant, and even friendly complexion, but always independent ... [and never anything to give France the idea that we are] crouching.... [This is because], we see that no consequences, however ruinous to them, can secure us with certainty against the extravagances of her present rulers.... Ask no favors, leave small and irritating things to be conducted by the individuals interested in them ... and then not push them to irritation.... No matter at present existing between them and us is important enough to risk a breach of peace.[33]

In a similar vein, Jefferson wrote Dr. Hugh Williamson on April 30, 1803 — ironically, the very day the U.S. *did* obtain New Orleans "for money":

> Although I do not count with confidence on obtaining New Orleans from France for money, yet I am confident in the policy of putting off the day of contention till we have lessened the embarrassment of debt accumulation ... till we obtain more of that strength which is growing on us so rapidly, and especially till we have planted a population on the Mississippi itself sufficient to do its own work without marching men 1,500 miles from the Atlantic shores to perish by fatigue and unfriendly climates. This will soon take place.... To have seized New Orleans, as our Federal maniacs wished ... would have produced a blockade ... instead of a paper blockade from New Orleans alone while the river remained open.[34]

This last letter is fully in line with Jefferson's cautionary note to Madison of March 17, 1803, regarding Livingston's various moves:

> I now return the letter[s] of Mr. Livingston.... I hope the game Mr. Livingston says he is playing is a candid and honorable one. Besides an unwillingness [by the U.S.] to accept any advantage which should have been obtained by other means, no other means can probably succeed there. An American contending by stratagem against those exercised in it from their cradle would undoubtedly be outwitted by them. In such a field and for such an actor nothing but plain direct honesty can be either honorable or advantageous.[35]

Within the space of a single month — in fact between April 10 and 30 — France was able both to decide on the sale of all of Louisiana and to sign agreements with the two American negotiators effecting that sale as well as settling the spoliations issue. (Actual signing of the agreements in their final, dual-language form was not completed until 9 May, but the documents retained the official date of 30 April.)[36] While the focus of American concerns, and the limits of the authority given to Livingston and Monroe, had been restricted to New Orleans and the Floridas, the Paris

3. The Monroe Mission and a Diplomatic Breakthrough 65

negotiations accommodated Napoleon's more far-reaching decision. Livingston described the situation along the following lines in a dispatch to Madison of 17 April that said, in part: "The commission contains powers only to treat for lands on the east side of the Mississippi." He had been pressing France "to yield us the country above the Arkansas." He did so to avoid France's ability to "draw off a prodigious population from our side of the river and from such a connection between the inhabitants of the western country and these new settlers, who would be their relations and friends." It was through "my private negotiations with Joseph Bonaparte" that he made his case that France should "give us that country."[37] His efforts "have had their effect.... Mr. Monroe, however, agrees with me that we will proceed as well as we can and, *as we left no copy of the commission, it may possibly escape unnoticed*" that their powers did not go as far as the French proposition. "I have been absolutely without powers to the present moment ... *and now they are unfortunately too limited* [emphasis added]."[38]

The concern of the Americans proved unwarranted, almost certainly because the French government was anxious for an agreement and consequently preferred not to take notice of the discrepancy between their powers and the three conventions under contemplation (the cession itself; the purchase price of 60 million livres; and the 20 million livres to be paid by the U.S. to American claimants against France, which would be quit of any and all other claims against it).[39]

Moreover, both negotiating parties fully recognized that the cession of all of Louisiana would be well received by the U.S. government, as indeed it was despite the constitutional questions it raised and the unexpectedly large financial amounts involved: Madison wrote Livingston and Monroe on 29 July that the administration was pleased with their reports of April 11, 13, 17 and May 13 covering the negotiation and signature of the conventions of 30 April.[40] A paraphrased summary of the last of these cited messages from the American negotiators, in which they explained that the first consul had already ratified the agreements, sanctioning Marbois's "conduct," is in order:

> Before the negotiation commenced, we were apprized that the First Consul had decided to offer to the U.S., by sale, the whole of Louisiana and not a part of it.... On that point we did not long hesitate, but proceeded to treat for the whole. We were persuaded that, by so doing, it might be possible, if more desirable, to conclude eventually a treaty for a part, since, being thus possessed of the subject, it might be easy ... to lead from a view of the whole to that of a part, and with some advantages peculiar to a negotiation on so great a scale.... We found, however, as we advanced in the negotiation, that M. Marbois was absolutely restricted to the disposition of the whole; that he would

treat for no less portion, and, of course, that it was useless to urge it. On mature consideration, therefore, we finally concluded a treaty on the best terms we could obtain for the whole.

Even if the two of them had obtained only New Orleans and West Florida, another power would have had the right bank and, therefore, "a divided jurisdiction" could have led to troubles "highly injurious to us in many of our most important concerns"; also, England would have been unhappy with the agreement the U.S. would otherwise have had to make with France, which would have demanded and received stipulations "of a permanent nature" favorable to it as sovereign of the right bank; therefore, it helped to "separate ourselves ... from the European world and its concerns, especially its wars and intrigues." Also, the U.S. internally would have an "increased parity of interests" and, therefore, the "bond of our union will be strengthened, and its movements become more harmonious."

The agreement was that the U.S. shall pay to the French Government 60 million of Francs, in stock, bearing an interest of 6%; and a sum not exceeding 20 more to our citizens ... and also to exempt the manufactures, productions, and vessels, of France and Spain, in the direct trade from those countries, respectively, in the ports of the ceded territory, from foreign duties for the term of 12 years. The stock is to be created irredeemable for 15 years, and discharged afterwards in 3 equal annual installments.... [Interest is to be paid in Europe] on it.... [The government of France could] sell it....[41] The debts due to our citizens are to be discharged by drafts on the Treasury....

Louisiana was acquired of Spain by France, in exchange for Tuscany, which latter is settled by treaty on the son-in-law of the King of Spain ... and was estimated in the exchange, in consideration of the revenue, at 100 millions of Francs." This exchange showed Napoleon's "high idea" of Louisiana's worth — at first, he demanded 100 million for Louisiana and also the write-off of the debts owed by France to U.S. citizens. Marbois's demand for 60 million was for cash, the whole in one year. He and Napoleon demanded "perpetual exemption from foreign duties." The previous year, the value of exports through the Mississippi was $4 million.[42]

CHAPTER 4

Factors Underlying the Breakthrough

The three men who worked together at Paris were well and favorably known to each other.[1] One episode earlier in Livingston's tenure as minister plenipotentiary will adequately illustrate the continuing value of his friendship with Marbois 20 years after its start during the Revolutionary War, when the latter was secretary of legation at Philadelphia. In October 1802, Foreign Minister Talleyrand had slighted Livingston on two separate occasions by receiving other visitors to his office who had arrived after him. The American, who resolutely ignored the likelihood that Talleyrand was acting at least in part out of understandable annoyance with Livingston's having in recent weeks widely circulated memoranda on diplomatic matters normally reserved for private conversation with him alone, was convinced this was a conscious snub — and an "indignity offered" to the United States itself — and accordingly sent him a stiff formal note on 19 October, as follows: "It is with regret, sir, that I find myself reduced to the necessity of transacting this business [regarding Leclerc's mistreatment of American sea captains] and all other in future with your office, by note till I shall receive specific instructions from the U.S."[2] Talleyrand had Marbois show Livingston a draft of his intended response, which, in addition to pleading untenably that both times he had simply not seen Livingston waiting in his outer office, accused the latter of lacking adequate knowledge of diplomatic procedures. Livingston, revealing a rather exalted strain of self-dignity that had run through his demeanor even with his own government from the very start of his renewed diplomatic career in 1801, rebutted through Marbois on 24 October that he himself had previously filled a position at the same level in the U.S. government as Talleyrand was now filling for France and therefore needed no lessons in matters of protocol:

> The minister has agreeably to my conception, treated me with disrespect. I tell him so by a formal note. To this, he makes me no other answer than assuring you and not me that none was intended [and] ... that he did not see me.... [His note founded] my conduct upon my ignorance of the diplomatic forms, and my having but lately entered upon duties that required a knowledge of them.... [That is, he wrongly presumed I was] disqualified to hold [my] station.... He should also have known that I have many years since had the honor to fill an office similar to his, which, he will admit, requires some knowledge of the diplomatic usages.... [He told me] that the President, who [has] more experience, will not justify my conduct.... [His] informal note [failed to include] ... the apology that he made you ... [It also failed to include] my note with it, which ... [under my assumption of an apology,] I had agreed to receive, because [of] my attachment to the French government and my respect for him.

Marbois managed to conciliate the two adversaries, both notes were withdrawn, and the two met and agreed to continue working together on an amicable basis. Livingston later would attribute to this episode (in retrospect so dangerously close in time to Napoleon's decision to cede Louisiana to the U.S.) a change for the better in the way Talleyrand treated him.[3] He also wrote Marbois on 2 November to thank him for his help in the affair, which was "satisfactorily finished, and, I may add, that it is an addition to that pleasure to have been indebted to your friendly interposition for its early termination."[4] On that same day, he wrote to Madison that his problem with Talleyrand "is satisfactorily settled," but, as it could be "misrepresented," the Secretary should know the details. Talleyrand had failed to return his note as the two had agreed, given Talleyrand's "apology" and the offer of "his hand" to him. Two days later, the letter continued, Rufus King (who was staying with Livingston on a visit to Paris)

> informed me that he had been applied to by a person in the minister's confidence who [had seen] my note and the reply that it was intended to make me and urged him, as this reply contained some things which ... were such as might hurt my feelings and lead to disagreeable [~~replies~~] consequences, to advise me to apply for my note that the matter might drop. This needed no comment and I without hesitation told Mr. King to say that the subject was too delicate for him to interfere in. I am confident Talleyrand dare not send me that note, or, if he did, I knew how to treat it.

A few days later, Livingston went on, "Mr. Marbois came to me," Talleyrand having shown him his intended note and assured him "that I had taken offense without just cause" and "that he did not see me." Marbois got Talleyrand to give him both notes, and "he prayed me to accept this apology and take back my note." Talleyrand's note lacked Livingston's reply in writing to his own. Marbois said that, as Talleyrand was both a vain man and "the friend of both" of them, what Marbois told him "ought not to have less weight than if it came from Mr. Talleyrand directly." Livingston, insisted on "some proof ... other than have words which were capable of misrepresentation," Consequently, enclosed was Marbois's letter, which was followed up by Talleyrand's greeting him at their meeting the next day "with many professions of personal regard."

All this, Livingston's letter concluded, was "a fortunate circumstance, since it will impress Mr. Talleyrand with a conviction that we are not disposed to submit to any species of disrespect."

Typical of the criticisms Livingston would later be subjected to regarding his performance in Paris, Marbois himself, in 1829, would write a book about the Louisiana Purchase that, while praising the Jefferson administration for having had the wisdom to wait patiently, and in a non-threatening way, for France to work out its policy toward that newly acquired territory, charged Livingston with lacking in that wisdom by having resorted to threats of war in order to prevent France from taking possession of it. Of course, this was a self-serving argument by Marbois, because it was in France's—and his own—interest to portray Britain, and not the U.S., its permanent friend, as having been the principal source of the military threat to any French attempt to return to the North American mainland. (Since Marbois's book has been treated as a primary source by surviving participants in the negotiation over Louisiana, as well as by historians of that activity, the present writer has provided a brief analysis of the book in Appendix C.)[5]

Still, it is true that Livingston in 1802 and early 1803 had written and widely distributed lengthy memoranda seeking in a rather unorthodox and even brazenly undiplomatic manner to prove that it was not in France's commercial, diplomatic or military interest to take possession of New Orleans and West Florida, and also implying that the U.S. would, either on its own or jointly with Britain, forcefully act to block such a French move.[6] In modern terms, Livingston would clearly be considered among the more hawkish members of the Jefferson administration.[7] Thus, he would complain to Armstrong on May 25, 1802, that Madison was totally ignoring his proposal that the U.S. institute an "embargo" on trade with St. Domingue given the French abuses there of American ships and personnel (who, not so incidentally, were supplying not only the French but also the rebellious forces there). On 2 June, he wrote Pinckney that, as regards the restrictions put at St. Domingue by the French on "American trade," he would adhere to any instructions he may receive from Washington, but, without them, he would "endeavor to impress the government here with a belief that, though we respect, we do not fear them, and that we will not tamely submit" to any abuses. Earlier, in March, he had written that colleague that, "if France should reduce St. Domingue, I should not be surprised if she sent her black troops to Louisiana, in which case I think a reduction [by the U.S. of either] army or taxes should be well considered."[8]

In a letter Livingston wrote King on June 8 he summarizes his feelings. Just as King, too, preferred, he had already urged by letter to the secretary that the U.S. government retain the appropriated $300,000 for the compensation of French losses due to American seizures of their property in order to let him use it as leverage with the government of France "to satisfy our demands." However, "the government" disagreed, saying "it was improper to betray any distrust, that good faith on our side would produce it here, etc." Livingston, on the other hand felt "satisfied that neither timidity or delicacy are calculated for this [meridian], ... and I have strongly advised such an arrangement of our affairs at home as shall enable us to be prepared for every event.... This is a critical moment with us, and the events of the armament in the islands will plead more for us than a thousand acts of generosity." Unlike the notes of Denmark, Sweden, etc., to the French government, his own were "answered" while theirs went "entirely unnoticed. They want us and can do without them." He had "insisted with Talleyrand upon a full explanation of their intentions ... founding my demand upon our rights under the Spanish treaty." Talleyrand answered that France was sending a minister to the U.S., and then the two of them (Livingston and Talleyrand) would be able to talk more substantively. Livingston concluded to King, "On the principles that you may collect from what I have said, I should dread a quarrel, but I should dread still more a degrading submission."

Similarly, on 30 June, Livingston wrote Attorney General Dallas of Pennsylvania that the U.S. must be ready to defend itself against European intrigues: "Should France ultimately succeed ... so far as to possess both the Floridas, common prudence will compel us to an enlargement of our military establishments in their vicinity"; the U.S. "has a unique meridian even as it shares latitude with many." By 12 November, Livingston foresaw that France's plans to increase its "strength" and "wealth" by a possession of Louisiana as supplier to "her West Indies" islands would "compel us to a much closer connection with her rival than she would wish."[9]

Livingston on occasion even directly admonished the secretary of state for being too passive in his instructions as to how to counter French plans to repossess Louisiana.[10] For example, he wrote Madison on May 28,

1802: "I wait impatiently some further instructions from you"; at present, the instructions he had been given prohibited his taking "such measures as may show any dissatisfaction.... If I do not hear from you soon, I shall present a frank memorial to this government ... that fairly and candidly [gives] our objection to their taking possession of the Floridas and demanding security for the rights we [have] by treaty with Spain."[11]

Livingston followed this message up with one dated June 8. He firmly believed France would force Spain to include West Florida. Therefore, "by way of parenthesis," the U.S. should "rely not ... too much on her affection or her justice, nor neglect from economy every necessary means of defence." Talleyrand was saying that France was definitely sending Otto as minister to the U.S., and he and Livingston would negotiate regarding Louisiana. "In the meantime ... do not neglect the fortification of your harbors, conciliate the affections of your western country, and put your militia on the best possible footing. Circumstances may arise which you cannot prevent. There are various causes of irritation at home that may compel the government to take a decisive line, and where that may lead to god knows. Be explicit in your instructions to me.... They will be strictly fulfilled."[12]

Of course, Livingston soon would receive Jefferson's previously-quoted 18 April "private" letter giving him the confidence to embark on a more aggressive campaign to obstruct French possession of New Orleans and the Floridas. Thus, Livingston's ever-more strident letter to Madison of 10 November 1802, in which he explained that the French authorities were telling him "nothing on ... their limits or of our rights under the Spanish treaty." But General Victor [the designated commander of the military expedition intended to leave for Louisiana], mistaking an American merchant "from Louisiana ... for a French inhabitant," revealed ignorance of U.S. rights despite Livingston's "many conversations" with Talleyrand and his "different notes." Victor planned "nothing short of taking exactly what they find convenient.... If I may judge by the temper that Victoire [Victor; Livingston regularly misspelled the name as "Victoire"] will carry with him, an attempt [will be made] upon the Natchez, which they consider as the rival of New Orleans."[13]

From his previous letters, Livingston wrote, Madison knew that he was urging "the necessity of strengthening yourselves as soon as possible, both by forces and ships at home and by alliances, including with England, abroad. No prudence will, I fear, prevent hostilities ere long between us, and perhaps the sooner those plans develop themselves, the better." In fact, as late as February 18, 1803, Livingston was still admonishing Madison:

> You have intimated the propriety of opening some other channel of communication with the First Consul than through the minister. This I have effectually done and have learned his sentiments thereon. I can have a personal conference with him when I choose.... I defer it for two reasons.... Never yet have [I received] any specific instructions from you how to act or what to offer ... [and] it is one of the traits of his character, when has once fully avowed a sentiment, not easily to change it.

To return to Jefferson's 18 April letter, the reasons for its timing have been the subject of conjecture by historians. It likely was due to: (a) ever more firm reports from Europe, and especially from King in London and Humphrey in Madrid, that the French and Spaniards had cemented their agreement on the retrocession; (b) its natural association with Jefferson's decision that month to take advantage of Dupont's planned return to France to use him as his unofficial agent; and (c) Jefferson's appreciation that Madison's guidance to the field needed strengthening.

In Livingston's justification, the tenor of Madison's earlier guidance to his ministers in Europe clearly struck a much less bellicose note than did even the earliest of Jefferson's parallel messages—and than even some of the president's publicly reported utterances regarding the importance to the U.S. of blocking at all costs a retrocession of Louisiana to France.[14] An early example is Madison's pre-departure guidance to Livingston of September 22, 1801, in which he said that if an agreement between France and Spain had already been made or could not be blocked, not to unnecessarily annoy "our future neighbors," or have them check the liberality they might be disposed to exercise in relation to the trade and navigation through the mouth of the Mississippi—everything being equally avoided at the same time which might "compromise the rights of the U.S. beyond those stipulated" in the Pinckney Treaty. If the retrocession to France could not be blocked, "it will deserve to be tried whether France could not be induced to make over to the U.S. the Floridas, if included in the cession to her from Spain, or at least West Florida." That would help "reconcile ... [the U.S. to an] arrangement in itself much disrelished by them to strengthen the returning friendship [between themselves and France] ... and, by affording a fund for indemnifying and soothing our fellow citizens who have suffered from her wrongs ... [would assure] solid justice" for them.

Madison reminded Livingston that West Florida was of "great importance" to the U.S., several of whose "rivers, particularly the important river Mobile, [emptied] themselves into the sea" through it. Assuming Spain needed also to be involved, as it, "too, must feel an interest in the good will of the U.S., and [that it] is responsible in justice for very considerable depredations on their commerce, there may [therefore] be the greater possibility of her joining in the measure." In any event, Livingston was to try to have France press Spain to cede the Floridas to the U.S., if "Spain alone is to make the cession."[15]

As Madison noted, the problem lay in France and Spain's ambiguity in the matter. French ships were bringing into Spanish ports their American prizes, which then were "condemned in Spain, sometimes by her tribunals, sometime by French consuls." The government of Spain was referring the Americans to the French "for satisfaction.... In justice, they are both liable." The policy of the U.S. government was "strict and honorable neutrality" in all "decisions and transactions relating to foreign nations." But

> What the motives of Spain in this transaction [the retrocession to France] may be is not so obvious. The policy of France in it, so far at least as it relates to the U.S., cannot be mistaken. Whilst she remained on that footing of confidence and affection with the U.S., which originated during our Revolution, and was strengthened during the early stages of her own, it may be presumed that she adhered to the policy which in the treaty of 1778 renounced the acquisition of continental territory in North America, and was more disposed to shun the collisions threatened by possessions in that quarter coterminous with ours, than to pursue objects to which the commanding position at the mouth of the Mississippi might be made subservient.[16]

Circumstances were no longer the same "despite our again being together [a reference to the U.S.-French treaty of 1800].... The confidence and cordiality that formerly subsisted have suffered a deep wound from the occurrences of late years." France was convinced that America's Atlantic states favored the British and, therefore, it feared a joint Anglo-American conflict against it. France also feared a British occupation of the mouth of the Mississippi and consequently wanted to preempt this because British control would also increase their "hold on the U.S." Furthermore, France wanted to add to "her commerce a monopoly of the immense and fertile region communicating with the sea through a single outlet."

Madison concluded that the U.S. approach to countering these French views was clear: (a) the Atlantic states were "not disposed" nor "in danger" of allying with Great Britain in any manner that would be "injust or injurious to France"; (b) the U.S. national interest precluded any such eventuality; and, (c) without American cooperation, the British could not seize "Spanish possessions on the Mississippi," and there was no way the U.S. would offer such cooperation.

But Livingston month by month became increasingly convinced that the only way to attract France's attention to American demands was to pressure it militarily. By December 1802, his thoughts, as expressed in a private letter, were as follows:

> As to our affairs, they are of a nature to progress but slowly. Money is not to be had [from the French government] and Louisiana is a very favorite object with the First Consul.... I have omitted nothing to obtain payment and to convince them of the inutility of their project on Louisiana.... But little can be done by [the U.S.] who has no means of impressing her demands. The voice of justice ... is very little attended to when it is unsupported by power.[17]

He would expand on the theme of "power" — perhaps partly as a rationalization of his pessimism that the U.S. could ever block a retrocession of Louisiana to France or obtain New Orleans and the Floridas from either it or Spain — when he wrote to an American citizen in Paris that he differed "from your memoire and from many of our most respectable countrymen" regarding Louisiana. Livingston continued that, in fact, he wished "Louisiana to be France's," and that France "may render it mportant, or at least may esteem it so ... on the persuasion of the importance that it is to the U.S. to have something at our command to serve as security for their good behavior." Yes, U.S. citizens could be "seduced by them" and have "a thousand quarrels with them," but, "as long as that colony is within our power, the French government at home will think twice before they engage in a war with us on every trifling pretence, and nothing but some security of that nature can keep us out of war half a year."

Livingston became especially strident at the very close of 1802 when he learned that Spain, although it already was in the process of preparing to vacate the territory in favor of France, had taken the extraordinary step of announcing the closing of New Orleans as a place of deposit for American goods without offering an alternative port, as required by its treaty of 1795 with the U.S. He wrote Joseph Bonaparte on January 7:

> [First was the] silence [of France regarding the] navigation of the Mississippi and the right of entrepot at New Orleans.... [And now] a circular has just come to my knowledge ... which cannot fail to drive the U.S. into some violent measure.... The New Orleans governor [on 20 October said that Americans] will not in future be permitted to make a deposit of their cargoes in New Orleans in conformity to the 22nd article of the treaty of 27 October 1795 which has expired.
>
> He has studied the treaty and the governor was wrong. Moreover, the Americans would see France as behind his move: The U.S. will rather hazard their very existence than suffer the Mississippi to be shut again. Of this you will easily be convinced when you learn that,

4. Factors Underlying the Breakthrough 75

when their numbers were but half of what they now are, and their means of defense infinitely less, their instructions to their ministers that made the first peace with Great Britain [interlineated: "i.e., September 3, 1783, and then Jay's Treaty"] was by no means to sign a treaty, even though deserted by France, without securing the free navigation of that river. [The Spanish move could well lead to an alliance between the U.S. and Britain] and perhaps to an immediate rupture with Spain.[18]

While Madrid by March 1803 would order the cancellation of that action (whose motives remain uncertain and which it had disguised as a purely local initiative by its intendant at New Orleans) it did create a political crisis for Jefferson during the fall and winter of 1802–03.[19] The president managed to finesse congressional and western pressure for immediate military action by sending Monroe, who was just leaving his position as governor of Virginia and who had been Jefferson's law trainee from 1780–83, on his mission to France and, if necessary, to Spain as well.[20]

In retrospect, Livingston would admit that he had been too aggressive during this tense period, when he and many Americans assumed that only French pressure on Madrid could have explained the closing of New Orleans to the Americans.[21] The evolution in Livingston's position regarding the crisis at New Orleans may be sketched through the following messages: (a) having been regularly advised by Pinckney, starting at least in the latter's letter of February 5, 1802, that French influence over Spain was "irresistible," he wrote his brother, Edward, on October 3, 1802, that Napoleon's "wishes make at present the law of Spain and indeed of [a] great part of Europe"; (b) once he learned of the intendant's October move, Livingston followed up his above-described note of January 7 to Joseph with one to Talleyrand on January 10, 1803, advising that, having just learned of the intendant's action, "It is peculiarly unhappy, Sir, that his circular should have happened at the very moment that France is about to possess that country," although he himself did "too much justice to the integrity of France to believe that she would approve of a breach of treaty, and render their first entrance into our vicinity an act of hostility"; (c) Livingston then wrote King on January 20, 1803, reporting that he had suggested to Talleyrand that the Spanish intendant's order "has been done in concurrence with France" and will lead to "precipitating measures in the U.S.... They solemnly deny all knowledge of the transaction.... We must look to energetic measures at home for the success of our negotiations here"; (d) on 18 February, he advised Madison that, "I cannot but seriously wish that you may have availed yourselves of the pretence that Spain has given you to take possession — it will be best to treat with the subject in our hand"; and (e), having in the meantime learned of Monroe's mission, Livingston again wrote Madison, this time rather egoistically, on 18 March:

> I cannot but wish that my fellow citizens should not be led to believe from Mr. Monroe's appointment that I had been negligent or too delicate of their interests on any of the great points entrusted to my care. [You should kindly assure that] my notes ... [to the French government were seen by] some of them.... [They showed I] perhaps ... [went] farther than my instructions would justify.... [I did so because] I dreaded the consequences of delay, if France should take possession and continue the policy of Spain.... [Moreover, as] the time of Mr. Monroe's arrival [was] uncertain ... [I decided,] on reflection ... [to send still another note to Talleyrand, on 16 March, in response to the] very unsatisfactory [one I received outlining the first consul's reaction to his proposals regarding New Orleans and the Floridas.][22]

In sharp contrast to Livingston's preferred approach, Jefferson and Madison, as noted previously, were more temperate and sought peacefully to deflate the crisis and thereby to calm western and southern calls for an immediate attack and seizure of New Orleans, by sending, not coincidentally, Monroe (who had the trust of those regions) to Europe.[23] The rationale for their action is contained in Madison's dispatch to Livingston of December 23, 1802, in which he noted that contrary to the Pinckney Treaty, the Spanish intendant at New Orleans blocked the "deposit there for our merchandise ... without an equivalent establishment being assigned." The "western people" were beginning to complain. By the time of "the descent of the boats in the spring, it needs to be revoked." U.S. policy was not "to resort for redress in the first instance to the use of force." The western people had the "sympathy of their Atlantic fellow citizens on the subject."[24]

By 18 January, Madison would write Livingston: "It has appeared to the President that the importance of the crisis called for the experiment of an extraordinary mission.... He has ... selected ... with the approbation of the Senate, Mr. Monroe, formerly our Minister Plenipotentiary at Paris and lately Governor [of Virginia. He] ... will be joined with yourself ... and with Mr. Pinckney in a like commission to treat, if necessary, with the Spanish government." He and the President hoped that this "prospect of accommodation," including an offer of 30 (later to be raised to 50, as we have seen) million livres for the purchase of New Orleans and the Floridas, would help "in postponing the expedition to Louisiana."

In a second message of 18 January, Madison advised Livingston that the president had "carefully underlined" to the Senate "his undiminished confidence in the ordinary representatives" of the U.S. and that instructions would be prepared whose "object ... will be to procure a cession of

4. Factors Underlying the Breakthrough

New Orleans and the Floridas" and "consequently the establishment of the Mississippi as the boundary" between the U.S. "and Louisiana," and also, if such a purchase proved impossible, "to reestablish our present rights" and "to promote arrangements by which they may be enlarged and more effectively secured" under the Pinckney Treaty.

It is clear from this that the Monroe Mission was not inspired in the first instance by a desire to displace Livingston and Pinckney as the key negotiators for the purchase of New Orleans and the Floridas from either — or both — France and Spain, although there can be no doubt that Washington for some time had felt the need to buttress those two ministers with someone more in their confidence. Rather, that Mission was a response to the specific "crisis" caused by the Spanish intendant's ending of American port privileges at New Orleans. Livingston fully understood this last, domestically oriented purpose of the Monroe Mission but came to resent its inevitable connection to his work in purchasing New Orleans and the Floridas (or, failing that, in protecting American treaty rights on the Mississippi). An insight into his attitude and diplomatic tactics between arrival of the news of the Monroe Mission and the arrival of Monroe himself may be obtained from his previously cited message of 22 March to Talleyrand, in which he stated he had been vested "with full powers to receive and make those arrangements" regarding the conduct of relations between the U.S. and France as the new possessor of Louisiana as may be required for the confirmation by France of U.S. rights under its treaty of 1795 with Spain, and that "[I]n the appointment of Mr. Monroe jointly with me minister extraordinary near the First Consul, it was by no means their intention, considering the variety of accidents which ['~~must precede every arrangement which it may be~~'] could suspend or prevent his arrival, to delay the express confirmation" of those rights. Livingston further expressed that, "This declaration must precede all arrangements that may be thought proper hereafter to enter into, and to which both Mr. Monroe and myself will so cordially lend our endeavors. A treaty takes a long time, while the above-cited declaration should be so readily seen as required that it could and should be quickly given" by France prior to negotiating a treaty. "It is not, Sir, to negotiate for this acknowledgment that an additional minister is sent." Rather, he was sent regarding arrangements that could be made if, as was "generally presumed, the Floridas should be added to the acquisition of France." As "the bearer of the strong sentiments of the people" regarding the action taken by the intendant at New Orleans, he was to help show to France "the uselessness of this acquisition and the mistrust it will create between the U.S. and France.... I can only lament the inefficacy of my representations." The minister was requested to express Livingston's appreciation to the first consul for the announcement of Mr. Monroe's welcome in France.

That Washington's policy succeeded — as regards its specific domestic goal of fending off congressional pressures for immediate military action and thereby finessing the threat to domestic U.S. tranquility due to the Spanish intendant's action — is shown in the contrast between the relieved tone of Madison's message to Livingston and Monroe of April 20, 1803 and the highly concerned one contained in his previously-cited April 18 message:

> April 18: Our latest authentic information from New Orleans is of the 25th of February. At that date, the port has been opened for provisions carried down the Mississippi ... [subject to a duty] if consumed in the province ... [and, if exported,] an additional duty ... with a restriction ... to Spanish bottoms, and to the external ports permitted by Spain to her colonial trade.
>
> April 20: Orders for the reestablishment of our deposit at New Orleans [have been received there].... We hope [these orders will] mitigate considerably the losses from the misconduct of the Spanish intendant; and they are the more acceptable as they are an evidence of the respect in the government of Spain for our rights and our friendship.... It would seem that the Spanish government regards the cession to France as either no longer in force, or not soon to be carried into execution ... [given that the government alluded to] a future agreement ... [between the U.S. and Spain regarding] an equivalent deposit.[25]

Livingston's own relief is reflected in his congratulatory letter to Pinckney of 20 April: "I am extremely pleased to find that you have arranged so satisfactorily the affairs of New Orleans." In that same letter, he reported that Monroe "arrived on the 13th [sic] at night [and] has not yet been received and cannot therefore act officially but will informally give every aid in his power."[26]

An insight into the later thinking of the president and secretary of state on what underlay Spanish policy may be had from a dispatch Madison sent to Pinckney on October 12, 1803, a period during which Madrid was raising additional difficulties with the U.S., this time regarding the French transfer of New Orleans to American sovereignty: "The conduct of Spain ... is not readily explained.... [Its present] yielding to the impulses of jealousy and adopting obnoxious precautions ... [will result in bringing on,] prematurely, the whole weight of calamity which she fears.... [and] perhaps ... [all Spain is seeking is] concession of some sort or other ... [from France or the U.S.,] or both." On 12 September, Madison had similarly written to the president that the conduct of Spain "can only be explained by supposing [she] wished to obtain a price for her conduct and contest the extension of Louisiana to the limits she knows we have in view."[27]

American dislike and distrust of Spain had deep roots in the experience of the American War of Independence and fed the U.S. determination sooner or later to revenge itself for that nation's coldness toward it during that war — Spain would be evicted from both East and West Florida by 1819 by the most forceful of diplomatic and military measures of the U.S. government. The first phase of that eviction would be completed by 1810 with the occupation of West Florida as geographically defined precisely by the previously-quoted French memorandum of 1803 to Madrid and as further defined in Livingston's dispatches to Washington (i.e., up to the Perdido River just to the west of Pensacola). But, as has been noted above in connection with that 1803 French memorandum, by November 1804 Talleyrand would be writing Napoleon *countering* the argument contained therein that West Florida properly should have been ceded to France as part of the retrocession of Louisiana and therefore now should be ceded by Spain to the U.S. (See Appendix B for a summary of Talleyrand's memorandum and a subsequent related one of May 1806.) It should be noted that, even there, Talleyrand was not necessarily opposing an *amicable* sale by Spain to the U.S. of the Floridas but was vehemently opposing the strong-armed tactics of the U.S. at Madrid and also its effort to insinuate the French in their argumentation by falsely, in Talleyrand's view, claiming that France's cession of Louisiana to the U.S. properly included West Florida up to the Perdido.

A good example of the post-purchase U.S. rationale is in Livingston and Monroe's joint message to Madison, June 7, 1803, which included:

> We are happy to have it in our power to assure you, that ... we consider it incontrovertible that West Florida is comprised in the cession of Louisiana. West Florida was a part of Louisiana when it was in the hands of France, and it was not in her hands in any other situation. The transfer of the whole was on the same day, November 3, 1762, [in the form of] ... preliminary articles [for the definitive peace treaty of February 10, 1763, which was signed] between those [two] powers and Great Britain.... The Treaty of 1783 between Britain and Spain ... put Louisiana in [Spain's] hands in the same state it was in the hands of France.... [The 1795 Pinckney Treaty between the U.S. and Spain] only tends to confirm this doctrine.... The U.S. should act on it in all the measures relative to Louisiana.[28]

As we have seen, the U.S. would do just that.

CHAPTER 5

A Nasty Competition for the Credit

We have seen that Livingston, in a most bold and entirely personal initiative in December 1802 and January 1803, made fresh written proposals to Joseph Bonaparte, his newly found private channel to Napoleon and someone he considered as "the only man who is supposed to have any sort of influence over him."[1] As he over-optimistically wrote King on 19 December: "I have indeed found a new channel to the First Consul by means of which I have got a very strong memorial under his eye. It has been well received, but what the effect will be I know not.... [Talleyrand gives me] a much more marked attention ... since our little difference ... [perhaps and/or because] he suspects that I have obtained another passage to his master."[2] This demarche by Livingston was fully in keeping with Madison's instruction to him of 15 October to go directly to "the chief consul" if Talleyrand won't give him straight answers; it would be worth upsetting that minister if that move got results: "No pains ought to be spared for putting an end" to the "unwise" project; a U.S. purchase of New Orleans and Florida would be, if on "convenient terms ... the happiest of issues ... to one of the most perplexing of occurrences."

In fact, Livingston continued to work through Talleyrand even as he developed his channel to Napoleon through Joseph; moreover, when Livingston finally wrote directly to the first consul on 27 February, it was arranged through the foreign minister, who on 24 February had even been given a draft of Livingston's proposed letter for comment, which was duly and expeditiously rendered to the American. To recapitulate the correspondence between Livingston and the foreign minister in the weeks leading up to Monroe's arrival[3]: On 10 January, Livingston wrote Talleyrand to explain that the implications for Franco-American relations of the Spanish intendant's action were "of a nature to call the immediate attention of

France to the several matters [he'd been raising,] the neglect of which has excited the liveliest sensations in the U.S." Therefore, and as the minister had invited him to do, enclosed was "the outline of treaty." Without the Floridas, Louisiana wasn't worth French possession; therefore, he presumed "the Floridas are in the hands of France." West Florida "includes the bay of St. Esprit [Tampa] and Pensacola." Only "Augustine" was more than "of the smallest importance in the west [sic] of the Mississippi." If France sent a large "emigration," that would be "such a drain to the wealth and population of France as will inflict as deep a wound to her agriculture and manufactures as that felt by her on the revocation of the Edict of Nantes or by Spain on the expulsion of the Moors." Moreover, they would one day revolt from France. In this regard, the minister was invited to refer to his earlier "paper, which you've read, for more details."

France should cede to the U.S. "so much of Louisiana as lays above the mouth of the River Arkansas," said Livingston.[4] That would create a U.S. "barrier" against a British attack and a French barrier between the U.S. and Mexico that would also serve to protect "the Spanish establishments against the ambitious views of any European power." France would also possess "East Florida as far as the River Perdigo." West Florida, New Orleans, and the territory on "the west [sic] bank of the Mississippi" would go to the U.S., which was seeking possession of "the mouths of the River Mobile and the other small rivers" in West Florida. This would "calm" its "apprehensions relative to the Mississippi." France could easily develop the site opposite New Orleans— Fort Leon — as its own ocean-going port.

Of great importance, wrote Livingston, was the fact that "The right of deposit, which the U.S. claims and will never relinquish, must be the source of continual disputes and animosities between the two nations and ultimately lead the U.S. to aid any foreign power in the expulsion of France from that colony," if it included New Orleans and West Florida. Furthermore, the U.S. would remove its major "commercial capital" from New Orleans to Natchez and make New Orleans "of little importance."[5] Any other course of action by France would surely leave Britain in control of "the whole of this establishment." From Canada, "15–20,000 troops plus a host of savages" could easily seize New Orleans.[6] If France possessed all of Louisiana, that would throw "the whole weight of the U.S. into the scale of Britain," which would then have all of the "New World" at her command.

Although France should in its own interest and "magnanimity" give these requested territories to the U.S. "gratuitously," America was "not unwilling to purchase them at a price suited to their value ... in the hope that France will at the same time satisfy her distressed citizens and the debts which they have a right by so many titles to demand." The minister was urged not to send to the U.S. a representative "only with powers to treat without being the bearer of anything conclusive."

On 24 February, Livingston sent Talleyrand for comment his draft letter to Napoleon.[7] He added:

> I will also, Sir, solicit your interference with him that some immediate step may be taken with respect to New Orleans.... There is unfortunately no medium, Sir, between a rupture and such declaration as shall satisfy the people of the U.S.; nor will the subject admit of delay. I have no doubt that Mr. Monroe's instructions will be precise and positive and perhaps they may on that account be ill-received here. If France really means to agree to our explication of the treaty [for the sale of New Orleans and the Floridas], every reason of sound policy will rather direct her to do it as an act of good will than as the result of any pressing measures on the part of the U.S. ... You will have the goodness not to consider this as an official letter.

We see here an early example of what will become an unattractive pattern of dissembling by Livingston in his effort to create a paper trail designed to prove he and not Monroe was the one who most merited the distinction of having brought the French to offer all of Louisiana to the U.S. In contrast to the clear evidence in this letter to Talleyrand that by 24 February he already knew of the Monroe Mission, he would write Graham in Madrid on 28 February that his letter to Napoleon of 27 February was sent "just before I heard of Mr. Monroe." One can be certain that, if Livingston had by 24 February learned of the Monroe Mission, so had the French. It would only be on 3 March that Livingston would write Madison acknowledging the latter's 18 January informing him of the Monroe Mission.

The fresh ideas Livingston included in his memoranda of December–January to Joseph Bonaparte provided for an arrangement by which the first consul would transfer "jurisdiction" to the U.S. over New Orleans, West Florida, and all of Louisiana north of the Arkansas River, in exchange for: (a) $2 million, and then only for New Orleans and West Florida; and (b), an equal ownership *with the Bonaparte family* of all the land in that right bank territory, the two partners to share in the profits from the sale of the land to private persons. While Joseph, contrary to Livingston's assertion to King, quickly rejected the proposals, it nevertheless had presumably been brought to the first consul's attention along with a set of similar proposals (minus the inducements for the Bonaparte family) which Livingston sent directly to Napoleon on February 27, 1803, and which entered the hopper of his ideas that would shortly thereafter indeed carry the U.S. to the west of the Mississippi.[8]

Regarding the 27 February letter to Napoleon, Talleyrand had advised Livingston not to combine in that letter a proposal for the cession to the U.S. of French possessions with a detailed financial discussion of the debt issue. Not surprisingly, when the foreign minister on 11 March, explicitly in the name of Napoleon, answered Livingston's letter, he admonished the American for having done just that:

> As concerns the second question raised in your memoire [the first question having related to American claims], which is in regard to Louisiana, the First Consul would have wished that you had made it the subject of a separate and distinct presentation.... It is totally contrary to the principles of the government of the Republic to mix together political matters of importance and delicacy with the calculations of balances due and of financial rates of interest. [It was this line of thinking that helps explain the three-tiered structure of the interlocking agreements comprising the Louisiana Purchase.]

To highlight Livingston's historically significant February 27 letter to Napoleon, Livingston stated it would be "easy to remedy" the debt problem: "If the plan which I've proposed regarding Louisiana is adopted ... [that would mean] the debt of the U.S. to France would be larger than the totality of the claims of the Americans....[9] [Therefore,] I'm ready to negotiate conditions assuring the French funds will not be diminished."[10] If the first consul preferred to negotiate regarding Louisiana without reference to these financial matters, Livingston said, "that would make it even easier to force the American creditors to appoint someone" to represent their private interests.

The change "which is ready to occur in Louisiana," said Livingston, had "aroused U.S. concerns, which are heightened by the silence which the governments of France and Spain have kept and still keep regarding the rights which the U.S. claims, and which for a long time enjoy at New Orleans." By that he meant, (a) "the right of entrepot"; (b) "boundaries agreed with Spain"; and (c) "the navigation of the Mississippi." It would be reassuring for the U.S. to have French confirmation, even though its rights were beyond limitation, because "distant officials often act in accordance with their own way of thinking and not that of their sovereign." The reaction of the U.S. to the intendant's action illustrated the great "interest" it had in that situation. As Livingston noted, "A spirit of resentment has been manifested all across the Union," and only the Spanish minister in Washington's "interposition" and the "disavowal" by the "governor of New Orleans [sic]," coupled with the "extreme solicitude of the American government to avoid" interrupting its "harmonious" relations with "all the powers of Europe," prevented the "American people from an immediate recurrence to arms."[11] Livingston still feared that the U.S. government could be "forced to follow the impulse of the people" once "the season arrives for the transport downriver of the products of the country."

Given these circumstances and prospects, he said, "I must press [for a] prompt and explicit declaration regarding our rights…. [Otherwise,] the future peace and harmony between our two countries will receive a terrible blow."

Here are Livingston's suggestions: (a) "appoint someone [later in this memoir Livingston specifies "either the Minister or someone else"] to negotiate with me…. That in itself would have the character of being an act of conciliation, and you would be able to direct the negotiation in which I trust nothing will be proposed on my part" [contrary to Napoleon's interests]; (b) "I must earnestly solicit some treaty explanatory of the terms on which France has received the cession of Louisiana from Spain, and recognizing the rights of the U.S."; and (c) as a mark of the first consul's "goodwill," France should "provisionally, depending on her taking possession of the Floridas ... [grant the] right of free passage in the rivers Mobile and Pensacola, and of deposit at their mouths, to citizens of the U.S."

This last suggestion would also help French commerce. River trade was "insignificant" right then, but could become "more important" later: "France would never have an advantageous role in the colonization of the Floridas and of New Orleans…. Even with all the advantages for New Orleans of foreign capital ... [and the] accession [to the trade of U.S. inhabitants that has brought] the number of free inhabitants there to about 7,000 souls, the total population east of the Mississippi hasn't gone beyond twice that number, most of whom are poor and miserable." There were "physical reasons" blocking the Floridas' development so long as they were "in European hands." They nevertheless were important for the U.S., because they include "the mouths of several of its rivers, which in itself will create constant disputes with any European sovereign there." The U.S. therefore was seeking Napoleon's approval of "the cession of this country." The U.S. was ready to make sacrifices to obtain that cession of New Orleans and the Floridas—a cession that would avoid "the only point of collision between our two nations, who moreover have so many common interests to unite them." It was in France's "own interest to make this cession."

Livingston concluded by saying, "Should this idea not be so fortunate as to meet your approbation, there are still a variety of views in which, by a partial cession, permanent commercial advantages may be acquired." The Floridas were "of slight worth" and "continually exposed to attacks by France's natural enemy, whether from Canada or from the sea." One final point: were French officials to fail to keep up Spanish payments to the "savages" east of the Mississippi, the resultant trouble [per Livingston's unsent English language version: "a universal massacre of all the planters will ensue"] could well lead to French charges that U.S. "intrigue" was responsible for it.[12]

In his 7 January to Joseph, Livingston had been even more direct regarding the military threat to a French colony in North America, having added a postscript making the point that his plan would "prevent the union between [the U.S.] and Britain which mutual fears will otherwise bring about." But Livingston fully realized that his efforts could not be put forward as representing the authoritative views of his government. As he had written Jefferson on October 28, 1802,[13] Joseph Bonaparte two days earlier, having previously been given Livingston's memoir on Louisiana, "begged" that any such future "communications ... might be informal and unsigned" in view of his need not to "appear to interfere with the minister." This discreet way was, said Livingston, "exactly what I wished, because I should act with less danger of committing myself and of course with more freedom."

Further evidence of Livingston's awareness that he lacked authority to speak with precision of his government's policies and goals regarding Louisiana and the Floridas surfaced once he learned of Monroe's appointment. In the previously-cited letter of 28 February to Graham, he wrote that he hoped "I have beaten the ground in such a way as to facilitate our combined operations when Mr. Monroe shall arrive ... [Of all] my different projects, [Mr. Monroe,] I presume, [will] have the only one that we must act upon."[14] Nevertheless, during the period between learning of the Monroe Mission and the 12 April arrival at Paris of that envoy, Livingston had "not hesitated to declare" to Talleyrand that, if the French "kept the port shut after the island is delivered up, the U.S. will not wait the effects of a negotiation," and to tell Bernadotte, the minister-designate to the U.S., that he shouldn't bother crossing the Atlantic "unless this business is previously arranged, as he will only have to return immediately."[15]

That Livingston's proposals in January and February 1803 to Joseph and Napoleon did not, in fact, receive the full support of his government is clear from Madison's dispatch to him of July 30, 1803.[16] There, the secretary explains that one reason Monroe and he were not given powers to seek land west of the Mississippi River was that it was only on 5 April that he had received Livingston's 29 January dispatch reporting his suggestion to the French government that it cede "the western country above the Arkansas." Madison added the criticism that Livingston's suggestion would still unacceptably have left France not only with "the possession and jurisdiction of one bank of the Mississippi from its mouth to the Arkansas,[17] but a part of West Florida,[18] the whole of East Florida, and the harbors for ships of war in the Gulf of Mexico." Madison also observed that, in any event, Livingston in that message reported French "repugnance to our views of purchase" [a report that very likely contributed to Washington's decision to harden its instructions to Livingston and Monroe in the supplementary guidance message of 18 April from Madison that has been previously described in this text].

Livingston never ventured to send as an integral part of his dispatches to his superiors in Washington the text, or the more sensitive details, of his proposals to Joseph Bonaparte.[19] The record shows the following: (a) Livingston to Madison, December 20, 1802: "I ... anticipated your wishes in finding another channel to the First Consul,[20] the consequence of which I have at this moment some very strong memorial under [his] eye and some projects that appear to be well received."[21] The details had to wait for "a safe conveyance." (b) Livingston to Madison, February 18, 1803: Only "unofficially" did he reach the first consul—by way of "the only man who is supposed to have any sort of influence over him." Livingston could not send his "notes" in this correspondence, "unless I can find time to put them in cipher.... You will, however, have them in the first letter I write to the President." (c) Livingston to Jefferson, March 12, 1803: "After full deliberations, my propositions so far as they related to personal advantages were not agreed to.... I was going to renew the idea, but as Mr. Monroe's appointment will render everything of this kind impossible, it is unnecessary to send you our [that is, his and Joseph Bonaparte's] correspondence as I had intended ... as the whole was unsigned and unofficial." (Note that this last to the president was sent one day after Livingston had received Talleyrand's unforthcoming and admonitory 11 March letter regarding his 27 February cession proposals. That letter, as noted above, was seen as very positive by Livingston but only as regards the American claims problem.)

This omission in Livingston's correspondence with Washington has created much confusion in the writing of the history of the Louisiana Purchase, not to speak of much sullying of his personal reputation. Therefore, it would be worthwhile to summarize here some of the more unorthodox aspects of that correspondence with Joseph that never entered at least the more accessible of the official records of the U.S. government. Perhaps the best way to introduce this correspondence is to highlight additional sections of Livingston's previously-cited message to Jefferson of October 28, 1802, in which he noted that Joseph had told him he shouldn't exaggerate his "power to serve me." Joseph had said Napoleon read "my notes on Louisiana ... with attention" and that he, Joseph, "had nothing more at heart than to be on the best terms with the U.S." Livingston had then warned Joseph of the danger of the local military in Louisiana getting into conflicts with the U.S. and proposed that (a) France first should give that colony back to Spain but retain New Orleans and also obtain possession of both Floridas; and (b) France then should give the western part of the Floridas to the U.S. along with New Orleans in exchange for its debt to American citizens. Livingston told Jefferson, "He asked me whether we should prefer the Floridas to Louisiana. I told him there was no comparison in their value, but that we had no wish to extend our boundary across the Mississippi, or give color to the doubts that had been entertained of the moderation of our views; that all we sought was security and not an extension of territory." Joseph answered that Spain would not make "any new [read: the Floridas] cession."

Livingston had then told Joseph that he was certain that France wanted to "procure ... some port in the Gulf from which they think they may secure their own and annoy the British commerce," and therefore he doubted that the U.S. could, in that event, win any cession of "east Florida." But, as Joseph pointed out to him, Spain was unlikely to cede it and "give France a command of the Gulf."

This remarkable letter warrants comment: (a) it is the first report of France's giving consideration to ceding land west of the Mississippi to the U.S.; (b) it makes crystal clear how far U.S. government thinking — and also that of Livingston at the time — was from seeking possession of that western territory[22]; and (c) it helps explain the origins of Livingston's proposal of December–January for obtaining U.S. "jurisdiction" over Louisiana territory north of the Arkansas River. In light of the above, one could justifiably credit Livingston's summer 1802 memoirs on Louisiana with inadvertently helping move French thinking in the direction that ended with the Louisiana Purchase.

As for the direct correspondence between Livingston and Joseph, the key message was dated 7 January and is summarized here. It was a follow up to that of 24 December, where, as noted above, Livingston had sought to find leverage by offering to have the U.S. delay agreeing to British demands for a "southwestern" Canadian border touching upon the Mississippi River. By 7 January, moreover, Livingston had heard of the action taken by the Spanish intendant at New Orleans against American goods and privileges. He understood the U.S. needed an "immediate arrangement," because the American people and government were agitated over reports of French plans in Louisiana, and by the "inexecution of that article of the treaty [of 1800] which provides for the payment of their debts," as well as "by the harsh measures at St. Domingue" against American ships, goods and personnel, and finally by the silence of France regarding "the navigation of the Mississippi and the right of entrepot at New Orleans." On top of all that, he wrote, "a circular has just come to my knowledge ... which cannot fail to drive the U.S. into some violent measure."[23] A French minister to the U.S. would have to answer: "Why has our minister been able in 14 months to effect nothing? Why has our debt remained unpaid? Why has he received no sort of satisfaction on any subject on which he has addressed himself to the government?" The U.S. would see French military moves in America and feel France was merely trying "to paralyze those measures of security that common prudence would suggest to the U.S. Is it not to stop the treaty which we are about to make relative to our western limits with Britain?"

Livingston continued with his concerns:"France apprehends ['fears'] that the rebels in her islands are being supplied with arms, etc., from the U.S. I trust that the apprehension has hitherto been unfounded."[24] But this could change and the U.S. could, "in its present state of agitation, consider the islands as the points in which she [France] is most vulnerable." However, the U.S. would respect any treaty provision blocking American help to the rebels: "As no chicanery, no crooked policy will mingle itself in our treaty, one may be concluded in a week, if the Consul shall be pleased to name yourself [Joseph], or General Bernadotte [the current minister-designate to the U.S. vice Otto], in whose candor and information I have great confidence."[25]

Livingston's "Essay Upon the Relative Maritime Power of France and Britain" had, he noted, "been honored by the First Consul's attention." The essay showed Livingston's high estimate of the Franco-American alliance of 1778, as had also been demonstrated "from the whole of my political conduct." Joseph's personal signature on America's treaty of 1800 "was considered a guarantee of that treaty." The solution to the problem of Louisiana could also be that for the problem of how to satisfy that treaty's provision for the payment of the French debt to American citizens. As discussed in his essay, the French "object" regarding Louisiana was to supply the West Indies and to send there the surplus population of France. It would be best for France to keep only that part of Louisiana that was within reach of "the sea" so as to avoid having the French there be "totally out of her control." Therefore, France could make use of the hinterland for building "her future connection" with the U.S. Only Pensacola and eastward would give France "ports for her marine," and with them "she will have the complete command of the Gulf." With that territory, and with "the free navigation of the Mississippi as well as possession of all of Louisiana lying to the west of the river and to the south of River Arkansas, comprehending a tract nearly as large as the old government of France," all that would surely meet fully France's needs and goals regarding that region, whose expanse "could support 15 millions of people." Surely, that level of population would be the maximum

France would wish to try to control. The population north of the Arkansas would have no cause to fear the French navy; moreover, a geographical separation between Louisiana and the population "to the east of the River Perdigo would afford France an additional security." In addition, because "both east and West Florida are barren tracts" and therefore would only serve as "military posts and commercial entrepots," they would attract a different type of population from that of Louisiana.

Livingston felt sure the American population in West Florida would help France "prevent any exertion on the part of the inhabitants of Louisiana, if they should at any time be disposed to revolt." The U.S. desired possession of West Florida, "not on account of the value of the land, for, except a very small quantity on the banks of the rivers [between the Mississippi and the Perdido], it was for the most part a sandy barren or a sunken marsh, but because it would give them the mouths of those rivers." France could only have a problem with the U.S. goal regarding New Orleans. But she could easily replace it by "fixing her capital on either side of the river." New Orleans was poorly located and endowed as a port, military or commercial; only historical accident explained France's choice of that spot on the Florida side of the river "where the settlement commenced." But a greater percentage of the population was now on the bank opposite to New Orleans, "where lands are richer and higher up and healthier." For example, Fort Leon "is in all things equal ... as a government house and barracks, etc. Should France retain the whole of the Spanish cession on both sides of the river, she will still find it absolutely necessary to remove her capital to the west side." Also important, three months out of the year New Orleans was not accessible from the west.

As to Britain's part in the matter, Livingston wrote:

> It cannot be doubted that the peace between France and Britain has been too disadvantageous to the latter to be of long duration.... The Cape, Malta and Egypt have already awakened the cupidity of Great Britain. Should she extend her views across the Atlantic (and what is to limit them?), the cession of Louisiana to France offers her the fairest pretence to invade that country either from Canada or by the Atlantic.... [Britain] felt no reluctance in leaving [the Floridas and Louisiana] to Spain ... [and,] having carefully removed every conflicting question and even conciliated by the liberality of her institutions ... it will be difficult to say what may be the extent of her influence [in the U.S.]

Moreover, a Britain also controlling "Louisiana and West Florida" would mean "no power in Europe would be in a situation to oppose her force.... The Bay of St. Esprit [Tampa] would become another Gibraltar," from which to hit "all French, Spanish and Dutch continental or island possessions in America." Livingston added, "She will monopolize the commodities of the West as she has already done those of the East Indies." France must place immediately "a barrier between the settlements that France may wish to retain in Louisiana and Canada." A French cession to the U.S. should also include "New Orleans and West Florida," and that would "take from [the British] the first inducement to attack that country." Even Spain would be best off to have a "neutral" [later: "who alone can defend them"] own the Floridas as the only way to keep them out of British hands. Note, he said, "the superiority of the British navy at the present moment." Therefore, why not "hypothecate the whole of east Florida for a term of years, for such part of the American debt as may remain unsatisfied?"

> [Livingston provided a clear course of action to Joseph:] Some permanent establishment for the First Consul's nearest connections which would not only contribute to their present ease but secure them against hazards however distant and improbable appears to me to merit your attention and that of the head of your family.... It is obvious that this cannot be found in France, nor in any colony dependent upon France, because these must be subject to the vicissitudes to be guarded against....[26] Louisiana inclusive of Florida [would be] a useless excrescent upon the body politic of France and which the bulk of the nation would see lopped off with pleasure, [and it therefore] happily presents itself as the means of affecting this desirable object [that is, of a safe-haven for the Bonaparte family]....
>
> This project [regarding the retrocession of Louisiana] will never flourish under the government of France.... Many of the men of influence among them are from the U.S.... Nothing but force will induce them to submit to the military [government] that will probably be established among them, nor will France retain them without the utmost difficulty in case of a war or when their population shall increase. Yet this colony, when by the consent of France it shall be incorporated with the United States, will probably be one of the most flourishing in the Union.... The value of land there will rise rapidly.
>
> [Livingston added a postscript:] [If the first consul] should consider it as an important object to retain a part of Louisiana with such parts as will give him a command of the Gulf of Mexico, [then] let him cede to the U.S. New Orleans and West Florida as far as the Perdigo, retaining East Florida, which will give him the only good harbors in the Gulf ... and leave to the U.S. the mouth of most of those rivers that run through that territory.... France will ... by running up the Mississippi to the mouth of the Arkansas River ... possess a territory of near 500 miles in extent from the mouths of the Mississippi ... while, *by a cession of what lays above, she enables the U.S. to execute such part of the plan as personally relates to his family* [emphasis added].[27]

The words "such part of the plan as personally relates to his family," as Livingston's postscript makes quite clear, referred only to that part of

Louisiana lying north of the Arkansas River, where, as he had put it earlier in the letter, that territory would be placed under U.S. "jurisdiction" while ownership of the "land" itself would be equally shared by the U.S. government and "those to whom the Consul shall transfer it, and sold on their joint account."[28]

In any event, Joseph's answer to Livingston on 11 January was short and sweet: "I can only repeat my oral answer"— Livingston should address his observations to the minister of foreign affairs, "who is the only one who can have the government's intentions made known to you."[29] This was in apparent response to a third-person note to Joseph, exact date uncertain but apparently sent between January 7 and 11, where Livingston wrote that he was sorry that he wasn't at home when Joseph called and even more so that Joseph declined "to listen favorably to an important part of [my] note, since there are duties which a man owes to himself and family which ought not to be overlooked when they can be performed without the smallest injury to the public," but that he was very "obliged" that Joseph had "submitted [his] observations to the First Consul." That note continued:

> Mr. Livingston conceives that there are a variety of modifications of his propositions which would tend to remove any possible objections and at the same time enable the First Consul to repay the services of some of those among his friends who have just claims upon the public without in the smallest degree burdening the community, always premising that this can only arise out of a transfer of the jurisdiction of the territory marked out, from which alone it can derive any value and greatly increase that of the portions kept by France, and from certain modifications in the payment of the debts which Mr. Livingston will point out.... Profound secrecy [is necessary to avoid] private speculation.

On 11 March, exactly two months after having received Joseph's advice to consult the foreign minister, Livingston received the following disheartening information from Talleyrand as a response to his 27 February letter to Napoleon: "[The first consul] appreciates your motives in setting forth the new relationships which could arise between the two republics, and informs you that, having now been alerted to the U.S. interest, although perhaps premature ... [but which was] at bottom natural and plausible ... [he] has decided to send directly to the scene a minister plenipotentiary to America so that he could, as soon as possible, send him a report that would enable him to have the information necessary to his making a decision on this matter." The first consul wished to assure him of his "attachment" to the U.S. and "his esteem and his personal consideration of the *premier magistrat* who governs it."[30]

On the day he received Tallyrand's response, Livingston wrote Madison that he had written directly to Napoleon despite the view of diplomats here that it would be "improper" and offensive to Talleyrand. "But our situation was such as to require something decisive." He sent it through Talleyrand, who "was pleased with this mark of confidence." Enclosed was "the answer" to his letter. It gave "such strong and such satisfactory assurances" regarding the debt that he has shared it with Americans in Paris to preclude their selling out cheaply.

The letter to Madison continued: While "Talleyrand had assured me, that no sale will be heard of," Bernadotte, once there, would better see that land as actually having less "value" for France, and see that French relations with the U.S. were more important. Bernadotte's "great object" was "to keep the British out of the river, and to secure as much of the carrying trade to France" as possible. Regarding Dupont's plan given to Consul Lebrun, "I have endeavored to convince those who may be consulted of the impractability of it.... I have hinted at making the island of New Orleans an independent state under the guarantee of Spain, France and the U.S., with a right of deposit to each." France was "the only manufacturing state of the three" and therefore would get the most out of it. Dupont's plan would hurt U.S. revenues. Livingston told Madison, "I should not have thought it worthwhile to mention this, had it not been that I gave an unsigned informal sketch of [Dupont's plan] to Joseph Bonaparte — it may possibly be given to General Bernadotte.... If, as I begin to believe, they do not get the Floridas, they will put the less value on New Orleans."[31]

By 18 March, Livingston had further discouraging contacts with Talleyrand, and he therefore more pessimistically wrote Madison that Napoleon's answer to him regarding "New Orleans ... is very unsatisfactory," and that he had at first decided not to respond to it but then "changed my mind and sent a note" on 16 March that once again underlined that (a) what the U.S. minimally wanted required no fresh information from Bernadotte in America but only a treaty reassuring the U.S. of its existing treaty-based rights on the Mississippi; and (b) that the U.S. would never "relinquish" its rights of "navigation" and "deposit" except "with their political existence."[32]

In a manner similar to Marbois' subsequent self-serving writings, most emphatically including his pro-cession role in the alleged two-man debate of 10 April before an indecisive Napoleon, Monroe would later claim that it was Napoleon's awareness of his appointment and arrival in France as "Minister Plenipotentiary and Envoy Extraordinary" that determined him to cede Louisiana to the U.S.[33] Both he and his biographers belittled Livingston's role in the negotiations as well as his influence with the French government or even with Marbois, and they characterized as counter-productive his preliminary efforts to influence French policy. For his part, Livingston, clearly never reconciled to the Monroe mission, stooped to a petty, and easily disproved, set of claims that he was on the cusp of success when news of Monroe's mission halted his progress. Examples of Livingston's lack of success prior to April 1803, and his consequent profound sense of failure about his mission, abound and include[34]:

1. Livingston wrote Madison on February 18, 1803, that he had impressed Talleyrand with the prospect that a revenue-less French Louisiana would be unable to pay "stipends" to the Indians, who would therefore "war" on the French with resulting "pain" for the first consul for having been "the means of the destruction of the white inhabitants whom it would be impossible to defend." Talleyrand's response was a discouraging one — that "I must consider the purchase of the country as out of the question, intimating that a sale was below their dignity, so that I fear my hopes founded on their necessities are frustrated."

2. Livingston wrote King on March 23, 1803, that he had been making good progress with Talleyrand regarding Louisiana when

> unfortunately, they received letters from Pichon informing them that the appointment of Mr. Monroe had tranquilized everything, and that they might safely defer their negotiations, in consequence of which I last nite received a very hasty note full of professions, and urging the necessity of waiting for Mr. Monroe, who may not be here till everything is arranged with Great Britain, in which case they may return to their old project. I believe that this appointment was necessary in the U.S., but as things have turned out, it has greatly embarrassed my operations.... Should they be sure of war [versus Britain], it will have its effect, otherwise not, and they may keep us negotiating as long as they please.

3. Livingston wrote Madison the next day: Pichon's dispatches led the French government to "substitute for the First Consul's note, which, as Talleyrand told me, arranged everything, for that enclosed, which contains nothing," so he answered Talleyrand with the enclosed note, and "only war or peace will determine its efficacy."

Livingston did not even shy from altering the dates of relevant documents, among other non-collegial actions more directly at Monroe's expense even after he arrived at Paris, designed to show that Napoleon's decision had already been made, and the negotiating process not only already begun but actually on the cusp of success, by the time that "extraordinary" envoy could enter into the negotiation (and then, according to Livingston, only in an unofficial, advisory capacity given that he would not be presented to Napoleon for accreditation until 1 May). Key correspondence in this early April period include:[35]

1. Livingston to Talleyrand, April 10 (following a meeting between the two): "[Were Bernadotte to arrive in the U.S.] without such dispatches from me as will give the American government just ground to say that a treaty [i.e., a negotiation] is commenced and that they may hope for a speedy and happy issue, that will have a very unpleasing aspect.... The time that will elapse before Mr. Monroe can arrive [at Paris from Havre, where he now was known to be] and be formally recognized is too valuable to be lost." The goal should be to curb pro-war elements in the U.S. and head off Britain's seizure of Louisiana on the basis of reports that no Franco-American agreement had been arranged. Enclosed was the draft of a note the first consul might empower him in the first consul's name to give Bernadotte for presentation to the U.S. government. It stated that France was willing to cede to the U.S. "the whole of Louisiana."[36]

Talleyrand was then urged, "after this note" to Bernadotte was approved, "to go on to open the treaty even before Mr. Monroe is formally received, as I shall have the benefit of his advice and as he will be made a party to it before it can be ready for execution. You will be pleased, Sir, to consider this as unofficial." (One reason for the latter request is clear from the following note to Madison where Livingston misleads the secretary by reporting that he had initially declined an offer by Talleyrand of the whole of Louisiana.)

2. Livingston to Madison, April 11 (with an April 12 postscript):

> The affair of New Orleans gave me two very important strings to touch.... The U.S. would avail themselves of the breach of the treaty to possess themselves of New Orleans and the Floridas; [or alternatively] Britain ... would immediately seize them as soon as the transfer [to the French by Spain] was made.... These reasons, with the probability of war [between France and Britain], have had, I trust, the desired effect.... Mr. Talleyrand asked me this day, [11 April] when pressing the subject, whether we wished to have the whole of Louisiana. I told him no; that our wishes extended only to New Orleans and the Floridas; that the policy of France should dictate (as I had shown in an official note) to give us the country above the River Arkansas, in order to place a barrier between them and Canada. He said, that if they gave New Orleans, the rest would be of little value.

Livingston said Talleyrand went on to ask what amount the United States would pay for "the whole. I told him it was a subject I had not thought of;

but that I supposed we should not object to 20 million [livres], provided our citizens were paid." Talleyrand's response was that this amount was inadequate and that the two should talk again the next day. "I told him that, as Mr. Monroe would be in town in two days, I would delay my further offer until I had the pleasure of introducing him."

Talleyrand then hinted to him that Napoleon's "resolution was taken in Council on Saturday" (9 April) to sell all of Louisiana to the U.S.[37] "I would rather have confined our views to smaller objects; and I think that, if we succeed, it would be good policy to exchange the west bank of the Mississippi with Spain for the Floridas, reserving New Orleans."

3. Livingston to Madison, 14 April (early A.M.)[38]: "I have just come from the minister of the treasury. [The matter was] so important [that] I fear that I shall not have time to copy and send this letter, if I defer it till the morning. By my letter of yesterday [actually, April 11–12], you learned that the minister had asked me on the 11th ... [whether the U.S. would want to] purchase Louisiana." On the 12th, he called upon Talleyrand to press the matter further. The latter then

> thought it proper to declare that his proposition was only personal.... As I expected Mr. Monroe the next day, he shrugged up his shoulders and changed the conversation.... He told me ... Louisiana was not theirs.... I smiled at this assertion.... I told him that I was very well pleased to understand this from him, because, if so, we should not commit ourselves with them in taking it from Spain, to whom, by his account, it still belonged, and that ... if Mr. Monroe concurred in opinion with me, we should negotiate no further on the subject, but advise our government to take possession.
>
> He seemed alarmed [at these words].... I told him ... that we were not disposed to trifle ... and that I did not know what instructions Mr. Monroe might bring.... I was very fearful from the little progress I had made that my government would consider me as a very indolent negotiator. He laughed and told me that he would give me a certificate that I was the most importunate he had yet met with ... [and that] I could rely upon the intelligence I had received of the resolution [by France] to dispose of this country [the whole of Louisiana].
>
> Monroe spent 13 April with him examining [Livingston's] papers, and while he and several other guests were at dinner with him during the early evening, [Livingston] observed the minister of the treasury walking in my garden.... While we were taking coffee, he came in.... We strolled into the next room [and had] one of those free conversations which I had frequently had with him.... He told me that ... something important ... had been cursorily mentioned to him at St. Cloud [a Napoleon residence very close to Paris].... I had better call upon him anytime before 11:00 that night. When Mr. Monroe took leave, I followed him [Marbois].[39] He told me that he wished me to repeat what I had said relative to Mr. Talleyrand requesting a propo-

sition from me as to the purchase of Louisiana. I ... stated the consequences of any delay on this subject, as it would enable Britain to take possession [and] who would readily relinquish it to the U.S.[40]

There followed "a long discussion of no moment to repeat. He said ... the Consul had said to him on Sunday [10 April] at St. Cloud" something regarding the sale of the whole of Louisiana to the U.S. that "had more of earnest than he thought at the time.... He told the Consul [at that time] that he had seen in the London papers the proposition for raising [by the U.S.] 50,000 men to take New Orleans. The Consul said he had seen it, too, and he had also seen that something was said about $2 million being disposed among the people about him" to bribe them, and then left Marbois.[41]

> Afterwards,[42] when walking the garden, the Consul came again to him ... and inquired how far I [Livingston] was satisfied with his last note [presumably, Talleyrand's disappointing 11 March answer to Livingston's 27 February letter to Napoleon, above]. Here, some civil things were introduced for which I presume I am more indebted to the minister's politeness than to his veracity, so let them sleep.... [Marbois] then took occasion to mention [to Napoleon] his sorrow that any cause of difference should exist between our two countries. The Consul told him in reply, "Well, you have the charge of the treasury; let them give you 100 million livres and pay their own claims and take the whole country." [Marbois] told the First Consul that the thing was impossible, that we had not the means of raising that. The Consul told him we might borrow it....
> I now plainly saw the whole business.... [Napoleon] distrusted Talleyrand on account of the business of the supposed intention to bribe and meant to put the negotiation into the hands of Marbois, whose character for integrity is established. I told him that the U.S. ... wished to remove [the French] to the west side of the Mississippi; that we would be perfectly satisfied with New Orleans and the Floridas and had no disposition to extend across the river; and that, of course, we would not give any great sum for the purchase.

Livingston underlined to Marbois the "extreme exorbitancy of the [First Consul's] demand, which would not fall short of 125 million livres [therefore, Livingston assumed 25 million would be needed to cover American claims]; that, however, we would be ready to purchase" the whole of Louisiana.[43] "He then pressed me to name the sum. [I responded that] this was not worthwhile.... If a negotiation was to be opened, we should, Mr. Monroe and myself, make the offer after mature reflection.... As he himself considered the [First Consul's] demand as too high, he would oblige me by telling me what he thought would be reasonable. He replied that, if I would name 60 million and take upon us the American claims to the amount of 20 million more, he would try" to get that amount accepted.[44] He told Marbois it was vain to ask anything that was so greatly beyond U.S. means and that would "render the present government unpopular and have a tendency at the next election to throw the power into the hands of men who were most hostile to the connection with France, and that this would probably happen in the midst of a war."

Marbois "feared the Consul would not relax" his demands and looked more positively for a solution to "the prudence of the President," saying,

> You know the temper of a youthful conqueror. Everything he does is rapid as lightning.... In a crowd, he bears no contradiction. When I am alone with him, I can speak more freely ... but this opportunity seldom happened and is always accidental.... Try then [to] come up to my mark. [You would then have] exclusive navigation of the river ... no neighbor to disturb you, no war to dread. I told him ... there was a point beyond which we could not go, and that [80 million livres] fell far short of the sum [100 million plus American claims] he [Napoleon] mentioned.... I asked him, in case of a purchase, whether they could stipulate that France would never possess the Floridas and that *she would aid us to procure them.... He told me that she would go that far* [emphasis added].[45]

Marbois also told him that, as the first consul knew of their personal friendship, he having several times had occasion to speak of him and his family and the principles they held, he (the Consul) believed that there would be no difficulty when the negotiation was somewhat advanced to have the management of it put into his (Marbois's) hands.

> Thus, Sir, you see a negotiation is fairly opened[46] and upon grounds which I confess I prefer to all others ... A simple money transaction is infinitely preferable [to "commercial privileges"].... The whole sum may be raised by the sale of the territory west of the Mississippi with the right of sovereignty to some power in Europe whose vicinity we should not fear.... [47]
>
> I speak now ... without having seen Mr. Monroe, as it was midnight when I left the treasury office and is now near 3:00 o'clock. It is so very important that you should be apprized that a negotiation is actually open even before Mr. Monroe has been presented in order to calm the tumult which the news of war will renew, that I have lost no time in communicating it....[48] Mr. Monroe will be presented to the minister [Talleyrand] tomorrow.

4. Livingston to Madison, April 17 (a report written over a several-day period): On 14 April, Monroe and Livingston met with Talleyrand, Marbois also being present. They had hoped Napoleon would see them

"this day, Sunday being a day of reception [only] for the civil officers of the government.... Mr. Monroe, having been compelled when here to be well with the party then uppermost and who are now detested by the present rulers, it will be some time before they know how to estimate his [~~value~~] worth, and Talleyrand, I fear, has imbibed some personal prejudice against him that will induce him to throw every possible obstruction in his way, that he can consistently with their own views."

Monroe was not oblivious to Livingston's machinations. As early as 15 April, he wrote a private letter to Madison:[49] "It is proper for me to mention to you in confidence some circumstances which I wish not to include in an official letter." According to U.S. Consul Fulwar Skipworth, Livingston was "mortified at my appointment [and] had done everything in his power to turn the occurrences in America, and even my mission, to his account, by pressing the government on every point with a view to show that he had accomplished what was wished without my aid; and perhaps also that my mission had put in hazard what might otherwise have been easily obtained....[50] Colonel Mercer, who was present" at Livingston's meetings with Talleyrand on April 11 and 12, told him that his travel from Havre to Paris was given Talleyrand only the next morning — that is, the 12th — at the second interview.[51]

Monroe explained that Livingston told him, at their first meeting, "that he had been with Talleyrand that day [April 12] ... and ultimately, on being asked what we would give, had actually offered terms."[52] At dinner the "next day,"[53] Livingston and Marbois "had a private conference.... He told me he was going [to Marbois's office] and the subject was 'to confer relative to the purchase of Louisiana.'" That "same day," Livingston told Skipworth at dinner that

> he regretted his misfortune in my arrival, since it took from him the credit of having brought everything to a proper conclusion without my aid....
>
> In strict propriety I ought to hold no communication or sanction one with this government till I am presented. Though my colleague considers my reception by the minister [Talleyrand on the 14th] ... and the information he gave us that a person would be designated to treat with us, with whom we might hold informal communications in the interim, as placing me on the ground of a person recognized...
>
> Under these circumstances, I have been driven by necessity, in private communications with [Livingston], to signing nothing or authorizing it on his part, to permit him to state to Mr. Marbois that I would assent to the purchase of Louisiana at the price we were willing to give for the territory to the left of the river, France relinquishing all pretentions to the Floridas, and engaging to support with her influence our negotiation with Spain for them....[54] All this attention to my col-

league, etc., may be an intrigue though on the part of Marbois.... The minister may suppose [Livingston] will be less reserved,[55] though it is certain till my appointment was known that [Marbois] often treated him with great neglect and even disrespect.... My colleague has now promised me in the most explicit terms to hold no further communication with Mr. Marbois or any other person, till I am received, and a person regularly appointed to treat with us. I do not know that any real injury will occur to the object of the mission by what has passed.

An additional complication for Monroe in getting his negotiation started was that, shortly after writing this letter, he would be kept out of action for several days due to a backache — even as late as 27 April, he was still so "indisposed" that Livingston and Marbois had to conduct a meeting at his residence so that, as he wrote in his journal, "I might repose as it suited me."[56]

There would be still another source of strain between Livingston and his government: He would soon strongly protest to an apologetic Jefferson and Madison (who actually resorted to a blatantly false plea of clerical error) the diplomatic title accorded to Monroe but not to him, a title he saw as invidiously lifting the former to a level higher than his own as mere minister plenipotentiary.[57] In fact, it is noteworthy that this issue of Livingston's rank actually preceded the latter's learning of the Monroe Mission. On February 18, 1803, he had written Madison: "I am not satisfied ... that I am empowered to do anything but the common routine of business.... I find that I have no precise diplomatic character, being not even an envoy ordinary or extraordinary, though it had been usual for the U.S. to grant the latter grade to gentlemen of less standing than myself." Livingston said that he only mentioned all this because Bernadotte was unhappy he couldn't have that title "while the U.S. only retains a minister plenipotentiary here."

Livingston returned to this issue in his "private and confidential" dispatch to Madison of April 17, 1803: "Since my letter of the 13th" (actually, as we have seen, the 14th) Monroe and he, prior to meeting with Talleyrand on the 14th, went over "our commission in which there are two circumstances with which I am not quite satisfied.... I have not the same rank.... My age and the station I have held" warrant the higher one accorded Monroe.

As mentioned, Madison on July 29, 1803, apologized to Livingston. He did so in the following terms: "The difference in the diplomatic titles ... was the result merely of an error of the clerk.... The President ... [had no intention of making] any distinction of grade." Of course, this explanation does not stand up to close examination: (a) even in his instructions to Livingston and Monroe of March 2, 1803, Madison wrote: "You will herewith receive a commission and letters of credence, one of you as minister plenipotentiary, the other as minister extraordinary and plenipotentiary"; and (b) Jefferson, in his communication to the Congress seeking authorization to commission Monroe for his mission to France and Spain, was explicit in his view that an "extraordinary" envoy was needed to meet the situation to supplement the efforts of the "ordinary" minister. But Madison did not merely rest on a defense of clerical error; his 29 July response went on to note that, according to the jurist Vattel, the two titles in fact were "precisely of the same grade." Still, Madison acknowledged that "it is said" French usage disagreed with Vattel on this point. The secretary also took the occasion to comment that Livingston's letter didn't repeat his earlier expressed desire to return to the U.S. and that he therefore hoped that meant "the interesting scenes which have since supervened may reconcile you to a longer stay" in France.

The various issues raised by the announcement of the Monroe Mission were subjects of public discussion in the U.S. For example, Gouverneur Morris' letter to Livingston of April 23, 1803, included the following:

> I did not write to you by Mr. Monroe, because he and I are not on terms of such intimacy [an understatement: Senator Monroe had bitterly protested Morris's appointment in 1792 as minister plenipotentiary to France] ... because I did not choose to put one in his care, and because I wished you to judge of things without any bias from comments on my part.... Not being in the confidence of our Cabinet, I cannot account for a conduct which in every point of view is so strange.... [Your] sacrifices ... [for the administration and your] rank in society ... all required more delicacy on the part of your political friends.... I consider [Monroe] as a person of mediocrity in every respect. Just exceptions lie against his diplomatic character and ... his appointment must appear extraordinary to the cabinets of Europe. It is in itself a most unwary step and will lower our government in public estimation.... I trust it will not be pretended that the application of money could not be as safely entrusted to your care and intelligence as to those of Mr. Monroe. The pretext that he is only joined with you in that commission is mere pretext and every discreet man with you will naturally consider him as the principal, the chief, and in fact the sole minister.[58]

(Morris enclosed with this letter a pamphlet he had written and anonymously published in March 1803 on this subject, *Munroe's Embassy*.)

That Livingston did not need Morris to stoke his fire of resentment at Monroe's rank and mission is clear from a remarkable letter written to that longtime friend five days prior to Morris' own. That letter, and those written by Monroe — one to Madison that same month (quoted earlier) and a second to his political friends in Virginia the following month — belie the public stance of these two men that reports of dissension and rivalry between the two of them were false. Here are excerpts from Livingston's letter to Morris of 18 April, in which he reported the delay in responding to his note of 10 October was

> not from want of affection ... but I confess my sins fairly, from that spirit of idleness and procrastination [familiar faults, which Morris and Jay both regularly charged their friend Livingston with during periods in the Revolutionary War when he seemed to be moping at his Clermont home]....[59] Contrary to your view, the U.S. stands higher than ever in Europe.... The spirit shown on the subject of New Orleans has also tended in a very peculiar manner to raise the national character. Perhaps had it been suffered to go the whole length and to change the sovereignty of that island and the Floridas, it would have had a still more beneficial effect. As it is, I have made the best use of it, and it has accelerated my operations here, which I think I should have terminated happily by this time had I been invested with powers (which I never have been), though I repeatedly requested them.

Nevertheless, "concealing this circumstance in the hope of receiving them," Livingston had "prepared everything, first, by creating a personal interest,"[60] second, by showing the "inutility" of transferring Louisiana to France, and by demonstrating the danger

> of suffering that country to go in the hand of Britain, which I considered as a consequence of the attempt on the part of France to colonize them. I had advanced so far as to have been upon the point of concluding when the appointment of Mr. Monroe stopped my operations. But, though this will retard, I trust it will not defeat them. On his arrival, he found me so far advanced that a treaty [that is, as the reader may recall, a negotiation] was informally opened upon the principles I had stalked out.... But it was neither in my power or in my inclination to proceed singly, for, though I trust that we shall render our country [~~the most~~] important services, yet I am not so ignorant of the malevolence of party spirit as not to be assured of a plentiful share of abuse. I am content if anything is done to divide the [~~honors~~] profit and loss with him, for I presume our friends will not be less liberal of praise than our enemies of censure. He has not yet been received, and I am very fearful that he will not be till the usual time of reception, which is the 15th of every month [in fact, as already mentioned, Monroe would be received by Napoleon on 1 May, when he also attended a diplomatic dinner hosted by the first consul]....[61] Till then, I can only have the benefit of his council. I am happy to find that we [he and Monroe] cordially agree in sentiment hitherto [regarding the negotiations.]

For his part, by May 25, 1803, Monroe — although now, as compared to 15 April, somewhat more philosophical and mellow about Livingston given the great accomplishment of his mission — was writing from Paris to political friends in America (the two Virginia senators):

> It is proper that you should possess a correct knowledge of the facts here which led to this result [of the Louisiana purchase]. I arrived at Havre on the 8th of April, which fact was known here on the 9th.[62] On the 10th this government resolved to offer us by sale the whole of Louisiana....[63] On the 12th, I arrived in town, on the 14th was received by the minister [Talleyrand], recognized by him, by order of the First Consul, and informed that ... a person would be appointed to treat with us with whom we might proceed [prior to his being] presented [to Napoleon]. The decision to offer us the territory by sale was not the effect of any management of mine, for it took place before I reached Paris; nor of my colleague or it would have taken place sooner: Being postponed until my arrival in France or indeed till the mission was known, is a full proof that it was the result of the cause above mentioned and of those only. I enclose you a copy of a letter from Mr. Livingston bearing date on the 10th of April ... which established the above facts....[64] Had the measures of our government ... failed ... all the responsibility would have been on the government and myself.... Personally, I pretend to nothing but zeal and industry after I got here, a merit which is equally due to my colleague.... I expect no misrepresentation from my colleague and ... I am happy to have it in my power to bear testimony in the most explicit manner in favor of his zeal, sincere and diligent cooperation through the whole of this business.[65]

By the following year, Livingston, too, would be mellowing regarding his relations with Monroe. In a private letter of May 5, 1804, to Madison, he wrote[66]:

> My public letters have shown you the state of our affairs here and the very disagreeable situation in which they are placed by the obstinacy ... of one, and the weakness of the other two [American claims] commissioners. I am now to acknowledge [having] received your friendly private letter. With respect to the correspondence of Mr. Monroe and myself on the subject of the guarantee [by the French and the U.S. of their respective American possessions] ... I think with you the less ['the letters'] are known the better, for be assured that I find none [of the 'sensibilities'] in myself that do not perfectly harmonize with the esteem I have for Mr. Monroe. We saw the subject [of the guarantee] in different lights.... Both the one and the other sought the public good, and notwithstanding the little artifices of some persons here [read: Sumter and Skipworth — see the following] to excite jealousies between us, I have never [!] felt them for a moment, and I trust that he is equally above them.
> Some circumstances make me fear that my friend, Marbois, is declining in favor.[67] Talleyrand is all powerful and does not love him

and has taken advantage of the bad bargain that he allegedly made with us to hurt him....[68] Last Sunday, at a public audience, [Napoleon] asked me when our elections come on? Whether Louisiana would be allowed to vote? and expressed in very strong terms his hope that there would be no change of President.... I assured him that he would meet with no opposition.

This episode regarding the Monroe mission was not the first occasion for Livingston to have complained on matters affecting his personal authority. During the greater part of 1802, he and Sumter, his secretary of legation, had bitter exchanges, including lengthy written ones, as to their respective job descriptions. Sumter had to resort to political support back in the U.S., including to the president, who had been the initiator of his appointment to Livingston's staff, forcing Livingston to write Jefferson that either Sumter went or he would.[69] In the end, Sumter did leave — to join *Monroe's* staff![70] As this problem would greatly preoccupy Livingston, take a significant part of his working time, be brought to the attention of the president and secretary of state, and also become entangled with the diplomacy related to the purchase of Louisiana, it merits summarizing here the highlights of the 1802 correspondence related to the Livingston-Sumter conflict, as follows[71]:

1. Livingston to Sumter, April 27: "I have just received with equal surprise and pain your letter of this day.... I'm submitting your letter to the President; he will, I presume, give such orders as he thinks proper." (Along with Sumter's letter complaining of such matters as "the nature and extent" of his "official duties," Livingston sent Jefferson a copy of another of Sumter's letters, where Sumter explained why he had declined to copy Livingston's response to Monroe's previously-cited request for two swords for Virginian revolutionary heroes — he did not consider the subject an official matter.) His letters "convince me, Sir, of your wish to make a breach between us." The president had assured him that "you would be ready to perform the duties of a private secretary" as well as secretary of legation. If he did wish to return home, "surely, Sir, it will be more for your interest and honor to assign some domestic reason for it than to see a cause in an imaginary [grievance] against me." (The letter concluded that he "reciprocated" Sumter's "professions of respect and personal friendship.")

2. Livingston to Jefferson, April 29: Livingston was sorry to have to write him on a personal matter "which I fear will not be less painful to you than it has been to me." From the start, he "never believed ... that [Sumter] would remain long in France, because nothing in the country ever appeared to please him.... The endeavor to make diplomatic characters by choosing secretaries of legation from among the young men of fortune or connection

from whom they expect support at home, and rendering them independent of their principals, will ... be ineffectual...."[72] As this letter may become the subject of [public] discussion," he wouldn't raise other subjects.

3. Livingston to Madison, May 12: Sumter had resigned "for reasons which I presume he will explain to the President.... I trust I will be able now to name my own secretary "[who shall be subject to my particular regulations]" [and the] system of appointing secretaries to the legation in which there are obvious inconveniences will be laid aside."[73]

4. Sumter to Livingston, October 24: "I have prepared a statement of our difference on the 22nd which is more full than yours of that date.... This difference must be judged by our government." As in the past, the difference was regarding "a question about the public and private agency of claims."[74] Regarding his threat of 22 October "to make Major Mountflorence your secretary," that will not be carried out "in my office...."[75] Thank God ... [he will not long remain as] secretary of the legation." Meanwhile, "I shall continue to refuse and to resist the employment of a person in it, who has not the confidence of our government." Livingston knew of this lack of confidence in him "on public authority as well as on my information, before you formed any connection with him."

5. Livingston to Jefferson, October 28: The enclosed "packet [was] ... very painful to me." It showed that Sumter saw himself "as my coadjutor." Livingston was on his own hiring a secretary. "If it continues to be the system of the government to give the ministers a secretary of the legation and no private secretary," then "I must explicitly request ... that my resignation may be accepted." The whole business would have cost Sumter less than a day's work from August. There was no way out of the problem given his belief that "he has a supporting interest at home."

6. Livingston to Madison, November 2: His private secretary was needed "to do the business of the office till I receive your direction."[76]

7. Livingston to Madison, November 10: "Having no one to copy" a long letter he had written him, he was sending him this on "the single object lest I should miss" the opportunity.

8. Livingston to Tillotson November 12: Regarding his "utmost difficulty" with Sumter, "either the President must recall him or me." (Tillotson's response of March 14, 1803, was that he was not surprised at Livingston's problems with Sumter, whose appointment from the start he disliked and who now could hurt Livingston's reputation in the south.)

Nor did it ease Livingston's plight in Paris that, as mentioned earlier, the Virginian Skipworth, his inherited American consul at Paris, fed Monroe inside information tending to undermine that visitor's confidence in

Livingston's competence and receptivity to his special mission. In effect, this brought to five the pairs of skeptical, if not outright unfriendly, southern eyes (increasingly including the president's) focusing on Livingston's every move. That Monroe made quick and effective use of Skipworth's information at Livingston's expense is clear from his letter of April 15, 1803, to a receptive Madison (previously quoted). Madison's response to Monroe of 30 July included a sarcastic reference to Livingston as "Magnus Apollo" and as "the ordinary minister" whose "appeal to the French government had been ... hackneyed." Madison in this message also expressed great irritation at Livingston for apparently orchestrating a campaign in the U.S.—through his American business friends having an interest in the spoliation claims against France—whose purpose was to demonstrate that it was precisely his various memoranda to the French government that most influenced Napoleon to cede all of Louisiana. That campaign, which denigrated Monroe's (and by implication the U.S. government's) role, culminated in newspaper publication of Livingston's printed memorandum of 1802 that contained conjectures about future military and economic prospects that Madison accurately predicted would lead to official protests from London. When directly confronted by Madison's complaint, all Livingston could lamely write in self-defense, on November 15, 1803, was that, as his memorandum was "not an official paper, as it is not signed or delivered in my public character, I do not see that it can ever be noticed on this side of the water as such; besides that, there is nothing in it relative to Britain that has not been told them officially by our government and by almost every maritime power in Europe."[77]

Chapter 6

A Balance Sheet

It was with a mixed sense of great accomplishment for his country and aggravation at his own government that Livingston in the fall of 1804 would hand over his legation to his successor (and brother-in-law, the future secretary of war, General John Armstrong) and return to the U.S. in the spring of 1805 to devote the remaining decade of his life apolitically at Clermont cultivating his interests in technology and agriculture, while Monroe went on to succeed Madison as both secretary of state and president of the U.S.[1]

A retrospective balance sheet on Livingston's mission to France might incorporate the following elements:

Positive Considerations

1. Livingston's activities were clearly within the framework of the policy of the U.S. government. As will be recalled, there is a rich irony here: Monroe — who now was basking in the glory of having played the key role in the Louisiana Purchase, overshadowing that of President Jefferson's faithful resident minister — had himself been, as minister plenipotentiary to France under President Washington, out of sympathy with his government's then policy toward France, notably as reflected in the Jay Treaty of 1794.[2] Accordingly, he had been peremptorily recalled from his post by President Washington, who ever afterward felt only enmity toward him, especially when Monroe, back in the U.S., published a version of the events that was strongly critical of the tilt of the second Washington administration in favor of Great Britain.[3]

2. As point man, so to speak, for the ambivalent policy of his government as between resorting to military threats or only using "peace and persuasion" to achieve the (poorly defined) goal of warding off a French presence on the continent of North America, Livingston naturally drew

much of the fire leveled against the U.S. by the French authorities and, at home, not only by political opponents of the Republican administration, but also by the mercantile interests who were unrealistically expecting more rapid progress in implementing the (weakly worded) provisions of the Franco-American convention of 1800 for French compensation to them for the "spoliations" of the recent quasi-war between the two nations.

3. As John Quincy Adams would write decades later, Livingston's impressive range of memoranda to influential French figures made the best intellectual case possible for the wisdom of U.S. policy. While difficult to document, it seems most probable that the analyses contained in those memoranda — not only of the rationale for his own country's policies but also of why it was in France's true interest to reach an accommodation with the U.S. — did have an impact on the thinking of Napoleon and his senior officials. After all, their final decision to carry the U.S. west of the Mississippi was consistent with Livingston's argumentation, as was the design of the agreements of April 30, 1803, to marry that decision to a settlement of the thorny problem of France's treaty responsibility to meet the demands of American citizens for compensation for their commercial losses due to French spoliations. Moreover, the 1806 memorandum from Talleyrand to Napoleon (contained in Appendix B) gives clear evidence that Livingston's memoranda were indeed closely read, contrary to the skepticism of many historians, such as Irving Brant and Lawrence S. Kaplan. In addition, recall that as early as October 1802 — that is, prior to the crisis caused by the Spanish intendant at New Orleans and prior to the certainty of French defeat at St. Domingue and to the renewal of France's war with Britain — the French were responding to Livingston's memoranda by hinting to him at the possibility of ceding to the U.S. not just New Orleans but all of Louisiana west of the Mississippi. Finally, it seems justifiable to underline the value for the ultimate American success regarding Louisiana of Livingston's long-established relationship with Marbois, whose own predisposition to promote close Franco-American relations was clearly strengthened by his confidence that Livingston reciprocated that attitude.

In fact, it is another irony of this story that, if one recalls his letter of December 11, 1802, to Mark Leavenworth, Livingston may have felt himself *too successful* in having influenced France to cede *all* of Louisiana to the U.S. Livingston's goal in early 1803 was, as he described it to Joseph Bonaparte and Talleyrand, a U.S. jurisdiction over the territory west of the Mississippi but above the Arkansas River, leaving France to share that river with the U.S. below that line and thus to expose itself to the leverage of a constant fear of nearby U.S. military power.

However that may be, Livingston, on balance, clearly took pride in the 30 April agreement and made strenuous efforts to assure that he personally would get the lion's share of the political — and historical — credit for the achievement. In the particular time-honored way of diplomats (witness John Jay's apologia for the record of November 17, 1782, from Paris to Secretary Livingston), Livingston set forth in the contemporary record the best case possible for his having been the one to have most contributed to the French decision to sell Louisiana. He did so in his previously-cited message to Madison of May 12, 1803, and the reader must be left to his own judgment as to the validity of the writer's claims, because much of them, although plausible, are difficult to document and are at times marred by a clear distortion of the record (such as Livingston's claim that his previous messages to Madison had reported that Napoleon had taken his decision as early as April 8 — that is, prior to news of Monroe's arrival at Le Havre).[4] Here is a summary of Livingston's 12 May letter[5]:

> You have seen in my late letter [presumably the one of April 11–12] the direct commencement of the negotiation previous to the arrival of Mr. Monroe, and, in our joint letter [presumably, the letter dated 13 May (i.e., one day after the date of the present letter)], its consummation. It will be a matter of curiosity, at least to you, to be more intimately acquainted with the exciting causes which have been long operating, and which I have hinted at in my letter to the President,[6] but which, from their extreme delicacy, I have not thought it proper to detail. As this goes with the treaty by a special and safe messenger, I will send you the papers I referred to in my letters to the President.[7]

Livingston then began to detail the events leading up to the purchase, beginning with Joseph Bonaparte, who started in 1802 to pass on to the first consul his proposals regarding Louisiana. While Napoleon advised, regarding that part of his ideas concerning "personal objects," that "he could not listen to it," he did approve "my [Livingston's] propositions, in part, but not to the extent I had proposed. I am satisfied that from this period [presumably December 1802–January 1803] they had determined to let us have New Orleans, and the territory above the Arkansas, in exchange for certain commercial advantages; and that, if they could have concluded with Spain, we should also have had West Florida."

Napoleon and Talleyrand soon thereafter made clear their "idea" that France must first take possession "of the country" and then it "could more advantageously treat with our government." At about this time, news arrived of the action of the Spanish intendant at New Orleans and of the appointment of Bernadotte as minister to the U.S., regarding which Talleyrand "assured me that Bernadotte should have powers" to treat with us along the previously-stated lines. Until Talleyrand's letter to Livingston of 11 March containing Napoleon's answer to his letter to him of 27 February, the French had a "disrelish" to sell the territory, preferring only to cede it "in exchange for commercial advantages." After that date, Napoleon — regarding the commitment he had personally and "hastily" made in that 11 March letter to discharge *fully and promptly* all debts France rightly owed to American claimants under the 1800 treaty — realized that he was "in no situation to fulfill [it], and yet knew not how to elude [it], as I pressed at every turn," making clear to all the authorities "that I had communicated it not only to the [U.S.] government but to the creditors." Livingston told Marbois he would "publish my letter to the First Consul, with his answer." Moreover, he had translated and given to the French government the text of Congress's hard-line resolutions. On top of all that came the likely "rupture with England."

These circumstances "produced a determination to sell, which was communicated [by Napoleon] to the Council, as I informed you, on the 8th of April." The reason why Talleyrand first "called on me to set a price" and then "pretended he spoke without authority ... was cleared the next day.[8]

> The subsequent measures you have in my letters and notes and in those Mr. Monroe and myself have jointly written to you as I believe that next to the negotiation that secured our independence this is the most important the United States have ever entered into; I thought every thing that lead to it might interest you and the President; I wished you to be minutely acquainted with every step I had taken, my verbal communications with everybody to whom I had access whose interest I conceived might be useful it would be impossible to detail. Nothing however was neglected on my part; and I sincerely hope the issue may be acceptable to our country.

Negative Considerations

1. Livingston was too importuning, too threatening, overly didactic in his written presentations to the French government. His having printed and widely distributed a major and candid analysis of French interests regarding Louisiana antagonized Foreign Minister Talleyrand and predictably ended up being published in newspapers in both hemispheres.[9] This, coupled with some of his other memoranda that became public knowledge, led to friction in relations between the U.S. and Britain, which naturally had taken umbrage at some of Livingston's invidious conjectures regarding the pros and cons of American alignment with it or with France.[10]

2. Had Livingston's overly bellicose reaction to the Spanish ending of the U.S. right of deposit at New Orleans prevailed in Washington, relations between the U.S. and France might have become too tense to have enabled events to proceed as they did in April 1803.

3. Livingston's personal qualities were not those of an ideal diplomat. His being hard of hearing; his lack of fluent spoken French; his overly strong personal political ambitions to return to his home state, where, aside from his obsessive interest in the steamboat matter, he apparently envisaged a run for the governorship; his unduly close association with private American citizens having a direct financial interest in settling the debt issue with France (one of whom was his own brother, John) — all these factors contributed to giving credibility to the broader basis for considering his tenure in Paris, up until the April 1803 breakthrough, as a failure.

4. Livingston had an exaggerated notion of the extent to which the Jefferson administration wished to endow him with authority to supervise policy in Europe, and this, beginning early in his tenure, tended to antagonize it. Madison simply ignored that newly appointed minister's proposals, made even before leaving for France, that he be given authority to intervene in such broad multilateral subjects as neutral rights at sea, piracy in the Mediterranean Sea, relations between the U.S. and rulers in central Europe and Italy, etc. Livingston further tarnished his image in Washington by patently absurd and falsified claims that he was on the cusp of success when the Monroe mission was announced. Perhaps a pithy summary of Madison's pique at Livingston can be gleaned from the secretary's note to Jefferson of April 15, 1804: Livingston "is again a volunteer in diplomatic projects.... [He] lacks modesty."[11]

Summary Assessment

The key conclusion must be that Napoleon's decision to cede all of Louisiana to the U.S. was due to *force majeure* growing out of the renewal of armed hostilities with Britain and the military disaster at St. Domingue.[12] His later memoirs report that he had originally envisaged a 25,000 "black army" moving on from that island to make war even on the U.S. in implementation of his plan for a new, revitalized French presence in the western hemisphere. But this does not mean that Livingston's and other American pressures and argumentation necessarily were irrelevant to the first consul's ultimate decision, or that they were potentially counterproductive to that happy outcome from the U.S. point of view. To the contrary, those diplomatic activities may well have sharpened Napoleon's thinking—as well as that of Talleyrand and Marbois—on the issue, enabling France to act not only quickly but also in a most timely fashion, before any "cannon" was fired in Europe with attendant implications for Jefferson's own military ideas.

Moreover, Napoleon at least theoretically did have one obvious alternative to ceding all Louisiana to the U.S.: simply canceling the Spanish retrocession. Of course, this alternative was fraught with costs to France and Napoleon himself both diplomatically—a loss of face given the public steps already being taken toward that retrocession—and militarily, in that a Spain now on the French side (especially once Madrid, too, declared war on Britain in December 1804) would not necessarily have been immune from British attack on its possessions. On balance, Napoleon clearly opted to make the best of a bad situation by creatively turning his overly exposed new colonial territory in North America into both an immediate bulwark against his principal enemy and a building block for his longer-term goal of converting the U.S. into a military and economic asset for France on the worldwide checkerboard of the balance of power. (Again, Talleyrand's memoranda in Appendix B reflect this thinking.)

As regards the more narrow issue of which American diplomat deserves the lion's share of the glory for the purchase, we have Jefferson's own judicious summary view that credit must be shared equally between his two negotiators (Jefferson to Horatio Gates, July 11, 1803: "I find our opposition is very willing to pluck feathers from Monroe, although not fond of sticking them into Livingston's coat. The truth is, both have a just portion of merit").[13] Of course, this judgment incompletely describes the president's full, well-justified view that it was his own policy—and especially his happy choice of Monroe to temper domestically the calls for military action by westerners and southerners spurred on by the Federalist opposition, and overseas the apparently harsh feelings that were at times present between Livingston and the French government—that most accounted for: (a) the keeping of the peace on the Mississippi border of the U.S.; (b) facilitating the decision of France to cede Louisiana to the U.S.; and (c), solidifying both politically and economically all the geographical regions of his still-forming country into a more permanent union. Indeed, Jefferson's own letter to Gates, even as it reflects his politically partisan perspective, well describes his overall assessment of his achievement. In it he stated that the U.S. government "from April, 1802" made clear that war was in prospect without a settlement with France. The opposition, in their day, "had a war; what did they make it bring us?" Therefore, they were wrong to say the cession of Louisiana was only due to the luck of a war between France and Britain: "Instead of making our neutrality the ground of gain to their country, they were plunging into the war.... They were for making their country an appendage of England.... They would now be at war against the atheists and disorganizers of France.... We are not hostile to France."

CHAPTER 7

Consequences and Controversies — An American Historical Perspective

When the French flag was lowered in New Orleans on December 20, 1803, it marked the second time in forty years that France withdrew entirely from the North American mainland, leaving it only a pair of small islands off the coast of Newfoundland as somber reminders of a once-great presence on that continent just over the horizon. Whereas the definitive peace treaty with England in 1763, alongside the cession of Louisiana to Spain the previous year, ended over two hundred years of deep-rooted French possessions in North America, their withdrawal from Louisiana in favor of the United States ended a mere twenty days of purely titular French sovereignty over that territory. For the American colonists of 1763, the forced French surrender to England of Canada, and the voluntary French cession of Louisiana (including New Orleans) to Spain, meant the welcome total disappearance from the scene of their century-old European enemy. It also meant the removal to a distant wilderness of the remaining, largely non-threatening Bourbon power, Spain. Under such conditions, those colonists were soon able to achieve independence from a mother country no longer needed to help protect them from the French and, in fact, now perceived as the new obstacle to their economic and political betterment.

France, following the U.S. termination in 1798 of the Franco-American alliance treaty of 1778, felt free once again to return, not only to North American territory never held by England, as had been allowed even by the 1778 treaty, but also to the Floridas, which had been England's from 1763 to 1783. However, France was able to regain from Spain only a Louisiana that was narrowly defined to exclude that strategically important strip of Gulf coast that had been part of eastern French Louisiana up to the Perdido River just west of Pensacola. Not surprisingly, when the Americans purchased Louisiana from the French and then tried to convince Spain that the former French territory east of the Mississippi was a legitimate part of that purchase, they found Madrid to be as resistant with them as it had been with the French. This proved to be the case even with France, as it had promised to do during the negotiations with Livingston and Monroe, lending a diplomatic helping hand to the U.S. in making the case for West Florida.

West Florida and Beyond

The manner in which the Americans satisfied their demand for the Floridas, east and west, set the pattern that historians have identified as also prevailing in subsequent territorial accretions in Texas, New Mexico and California. That is, building on a relatively large, privately initiated influx of "Anglo-Americans" into the target territory, the U.S. government would encourage a movement of "independence" by those migrants, and then would show receptivity to calls for annexation into the federal Union. In doing so, the government would not hesitate to use its own force, whether to (a) dispossess from power overly demanding Americans, as was notably done in the 1810–11 occupation of the western part of West Florida; (b) evict the Spanish authorities, as was notably done by General Wilkinson in the 1813 occupation of the Pensacola region of West Florida; or, (c) coerce into capitulation by treaty, as was done by General Jackson in the period leading up to the 1819 termination of Spanish sovereignty in the rest of Florida.

For our purposes, the case of West Florida warrants further examination, because the claim to that land also proved to be the subject of diplomatic controversy between the U.S. and France as well as Spain. As made lucidly clear in Talleyrand's two post-Purchase memoranda to Napoleon (Appendix B), the issue with the Americans wasn't about their claim, per se, but rather over the line they took that implied, in Talleyrand's view, France was not living up to the terms of the 30 April treaty. By that treaty, according to the Americans, France was bound to include West Florida in the cession of Louisiana.[1] Talleyrand more accurately, and based on painful negotiating experience with the Spaniards, maintained that neither the various treaties between France and Spain since 1795, nor the oral and written commitments France made to the U.S., justified the point of view that Spain's retrocession of Louisiana to France, or France's sale in turn to the U.S., included anything east of the Mississippi River — except for New Orleans.

All this did not mean that France failed to support U.S. arguments to Spain in favor of turning over at least that part of eastern Louisiana that had been under French control prior to 1762–63. To the contrary, as documented in both the text and the appendices of the present work: (a) France provided Livingston an analytical paper on the historical background of the Florida issue demonstrating that it basically was only due to a technicality and to diplomatic courtesy toward Spain that France's November 1762 cession of Louisiana to Spain did not include West Florida up to the Perdido River; and (b), the technicality was that the English in any event were to be given that territory, along with the Spanish part of Florida, as an integral feature of the terms that were simultaneously being agreed upon by all three of those powers for the preliminary peace treaty of that same month and year. Accordingly, the French cession of Louisiana to Spain only concerned the territory west of the Mississippi and, after difficult French negotiations with the English, New Orleans as well. In sum, these three cited French documents illustrate that France truly shared some of the U.S. thinking as to the legitimacy of including West Florida within the boundaries of retroceded Louisiana.[2]

That France backed the American demand for West Florida and, if the Spaniards were willing, even for the rest of Florida, should not be surprising. For its own strategic reasons, it *wanted* the U.S. to have a strong presence in the area as a natural element in its overall policy of transferring Louisiana to that unthreatening young country. Moreover, as vividly shown in the analytical paper found in Livingston's papers, there also was a more emotional French motive for assisting the U.S. in its effort to obtain at least West Florida. That motive was France's disdain and resentment both for the military performance of Spain as its ally during the American War of Independence, and for Madrid's having dragged out the multi-year negotiations over Louisiana and Florida. This last point especially disgruntled the French, who plausibly believed that, had they been able to move years earlier than 1803 into Louisiana, the entire strategic situation might well have been altered, precluding the cession to the U.S.

Issues of Constitutionality and Governance

Circumstances overrode whatever qualms Jefferson had regarding the treaty with France as an act requiring constitutional amendment. While he never changed his view that such an amendment was necessary, he came to appreciate, between the time of the arrival of the treaty in July and its formal submission to the Senate in October, the need for urgency in U.S.

ratification. Based on reports from Livingston and Monroe, he had reason to fear that the mercurial Napoleon might change his mind notwithstanding his own ratification of the treaty days after its signature in May. Moreover, the military situation in the world had changed with resumption of the war between France and England. This argued in favor of America's completing the Louisiana transaction as rapidly as possible while the path was still clear for it to do so. In any event, all he was required to do as president was submit the treaty to the Senate — the prescribed procedure for a constitutional amendment leaves that initiative to the Congress and the States with no specified role for the president. Similarly avoiding the constitutional issue, the Senate, dominated by Jefferson's Republican party, approved the treaty overwhelmingly in two days of debate. This allowed the transfer of sovereignty to take place, as noted, before year's end. That the purchase and its legal handling by the administration was broadly approved by the people is clear from the results of the following year's presidential election. All but Connecticut and Delaware gave their electoral votes to Jefferson and his new running mate, Governor George Clinton of New York. Their opponents were Charles C. Pinckney and our now familiar Rufus King.

As increasingly noticed by American historians, the more difficult issue posed to the country by the Purchase was, how to govern a territory whose population — in keeping with the fact that the land itself had been beyond the boundaries of the United States— was comprised largely of those who were considered, at least for the foreseeable future, as not qualified for citizenship and self-government? In that year, 1803, the bulk of the inhabitants was still of French or Spanish origin, with a motley mix of free people of color, native Americans and African slaves; relatively few of the permanent residents as yet were "Anglo-Americans." The congressional debate on this governance issue was by far more divisive and time-consuming than was that regarding the constitutionality and ratification of the purchase treaty itself.[3]

It would be only by trial and error, including the weighing of a "Remonstrance" reminiscent of *Ancien Regime* days in France that was carried to Washington by representatives of the New Orleans population, that the Congress in these early years developed a set of compromise procedures. These were designed to avoid, on the one hand, the creation of a purely colonial situation between the U.S. government and its new possession, and, on the other hand, the bestowing upon the inhabitants there of the same political rights and privileges as those prevailing in the country's original non-state territories, notably under the Northwest Ordinance of 1787. Thus, the Congress moved from an initial law depriving Louisianians of any self-governing bodies or elected officials to one under which, for example, the most senior officials remained appointees of Washington but junior ones were elected locally. Also, a representative assembly was established, although with limited powers; and, for the southern part of the Louisiana territory, a promise of statehood was made, but on condition that it attain a population level of 60,000.

In the event, with the crisis over England's actions at sea against U.S. merchantmen rapidly coming into view, the process of statehood was accelerated, and the State of Louisiana was accepted into the Union in 1812 in order to help assure the inhabitants' loyalty to the American cause. By that time, the target level of 60,000 qualified residents had been surpassed, due partly to the influx of Anglo-Americans into the newly acquired territory, and partly to the turmoil in the Caribbean islands, where the repercussions of Napoleon's invasion of Spain in 1807 led to relatively large population movements that inevitably included refugees of European origin coming ashore in Louisiana.

The Special Issues of Slavery and Treatment of Native Americans

The pragmatic U.S. approach to solving the sundry governance problems associated with the acquisition of Louisiana allowed the Union to remain stable despite the political shocks it had to absorb as new territories evolved from ones of direct control to those of self-government, and finally to statehood. But one issue was a constant from the start, as reflected in strategic decisions stretching from the Missouri Compromise of 1820 to the Kansas-Nebraska Act of 1854: How to resolve the sectional conflict over slavery. As Roger Kennedy notes, the die was really cast between 1802 and 1820, when policies were adopted by the U.S. government and the Congress virtually assuring that the slave-owning planter class would dominate the newly acquired southern territories.[4] Thus, the original governance laws for Louisiana banned only the introduction of foreign slaves into the territory, leaving it legal for residents to bring in slaves from the original territory of the U.S. While this arrangement facilitated the ability of certain states of the Union who wished to do so to reduce their slave populations by sales to Louisianians, it nevertheless kept alive and well the basic problem the Union eventually proved unable peacefully to resolve — i.e., how to balance out and reconcile the political and cultural incompatibilities between slave states and free states. Obviously, as new states were added west of the Mississippi River, this problem inevitably became exacerbated, despite the various attempted compromises.

In this scheme of things, another human tragedy was looming in the form of the fate being determined for the Native Americans, initially those residing east of the Mississippi. While their role regarding the future stability of the federal Union was not the destabilizing one played by the institution of slavery, it did pose then, as now, moral and political issues of the first order. The strategy adopted by the U.S. government from Jefferson's administration onward was quite explicit: Move the "Indians" around as required by the security and growth needs of the country. Thus, Indians initially were to be given rather free rein in the northern part of the Louisiana territory, while the focus of post–Purchase national development was to be east of the Mississippi and the New Orleans region, where Indian-held territory was to be purchased or otherwise obtained for white settlers, including by the forced transfer of entire tribes from their ancestral grounds to the newly acquired open spaces northwest of the river. The idea — and it proved workable as the century unfolded — was gradually to dispossess the Indians even of that western territory to the extent required as the white population expanded toward the Pacific.[5]

In light of these two issues, one can only look with some hesitation at the label Americans have frequently put on their new possession: "The Empire of Liberty." If one can set aside these two aspects of the matter, there would be justification for such a self-congratulatory designation. A large part of that justification is based on the manner in which much of the federal land was utilized. Always excepting the large, slave-based plantation economy in the region from southern Missouri to the Gulf and from there westward to and eventually including Texas, that manner was to follow the admirable procedures established for disposal of much of the land between the Appalachians and the Mississippi. The land there was sold in relatively small lots to anyone who could afford it. This provided the basic pre-conditions for the spread of a democratic form of government as contrasted with the kind that had been the case in the French, Spanish and English colonies, where the land often was disposed of in large chunks on the basis of social hierarchy and political favoritism.[6] As John Adams famously said, "Power always follows property."

Security and Political Issues

The Louisiana Purchase is also seen as having in the short run provided the domestic political basis for a nation reasonably united as it entered the War of 1812 against England and its policy of impressing American sailors. The point is that there was a trade-off between New England's particular goal of absorbing Canada into the Union and the South's particular goal of extending its slave-based institutions beyond the original boundaries of the U.S. While that war had several positive results (although not regarding Canada), it did leave New Englanders, especially the states-rights and secessionist-minded ones in the Federalist party, feeling in a more weakened position than ever in what they saw as a growing domination of the Union by those opposed to their economic and political interests.[7] This view culminated in the calling of the ill-fated Hartford Convention in December 1814, a most untimely moment to consider even a gradual secession from the Union just as the country was on the cusp of the victory at the battle of New Orleans and just as the satisfactory peace treaty of Ghent was concluded and being made public. If anything marked the end of the Federalist party as a major political player in the nation it was that Convention.

The War of 1812 had followed upon Jefferson's failed effort, 1806–09, to counter attacks on American shipping, notably by his embargo policy, which proved only to be harmful to American economic interests, especially those of the northern states along the Atlantic seaboard. That American policy did not at all dent the offending maritime policies either of the English, who were blocking even neutral trade with Napoleon-controlled Europe, or of Napoleon, whose Continental System, to which the English had reacted, effectively ended all trade between Europe and England, including that carried by merchantmen from neutral states, such as the U.S. This failed Jeffersonian effort deepened the friction between north and south even as issues growing out of the Louisiana Purchase were, as noted above, beginning to generate national discord.

If the international situation in the years immediately after the Purchase brought anything positive for the U.S., it was the defeat in 1805 of the combined French and Spanish fleets off Trafalgar, Spain, by England's Admiral Nelson.[8] That defeat, so reminiscent of the result of other sea battles between the Bourbons and the English, ended residual concerns in the U.S. that Napoleon — once victory at sea and perhaps in England itself was assured — was planning to revive his original plan of an empire in the western hemisphere, with Louisiana at the top of the agenda not withstanding his April 30 treaty.

Sidelights: Hamilton and Burr and Livingston

Hamilton and Burr: To follow on the account given directly above of the impact of the Purchase on secessionist trends in the north, a related human drama concerns the 1804 duel between these two New Yorkers.

Burr had been roundly defeated as candidate for governor in the election that coincidentally was held the very month of the Louisiana Treaty's negotiation. When coupled with his previous loss of favor in the Jefferson administration, Burr's only political future now rested with assuming the leadership of a northern secessionist movement that was accelerating in reaction to the implications of the Purchase. As most recently put forward by Thomas Fleming, who had earlier made a special study of the duel, Hamilton was his main competitor for this leadership, and, in order to eliminate him, Burr purposely picked the fight that ended in Hamilton's death in July 1804.[9]

Were one to accept this line of historical analysis, it would be tempting also to conjecture and lay some of the blame directly on the Purchase for Hamilton's own actions leading to the fatal duel. Having so publicly and boldly urged a military solution to the twin problems of Louisiana's retrocession and the Spanish closing of the deposit at New Orleans, Hamilton surely lost political credibility as a result of the peaceful and happy outcome orchestrated by Jefferson.[10] As issues of face and reputation played an important role in the high society of that dueling period, it may very well be that this experience, along with other recent personal disappointments and tragedies, so upset Hamilton that he became reckless as to his fate. (On the substantive issue of how the U.S. managed to obtain Louisiana from France, Hamilton attributed it entirely to lucky events outside American control in Europe; but, if personal credit had to be given, he would assign it not to the leaders in Washington but to the diplomatic skills of Livingston.)[11]

Returning now to Burr's relationship to the Louisiana story, he moved his ambitions westward and descended the Mississippi River in 1805 while gathering some 1,000 arms-wielding local Americans in an ostensible plan to bring independence to Texas and Mexico. But the plan was so ambiguous as to allow his supporters to read into it a scheme also for bringing New Orleans itself into his breakaway territories. It was especially this latter aspect that determined Jefferson to capture him and bring him to trial. This was accomplished, but the result was not one the president would have wished. The trial was conducted by the U.S. Supreme Court under Chief Justice Marshall, and it ruled that there was insufficient evidence to convict. Marshall, it is thought, may well have been influenced by his longstanding personal dislike of Jefferson. In any event, this enabled Burr to leave the country for a few years, returning to it from England and living out his life in relative obscurity.

Robert Livingston: It is ironic that the man who continues to be seen by many as having been "in the pocket" of the French as their hand-picked foreign secretary during the American War of Independence is also the man who many then and now also recognize as having been a key U.S. negotiator in one of the great diplomatic achievements in American history — and at the expense of those self-same French. If scholars can, as they do, uncontroversially label Marbois as "the man who sold Louisiana," and label Gouverneur Morris as "the man who wrote the Constitution," then surely the present writer could be excused were he to label Livingston as "the man who bought Louisiana." Of course, in all these three cases, hyperbole applies: Marbois was merely the agent of Napoleon, Morris of the members of the Constitutional Convention, and Livingston of Jefferson and Madison.[12] And yet, did Livingston not, at his fateful, late-night meeting with Marbois, agree to that purchase?[13] And did he not do so in the absence of written or even informal authority from his government, and even prior to any substantive contact between Monroe and the French government? And finally, was this event not attributable in part to the "importunities," to use a word suggested by Talleyrand himself, with which Livingston pressed his own ambitiously creative ideas on the French, who, by the evidence presented in the present study, were influenced by them?[14]

Worth noting is that, to the extent that the achievements of American negotiators at Paris in both 1778 and 1782–83 have reasonably, if demeaningly, been ascribed in part to their skill in merely not interfering with the flow of larger world events (that in and of themselves were of benefit to U.S. diplomatic strategy as regards obtaining an alliance with France and later a liberal peace with England), so might we similarly ascribe the achievement of the Louisiana Purchase to the consequence of an international situation in which the U.S. was largely but a bystander. Still, there is room in this scenario to give appropriate credit to the policies and qualities of the American officials both at home and at Paris. Surely, for example, had a more belligerent Jefferson administration bent to domestic pressures and, as Livingston so dearly wished, sent a military force against New Orleans in early 1803, that would have altered the situation so basically as plausibly to have precluded a proud Napoleonic France from ceding the rest of Louisiana to the aggressor. Furthermore, surely the hard work of Livingston in repeatedly demonstrating by sharp analyses the strength of American opposition to a return of France to North America added to whatever the young and junior French diplomat Pichon was reporting from Washington in helping the French authorities reach the conclusions they did that April.

Had Livingston, as he personally wished, left France immediately following the signing of the Treaty, his subsequent reputation would have been much better than what it actually became. The clumsy and imprecise procedures established for discharging the French debt to U.S. claimants unfortunately assigned the U.S. minister a direct, operational role in the decisions as to who got what.[15] This inevitably embroiled first Livingston and then his successor and brother-in-law, Armstrong, in endless friction with both French officials and Americans in both the private sector and government.[16] It also, when combined with the fact that other close relatives of Livingston were among the claimants, lent itself to charges being levied to the present day that the Livingston "clan," as Kennedy pejoratively likes to put it, with Robert at its head, had been involved in illicit and unethical schemes for personal profit at taxpayer expense — charges the evidence fails to support.[17]

On top of all this, and more justifiably, as we have seen, Livingston is charged with falsifying records in the hope of giving himself full credit for the Treaty. This show of remarkable human weakness flew in the face of his own words regarding the behavior of some of his associates during the Revolutionary War: "The culture of laurels is the most expensive husbandry." Not that he wasn't provoked and tempted both by the incredibly tantalizing change for the better in the situation at Paris, and by the self-important attitude adopted by his unwelcome colleague, Monroe — who, for added salt in the wound, had come bearing the more senior title of envoy "extraordinary."[18] (It should be recalled, however, that Livingston *did* recognize from the start of Monroe's mission that it had ample justification from the American domestic point of view.) If a judicious judgment as to the respective contributions of these two American ministers may be allowed two centuries later, it would be that to *Livingston* belongs the lion's share of the credit for the Treaty itself, but to *Monroe* belongs the credit for protecting the validity of that Treaty when it was placed in doubt months later by a Napoleon reportedly having second thoughts. Monroe did so by taking upon himself in August 1803 the responsibility for authorizing the advance to the French of the $2 million Congress had already appropriated in February in the hope of facilitating the negotiation for New Orleans and the Floridas.[19] Here was another example of the advantages, as discussed in the text above, of having a negotiator come directly from Washington with a full and informal understanding of the policy and degree of flexibility of the president. Livingston, not having that advantage, would likely not have felt authorized to take that pre-ratification initiative — which, however, he did fully endorse and help execute once Monroe authorized it from his London post.

No less harmful to Livingston's historical reputation, aside from his unethical behavior in competing for credit and his unfortunate involvement in the implementation of the claims convention, is a third matter: His having tried to create what he cryptically kept calling in his dispatches a "personal interest" for the benefit of the Bonaparte family.[20] This matter is not at all about an indifferent question of what was the *location* of the particular land he was offering for revenue-sharing sales with a partnering U.S. government. It truly does matter whether that land was in the virgin territory west of the Mississippi and north of the Arkansas, or in the Floridas. When wrongly tied to the latter region and to that of New Orleans, Livingston's efforts become intertwined with charges of misuse of taxpayers' funds, shifty deals assigning land ownership to insiders at the expense of more legitimate, existing and prospective American investors, or payoffs to the well-known venal French, with Talleyrand at the head. When, as documented in the present study, Livingston's offer to the Bonapartes of a "personal interest" is more accurately tied to the trans–Mississippi northern parts of Louisiana, it more properly is seen as free of all these blemishes and, as Livingston put it at the time in a key defense of his ploy, as an offer that would not have required of the U.S. government a single penny's appropriation of funds or any loss of its sovereign rights in the affected territory.[21] (Rewarding Frenchmen with land owned by the U.S. government was not unheard of—the reader will recall that Lafayette, for example, in the early 1800s, with congressional authority, was granted property in lower Louisiana, which he then sold for badly needed cash.)[22]

Sidelights Regarding Other Personalities

Worth commenting on first is the role of du Pont. Interestingly, the totality of his memorandum to Consul Lebrun following upon the public announcement of Monroe's mission seems never to have been made available hitherto in English. Perhaps for that reason, the contemporary and subsequent debate as to the utility of his role leaves out this plausibly key element in the developments leading up to Napoleon's decision to sell Louisiana. This would be in addition to du Pont's known influence with Jefferson throughout the months leading up to the Purchase; for example, it was du Pont's correspondence that provided the basis for the inclusion in the 2 March instructions to Monroe and Livingston of authority to go as high as $6 million in the negotiation for the purchase of New Orleans and the Floridas. (Incidentally, there is a long-standing myth—perpetuated in extravagant terms by Dumas Malone—that du Pont, in Malone's words, "negotiated, with the secret envoy of Great Britain, the basis of the treaty which recognized the independence of the United States in 1782.")[23] As regards the pair of U.S. secretaries of legation at Paris and Madrid: Sumter ended a minor diplomatic career at a post in Brazil (even as his 70-year-old father, a South Carolina senator, had turned down Jefferson's offer in 1803 of the governorship of Louisiana). The more able and universally respected Graham went on to become assistant secretary of state under President Madison. He was in that leading position at the time in 1810 when Madison was solving the problem posed by the activities of Skipworth, who was now a plantation owner in West Florida and the leader of a very briefly lasting independent state there with its capital at Baton Rouge.[24] Skipworth's tactic was to try to convince Washington to negotiate with him on the terms and conditions for West Florida's annexation by the U.S. Madison simply overrode that demand by sending in troops and occupying the country.

Both Talleyrand and Marbois survived their service under Napoleon by returning to high office when the Bourbons were restored to power under Louis XVIII. Talleyrand had resigned in 1807 in opposition to Napoleon's diplomatic policies, notably toward Austria.[25] Marbois was finally dismissed around that time by a Napoleon perhaps tired of having such an honest official in charge of his treasury.[26] It has been well said that, whereas Talleyrand had actively worked for the Bourbon downfall during the French Revolution, making his return to that monarchy's service rather hypocritical, Marbois had never sought to undermine Louis XVI and so his return to Bourbon service is much less of an inconsistency.[27]

Some Still-Open Historical Questions

1. Despite the consensus that Madrid had indeed ordered the closing of the New Orleans deposit in 1802, and despite the absence of evidence that Charles IV did so at French behest, a suspicion remains even among the most informed historians as to whether the French did, in fact, somehow urge that step, which they were quite willing to live with once it was taken.[28]

2. How sincere was Jefferson in his stated readiness to act militarily, with or without England as ally, in seizing New Orleans under certain circumstances? Even the desparate, final instructions sent by Madison after Monroe was already in France leave room for doubt that the administration was really ready to resort to war in the absence of an absolute closing of the Mississippi River itself to American shipping.[29]

3. Was Talleyrand's erratic (and, in the view of some, possibly obstructionist) behavior of April 11 and 12 attributable to his alleged role in

England's bribery effort, or was it due to the circumstance that Napoleon had decided to assign the negotiation to Marbois, as described in the previous text? The two Talleyrand memoranda contained in Appendix B strongly support the latter explanation, given that Talleyrand is seen as a quite willing backer of Napoleon's decision to sell Louisiana to the U.S. In further support of it, recall that Talleyrand, already in the post–XYZ period, saw merit in cultivating a French friendship with the U.S.[30]

4. How reluctant was Spain to give up Louisiana or the Floridas? As for Louisiana, the evidence is strong that, for the right price in Italy, it was willing to be convinced that Napoleon's France could more effectively and cheaply defend that important buffer zone from seizure by Anglo-Saxons with eyes on Texas and Mexico itself.[31] But Florida was another matter. Unlike Louisiana, it had always been Spain's, at least westward up to the Perdido River, until England took it in 1763. And, it was partly regained by Spain during the American War of Independence by its own successful military operations at Mobile and Pensacola. It remained Spain's policy in 1802 to keep the Gulf of Mexico a "Spanish lake," even as it was ready to grant its French ally a return presence there. During the peace negotiations of late 1782 with England, Spain agreed to recede on its key war aim of recovering Gibraltar once England made its formal offer to return the Floridas to it (along with Minorca and other captured Spanish possessions)—it was that specific offer that is generally considered as the dealmaker allowing for the preliminary peace treaty of January 1783. As we have seen, it took a series of hard-line U.S. military and diplomatic pressure over a 16-year period before Spain with great reluctance finally gave up all of Florida to it.

As for English policy toward having a permanent, sovereign presence in the Gulf, once London recognized that it could not keep for itself the militarily essential ports of West Florida, whether due to French, Spanish or American opposition, it lost any interest it may have had in obtaining possession of Louisiana itself. It was with this outlook that, in 1801, the English assured the U.S., through Rufus King, that they would cede New Orleans to it were they to capture it from the French in any upcoming war.[32]

APPENDIX A

Summary of Livingston's Louisiana Memorandum, July 1802

Livingston's July 1802 memorandum, "Memoire sur cette question: Est-il avantageux à la France de prendre possesion de la Louisiane?" ("Memorandum Concerning the Question: Is It Advantageous for France to Take Possession of Louisiana?"),[1] *outlines his case for cession of Louisiana to the United States. Distributed in English and French, it argues that France's continued possession of Louisiana serves none of the country's interests — commercial, military or diplomatic. The memorandum proved highly influential in France and America, and may have affected Napoleon's decision to cede all of the territory to the United States.*

The importance of this document warrants its appearance in this text, but in view of its length and complexity I have taken the unusual step of summarizing it in order to focus on the points most important to this book's discussion. Words not in brackets are Livingston's; words in brackets are my summary.

The population of France, though very considerable, has by no means attained the point which renders it necessary to colonize.... [What France needs is more capital — witness Britain's success.] Overseas colonies add nothing to the strength of a nation. They are, on the contrary, weak points.... [France will have all she can handle merely to develop St. Domingue and her other existing colonies without taking on Louisiana.] For it is obvious, that whatever is placed in one is taken from the other. France is short of capital at home and abroad....

[The United States is increasingly adding to its capital and becoming less dependent upon the capital of British merchants.] It is equally obvious that the national expense must be increased by the increase of its establishments, and that the points of attack and defense must be multiplied in the same proportion in case of war.... [For example, Louisiana's problems include that it will need slaves. There would be no commercial advantage to France from what Louisiana can produce, since most of those goods can be produced on France's islands, which if] ... well cultivated, are equal to every demand of France, and, indeed, of Europe. [Livingston names wood and rice as perhaps the sole exceptions but notes that producing these in Louisiana might be too expensive to be worth it; for example, wood supply comes not from southern, but from northern states in the U.S., where] ... the labor of free hands is content to work for small profit.... [The West Indies' molasses is a cheap way for France to pay for wood.] Even England, with all her enterprise, her right to the navigation of the Mississippi, and the prejudice of Americans in favor of her fabrics, has never ventured to send her commodities [to the west] by that channel [that is, by way of New Orleans], well knowing that through Baltimore and Philadelphia they will find an easier entrance [by way of rivers and canals and roads. Therefore, France should put New Orleans into U.S. hands]... stipulating, at the same time, that it shall ever remain a free port of entry to French ships and French fabrics, subject to no greater duties than those paid by American ships.... [Also worth noting is that the U.S. would out-compete England for the Spanish American trade, and this, in turn, would help promote Franco-American commerce. The] ... commercial capital now in Orleans [is] principally American and British....

[A French Louisiana must be under a military government.] In case of a war between France and Spain ... supposing Britain to maintain her naval superiority (which I have upon a former occasion shown that she will, unless the commercial system of France shall be more liberal than it now is) ... the U.S. will acquire advantages [over France in Louisiana] from the war.... Louisiana, though settled near a century, has flourished neither in the hands of Spain nor of France.... At least half the trade of Orleans is carried on upon the capital of citizens of the U.S., under the faith of their treaty with Spain.... [This capital will go elsewhere on the Mississippi, if France takes Louisiana. Politically, a French Louisiana would be even more contrary to French interests.] The relative position of [mainland] France, which precludes all idea of danger or rivalship, either by sea or by land, between her and the U.S., has made them [the U.S.] view her as a natural ally, and consider the measure of her power as an additional pledge for the safety of their commerce and their future tranquility.... [French] statesmen ... at the end of a successful war, conceived it more advantageous to France to insure the lasting friendship of the U.S., than to acquire territory which might excite their jealousy, and throw them back into the hands of the nation from whom they had but just aided

Summary of Livingston's Memorandum

to liberate them.... [Livingston notes his awareness that raising this latter point risks giving "umbrage by freedom" to speak out] which haughty spirits may construe into menace.... [America's making a threat would be a "ridiculous" idea. France has made "united Europe" bow to her power.]

[There is no nation at present on the globe whose consumption offers such encouragement to foreign manufacturers as that of the United States. France should not easily act in a way that would make of the United States an "open enemy," which it would be if France possessed New Orleans. The U.S. would eventually have to form] ... cautionary connections with Britain ... [which] by this connection ... will hope to retain the commerce of America, which she almost exclusively possesses.... [Britain will do all possible] ... to prevent that commercial and maritime union between France and the U.S. on which alone France can hope to engraft a naval superiority ... [that is, a Franco-American alliance replacing the old Bourbon alliance of France and Spain against the British navy. Britain has wisely given up all] ... posts on the south side of the Lakes [and] ... Upper Canada is principally settled by emigrants from the U.S., who, in case of a rupture, would probably join [the U.S.] if the spirit of the American government did not prohibit an extension of [the U.S.'s] limits....[2] One third of the mercantile houses now employed in New Orleans belongs to the citizens of the U.S.... [Natchez can receive any size vessel New Orleans can.] Large vessels have already gone from France and unloaded their cargoes there without any difficulty.... Therefore, the market is always the better the further you advance.

Appendix B

Two Talleyrand-Napoleon Memoranda

I. Text of a Report by Talleyrand to Napoleon Written on November 19, 1804, Entitled "On the Subject of the 'Memorandum on the Floridas' Submitted by Monroe"[1]

The U.S., which desires under the auspices of France to negotiate at Madrid the acquisition of Florida, has earned few titles to the good offices of His Imperial Majesty by the bitter tone and the lack of respect with which it has conducted itself with Spain.

Several disputes having arisen last year over the right of deposit which it enjoyed at New Orleans, the U.S. threatened to send an armed force into West Florida and moved some troops toward that frontier.

Ever since the acquisition of Louisiana, the U.S. has arrogated to itself in that same part of Florida some rights regarding customs, navigation, and sovereignty which justifiably offended His Catholic Majesty, and it is only due to the strong representations of the Madrid court that the U.S. has not implemented the measures which it has decreed.[2]

Now, seeking to give a legal character to its plan to usurp West Florida, the U.S. claims that this province was included within the cession that France made to it of Louisiana, and, without concerning itself over whether this assertion could compromise France with Spain, or whether it might not result in an impression that France has been lacking in good faith either toward it or toward Spain, the U.S. proposes to make good on those claims at Madrid and to present itself there as the sovereign over one part of the Floridas—without doubt with a view to acquire the totality of it at the best price.

The U.S. has still other points of disagreement to resolve with Spain. It is demanding from it indemnities for the losses that the temporary suspension of its right of deposit at New Orleans has caused to its commerce; moreover, it insists on the ratification of a convention by which Spain had promised to indemnify it for the American prizes brought by French cruisers during the last war into Spanish ports, where they were condemned.[3]

This last claim should have been considered as set aside by the convention that France had signed with the U.S. on September 30, 1800, because that convention stipulated that no indemnity shall be accorded for the respective prizes taken in whatever area and brought into whatever port. For the U.S. to demand of Spain an indemnity for the prizes taken into and condemned in Spanish ports is to go back on a part of the general renunciation that it had made.

It also seemed that all the disputes relative to the right of deposit at New Orleans should have been ended by the treaty in which France ceded Louisiana to the U.S. The acquisition of an immense territory could well cancel out a few earlier losses. France, in ceding Louisiana, had in further view the consolidation of good relations between Spain and the federal government, between whom it seemed that this measure left no further subjects of disagreement.

But the U.S., deceived by the ascendancy which it now has in the New World into forgetting about the position it should conserve in the Old, seeks to reopen with Spain the least plausible matters of disagreement. It mixes threats of a rupture with proposals for an arrangement, and Mr. Pinckney, the U.S. minister at Madrid, after having written notes containing arrogant [*ton de jactance*] and sharp language ill-suited to a new state addressing an old and respectable monarchy, has requested his passports for a return to America in the event Spain does not immediately agree to ratify a convention which had been unexpectedly imposed on it.

Were these various points of disagreement between the U.S. and Spain substantively irrelevant to France, our interest in seeing them resolved might have been limited to the interest we naturally have in reconciling two powers with each of whom we maintain friendly relations. But the claims of the U.S., particularly those which have as their object the seizure of West Florida on the grounds that land had been ceded to it by France along with Louisiana, being a kind of affront to France's dignity and her good faith, His Imperial Majesty will doubtless believe it necessary to express his discontent to the U.S. when, after the developments which I shall now have the honor to report to him, he will become convinced: (a) that Spain, when she made the retrocession of Louisiana to France, did not at all include in it West Florida; (b) that she expressly refused to alienate any part of the Floridas; and (c), that France, when she negotiated two years later with the U.S., never offered the cession of West Florida, regarding which she neither had the right nor the intention to transmit to it, and never inserted anything in its treaties which could serve as a plausible pretext for America's claims.

The historical record of the French negotiations with Spain does not allow any doubt regarding this matter.

When general Berthier was charged toward the end of [1800] to negotiate a treaty with Spain for the retrocession of Louisiana, he also carried out his instructions to try to obtain the Floridas; but the King of Spain consistently refused to concur, and M. d'Urquijo, the then-minister, declared that "at this time, His Catholic Majesty was so much against the cession of any part of Florida that it would be both useless and impolitic for him to speak of it." However, d'Urquijo made it clear that, "at the general peace, the King could possibly decide to cede a part of the Floridas between the Mississippi and Mobile Rivers pursuant to a specific request that might be made of him at that time by the First Consul."

The acquisition of the Floridas not having been inserted in the treaty of [St. Ildefonso of October 1, 1800], General Beurnonville was instructed, upon going to Spain in [1802], to reopen the proposition and negotiate a treaty by which Spain would cede the Floridas to France in exchange for the Duchy of Parma, which would be added to the States of the King of Etruria. This new negotiation proves that France had not as yet obtained any part of the Floridas. The proposals made to Spain by General Beurnonville did not lead to any treaty: the rupture of the treaty of Amiens ended efforts to obtain the Floridas and, far from seeking their acquisition, it was then France which transferred Louisiana to the U.S. with the same rights and in the same form that she herself had obtained it. In order to express with greater precision the extent of the cession made to the U.S., there was inserted in the treaty concluded with it the article contained in the treaty of St. Ildefonso which served as the foundation for this alienation.... [The reference is to Article 3, whose text Talleyrand transmits here. That Article stated that the retrocession involved Louisiana as it was transmitted to Spain by France in 1762.]

The limits of Louisiana were not literally spelled out in the St. Ildefonso treaty; but it sufficed to identify them by consulting the prior treaties.

France, which had possessed Louisiana until 1762 and which had ceded it to Spain, had only included in this cession the western side of the Mississippi plus the island of New Orleans, located at the mouth of that river. By the terms of the preliminary treaty signed that same day with England and confirmed a few months later by the definitive treaty, France ceded to England all that she possessed on the eastern side of the Mississippi and of the d'Iberville River, and the course of these two rivers was assigned as the limit between Louisiana and the British possessions.

Spain could only retrocede to France in [1800] what she had received from her in 1762, and a comparison between these two treaties sufficed to show the extent and the limits of the retrocession.

The U.S., in order to establish that the acquisition it made should be seen as extending on the eastern side of the Mississippi up to the Perdido River, that is to say, a length of ____ miles, alleges that Louisiana, during the period of French possession, had extended up to that point: but Louisiana also extended up to the Great Lakes of Canada and up to the Allegheny Mountains. The issue does not at all concern a return to these old limits which several treaties have altered: it only concerns having to recognize the extent of the country that France had given to Spain and that the latter has returned to us.

For a long time, all the territory situated to the south of the U.S. has been known solely by the names of East Florida and West Florida. That is how it had been designated by England, which owned them until 1783. That is how it had been designated until now by Spain, which has owned them since that time. That is how it had equally been named in the treaties concluded between Spain and the U.S., which today claims that a large portion of this territory is part of Louisiana.

In 1795, the U.S. agreed by treaty that the southern limit which separates its territory from the Spanish colonies of the two Floridas, East and West, would be defined by a line which would begin on the Mississippi River. The U.S., therefore, recognized at that time that the Floridas extended up to that river.

The same opinion is expressed in the several notes Mr. Livingston addressed toward the end of [1802] and the beginning of [1803] regarding Louisiana. He said: "I speak of Louisiana proper, in which I do not include the Floridas, because I think they do not form part of the cession" (Note of 1er fructidor An XI).

In a second memorandum, that minister requested that, in the event France may have acquired the two Floridas, she should cede West Florida to the U.S. from the Perdido River up to the Mississippi (Note of 20 frimaire An XI).

In a third memorandum, he requested that, in the event of a cession of the Floridas to France, she should accord to the U.S. free navigation on the Mobile River (Note of 4 ventôse An XI).

Finally, following the conclusion of the treaty of [April 30, 1803] ceding Louisiana to the U.S., Mr. Livingston announced that Mr. Monroe would be going to Madrid to negotiate the acquisition of the Floridas in whole or in part, and he requested for this plenipotentiary a letter of recommendation to the ambassador of France at Madrid.

One can conclude from these examples that the U.S., having constantly distinguished Louisiana from the part of the Floridas which it is now pleased to include within it, has itself demonstrated the slight foundation for the claims that it is putting forward.

On the basis of the above comparisons, one cannot suppose that the U.S. is truly convinced of the justice of its claimed rights, and one is justified to think that it is really by the effect of its confidence in its military power, its ambition, its ascendancy in America, that the federal government is putting forward claims for a part of the Floridas with the expectation that by those factors it could be even more demanding upon Spain.

His Majesty will surely agree that his sense of justice cannot accept such claims. If he facilitated by his good offices an arrangement between the U.S. and Spain, he would want good faith and impartiality to be the basis for it. That could only be the case if the U.S. desisted in its unjust claims on West Florida, and, in the event of its returning to ways marked by due respect and the proprieties, regarding which governments should never stray in their relations with each other, His Imperial Majesty could then lend himself to urging the Madrid court to accept the U.S. proposal for the acquisition of the two Floridas. Perhaps at that time His Majesty could consider that this territory is less suitable *[convient moins]* to Spain since its separation from the other Spanish colonies; that it is suitable for the U.S., because a part of the rivers which flow in its western states pass through the Floridas before emptying into the Gulf of Mexico; and finally that Spain could find that its present position and its prospective expenses in the upcoming war are reasons to consider the offers of the federal government.

II. Text of "Report of Prince Talleyrand to Emperor Napoleon," Written on May 6, 1806

The mission given to Messrs. Armstrong and [Bowdoin] to settle by an arrangement with the court at Madrid the differences between the U.S. and that power makes it my duty to put before His Majesty the reasons for these differences. The issues which are to be treated at Madrid are too closely tied to events in which France had been involved to avoid Your Majesty's having to decide some of the limits beyond which the negotiations between the U.S. and Spain should not be allowed to go.

During the last war between France and the federal government, some American ships were stopped by French privateers along the coastal waters of Spanish possessions. The U.S. demanded satisfaction from Spain for having allowed this violation of its neutrality and of its jurisdiction, and Spain committed itself in a convention to give it some indemnities (August 11, 1802).

This convention was to be ratified within three month, but the U.S. only did so two years later; and till today Spain has still not ratified it, and *I believe that it is in the dignity and interest of France that this incompleted act remain forever unexecuted.*

France had stipulated in its convention of [September 30, 1800] with the U.S. that the latter would receive no indemnity for the prizes seized during the period of discord which had taken place. This provision applies to all circumstances and to all places where these prizes had been seized. The ships captured along the Spanish coasts are therefore included, and Spain has no obligation to indemnify the Americans for their ship losses, because Spain itself has no right of recourse to France, which has freed herself by her treaties from all obligations on this point.

The question of indemnities had been settled with France, and it was only with France that this could have been done. The U.S., in reopening this issue with Spain, had hoped to bring France into some accommodation; but His Imperial Majesty perhaps will think that it would not be in keeping with his sense of justice to lend himself to this.

The second subject of disagreement that the U.S. has raised with Spain concerns the possession of the Floridas, which the U.S. has contested for some time with Spain and which it now is seeking to acquire.

The U.S. at first supposed that West Florida was part of the cession of Louisiana made to it by France; but this claim could not survive the slightest examination. Louisiana as it was ceded by France to Spain in 1762 only included the territories to the west of the Mississippi: the Louisiana that France returned to in 1801 [?] had the same extent. It is in this state that it was ceded to the U.S.: no part of the Floridas was joined to it, and Spain had firmly refused to cede them to France.

These explanations [or analyses—*explications*] have been so often given to the U.S., they are so much in accord with the terms of the treaty of cession concluded with it, that it is not to be presumed that it will continue to insist on this point with the French government. *Nor should it so insist with the court of Madrid, because it is not up to that court to give any explanations regarding the treaty which it* [the U.S.] *had concluded with France.*

If then the American negotiators who are going to Madrid plan to reopen the argument over their government's alleged right to West Florida, I think that the ambassador of His Majesty the Emperor should positively oppose this claim and maintain that only France is competent to judge it; but if the negotiators limit themselves to a friendly negotiation looking toward the acquisition of Florida, the discussion then would be within the bounds that it should have, and it is truly to Spain that the U.S. should address itself.

Here, I should examine the consequences that a cession of Florida to the Americans could have for the U.S., for Spain, and for the French colonies; this should enable His Majesty to judge if it is suitable to his purposes and interests to support, as the Americans desire, the approaches that they plan to make at Madrid.

West Florida, the only part which they have in view [!], is a territory having 80 lieus [about 240 miles] in length and 45 in width, located between the Mississippi and the Perdido River, and between the Gulf of Mexico and an imaginary line which follows that of 32° latitude.[4] Several rivers, a large part of whose course run within the U.S., pass through Florida before emptying into the Gulf of Mexico, and, as they offer American commerce a natural outlet, the federal government necessarily wishes to be the master of their mouths and of the country which surrounds them. Moreover, this country is nearly entirely uncultivated, covered with sand, poorly populated, offering few resources for exploitation; but its position on the Gulf of Mexico could turn it into a commercial area. The entrance into the Mobile River, along with a few other parts of this coast, offer some good ports. Florida would quickly be developed by the U.S. as a territory for warehousing of goods and for transshipment, and its population, which doesn't amount to 20,000 souls, would be rapidly increased.

Under the domination of Spain, Florida could not have the same prosperity. It is separated from the other Spanish possessions and so cannot make any commercial contribution to them; nor could it itself receive any advantage from them. If it is useful for Spain to keep it, it is less to extract some direct utility from it than to prevent other powers from establishing new ports on the Gulf of Mexico.

But the acquisition of Louisiana by the Americans gives them access to this Gulf, and this eliminates the basis of the previous Spanish policy of excluding other powers from those waters.

Sooner or later, West Florida will become a subject of military quarrel between Spain and the Americans, because there is no natural boundary between the two, because the Mississippi isn't adequate to meet the transportation needs of American commerce and Florida blocks that commerce at many other points, and finally because the American population near the frontiers of these two countries will continue to increase while that of Florida will remain stationary and without hope of increase under Spaniard rule.

Therefore, the U.S. will have a greater incentive to acquire West Florida than Spain would have to keep it, but still to be considered is the how this question relates to the interests of France.

His Majesty did not judge that it would be contrary to his interests to procure for the U.S. a fresh aggrandizement of its territory by ceding Louisiana to it. He could have thought that the solidity that he'd thereby give it would contribute to a weakening of England, that the cession would lead to some sort of military or commercial rivalry between those two countries; that, moreover, by increasing the territory of the Americans, that very operation would prevent too-large an expansion of their political power; that such an increase would result in separating the interests of the Eastern States from the Western ones and would perhaps prepare the moment for their separation into two powers.

The same motives that His Majesty had for ceding Louisiana to the U.S. can now lead him not to oppose the plan it has to acquire West Florida.

But it remains to consider if His Majesty should himself have some plan for the two Floridas, whether to acquire them in a period more or less distant from now, or whether to make use of them as compensation in some later negotiation. Only His Majesty can express his views on this point.

I have tried to establish in this report, regarding the issues the U.S. has with Spain, that it lacks the right to demand of the court of Madrid an indemnity for the American prizes that our privateers had taken on the Spanish coasts during the last war.

I have added that the U.S. lacked the right in its negotiations with Spain to reopen the question of its alleged right of sovereignty that it asserts for itself over a part of the Floridas.

If Your Majesty approves the observations that I have had the honor to present to him, I will write in that sense to His ambassador at Madrid.

As regards the negotiations that the U.S. would like to open with Spain regarding the acquisition of the Floridas, I beg His Majesty to inform me whether His ambassador at Madrid should go along with or should actively oppose the proposed arrangement, and whether the convention which might then be concluded shouldn't at the same time define the boundaries which are still undetermined between Louisiana and Mexico so that there would no longer remain any points of contestation between Spain and the U.S.

The correspondence of General Turreau [France's ambassador to the U.S.] has often given occasion to notice that, in its discussions with Spain, the U.S. has betrayed but slight willingness to conciliate, and that it did not fear to allow those talks to result in a rupture if it could throw the blame on the court of Madrid. It is in this spirit that it bitterly complained about a few acts of violence made without official authorization on the borders of Florida, and that it enjoined M. d'Yrujo, the Spanish minister plenipotentiary, to leave the U.S.[5]

General Turreau even believes that the federal government had knowledge of the plan organized by Miranda [a co-conspirator with some Americans having an eye on seizing Spanish territory] against the Spanish colonies of Caracas and Venezuela, a plan initially conceived by England and for the execution of which Miranda had gone to arm three ships at New York. The first two ships left toward the end of last December; the third, named the *Léandre* and carrying 18 cannons, left on the third of February giving a false destination and heading for some groups on St. Domingue. It was only after the departure of this ship with Miranda himself aboard that the government of the U.S., pressed by the complaints of General Turreau, began to pursue those in New York who had lent themselves to this plot. Mr. Madison had even assured Turreau that until then he had absolutely no knowledge of the plot, although Miranda, prior to his New York expedition, had come to pass a couple of weeks in Washington and had seen members of the government.

Whatever the merits of Mr. Madison's assertions, Spain has no less reason to complain of an expedition organized against its colonies in a port of the U.S. It is the duty of neutral powers to keep an eye on secret conspiracies as well as to prevent open attacks directed from their ports against another power.

Prior to this Miranda expedition, whose results are still not known[6] and against which the U.S. seemed only to open its eyes after its departure from New York, the President had complained in a message to Congress of the conduct of Spain toward Americans, of the obstacles that it put on American commerce in the port of Mobile, of its refusal to agree to an arrangement regarding the boundaries of Louisiana, and of the properties seized by Spain that were owned by American citizens.

The complaints of the federal government were then repeated in all the American newspapers; the goal was to excite public opinion against Spain and to render nationwide the war which they hoped would occur.

Since that time, the government of the U.S. has seemed to moderate its complaints: it has entered into negotiations regarding them; it wishes to have France support its opinion at Madrid; it has become more accommodating to France herself: it has agreed to prohibit all U.S. trade with the rebels at St. Domingue: it has gone so far as to express a desire to make

England respect its rights as a trading neutral, and it could be presumed that His Majesty the Emperor will agree to show his satisfaction toward it for these last two actions, even though one perhaps should attribute them to the news of His Majesty's victories.[7]

The modifications in the opinion of the American government resulting either from reflection or from those victories lead us to presume that its differences with Spain might be settled amicably, but one can foresee that the importance which the U.S. attaches to the acquisition of West Florida might lead it sooner or later to attack this colony with military force if it is unable to acquire it now by negotiation.

His Majesty perhaps will judge what small interest France has in maintaining between the U.S. and Spain a source of friction which perhaps could run a greater risk for the Spanish colonies than for the Americans. But if His Majesty goes along with the cession of Florida, He'll believe that Spain should not cede it except under advantageous conditions, and that France, having to bear the burden of the war, should be relieved of its costs by seizing the occasion to avoid having new taxes imposed on it.

Appendix C

Summary and Analysis of Selected Sections of Marbois's *Histoire de la Louisiane et de la Cession...*[1]

> *This book by Marbois has been treated as an original, historical document: as a primary source. It was written by a very interested party having a personal record of falsifying history, as in his post–Seven Years' War Letters of Mme. Pompadour; moreover, it was written too many years after the Louisiana Purchase to be dependable in its details even if its writer had the best and most honest of intentions. Nevertheless, the book, if read with appropriate caution, contains valuable insights and useful data. Following is the present writer's view of its more interesting contents and its biases and factual errors that are most relevant to the present study. It is presented here for the convenience of readers who find it difficult to obtain a copy of the book.*

"Part One: Louisiana Under the Domination of France and Then Under Spain"

    1. France is at this writing getting more out of the great economic growth of a free Louisiana than it would have had it chosen to control, monopolize and defend it.

    2. U.S. independence "is like a second discovery" of a new world by the old, whose fate has been greatly influenced by both discoveries.

    3. Genet's instructions and subsequent actions in the U.S. "breathed hatred" of George Washington, who, the French authorities believed, was unreservedly pro–English. In the face of this situation, the U.S. government conducted itself with "firmness and dignity." Genet accused

Washington of "violating the Constitution" and tried to establish the west as an independent nation but with part of the territory to be under the French Republic. While Washington forewarned the governor of Kentucky of the pending arrival of Genet's agents, the governor answered that he could not "block the people from asserting their rights necessary to their survival." Therefore, the U.S. government in the fall of 1793 demanded Genet's recall. His successor soon arrived and assured the U.S. government that France rejected Genet's conduct. Nevertheless, his legacy showed the government that its western population was unhappy and "disposed to insurrection."

4. The French Convention and its Committee on Public Safety failed to see that the U.S., in this threatening situation to its territorial integrity, would always demand free navigation of the Mississippi along with sovereignty over "eastern Louisiana." Therefore, France continued to try to obtain the entire "province" of Louisiana back into its own hands, as in its 1795 instructions to the Basle negotiator, Ambassador Barthelemy, to "demand the restitution of Louisiana, or the cession of the Spanish part of St. Domingue, or the retention of the Spanish province of Guipuscoa, namely, of Fontarabie and St. Sebastion, "conquests of French armies." Spain at that time preferred keeping Louisiana and giving St. Domingue. The newly established Directory's focus was on European affairs and consequently looked upon the Spanish offer with indifference. The Directory was "as incapable of managing the affairs of a great state as had been the Committee on Public Safety." The 1798 XYZ affair was the low-water mark for the "baseness" of the Directory-led France. John Adams on May 28, 1798, stated that the U.S. would reseize former American ships in French hands and would, in American ports, also seize French ones. In 1799, Congress ended all trade with France and stated that all treaties were no long "obligatory."

5. "The U.S. was getting involved in the [30-year "maritime war" between France and England] due to a pro–English party there and despite governmental efforts at keeping the country neutral and drawing great advantage from that." England and France each competed for the U.S. to side with it, but the Directory's "imprudence" made a French-U.S. "rupture inevitable." It failed to follow the "foresightful policy" of the 1778 alliance treaty with America of "not imposing unequal and onerous conditions" and, therefore, the U.S. Congress, "following the most offensive of provocations, took the decision in 1798 of declaring its treaties dissolved and broken." Thus, the Directory "ended up by breaking the alliance, that precious fruit of the policy of Louis XVI's Councils."

6. "Louisiana in this period had rather gained than lost under these conditions so favorable to illegal trade." Spanish local and Madrid authorities turned a blind eye to this trade and even extended liberality to other Spanish American colonies.

7. Prior to seizing power, Napoleon[2] was "uncontestably ... the first among famous men; one can doubt if posterity will place him among the greatest of men." His coming into power "entirely changed the face of things" regarding Spain and Louisiana. Napoleon got a naive and uninformed Spain to approve an agreement the Directory had let drop (i.e., "the cession of Louisiana"). He wanted to gain revenue — later, his policy would change in favor of "forced imposition of taxes on a Europe which had been voluntarily paying to industrial and shipping elements." His goal in this earlier period was for France to be "preponderant in America by means of possession of Louisiana." In this, he was supported and encouraged by French port interests, which had always opposed the 1763 cession of Louisiana to Spain.

8. With English[3] help and agitation, St. Domingue's rebelling slaves forced France, according to Napoleon, "to make of St. Domingue a great camp with an army ready to bring the war to England's own colonies." But Napoleon soon changed his mind following the Marengo victory of 1800 and the opening of negotiations with Spain, which quickly agreed to cede Louisiana as a defense against English use of Louisiana as "a boulevard towards Mexico and as a French guarantee of the tranquility of the Gulf of Mexico." The third article in the St. Ildefonso treaty of October 1800 provided for "the retrocession ... six months after the above-cited conditions and stipulations ... regarding Parma, of the colony or province of Louisiana, with the same extension that it presently has in Spanish hands, and that it had when France possessed it and as it should be according to treaties signed since then between Spain and other States."

9. The Madrid treaty of March 1801 renewed these provisions, and its first article specified that the Duke of Parma would have sovereignty over Tuscany, to be known as the Kingdom of Etruria, in compensation for his loss of the Duchy of Parma and for the cession of Louisiana. However, these conditions could not be met, leading to "much cause of grief by the Spanish" and to Louisiana's "remaining for a time" in Spanish hands. "The nearby French, who for a century had totally failed to develop French Louisiana, seemed to Spain less a cause of fear than that of the U.S." as regards keeping Louisiana as a barrier protecting the rest of Spanish America. But Spain conditioned retrocession with a stipulation that it would have preference in the event France would wish to retrocede Louisiana in its turn. "This will cause much difficulty, as we shall see."

10. John Adams, perhaps against his own desire, and "ceding to popular opinion, had opened negotiations with the Directory. These took on more substance when Napoleon took the reigns of government" and led to the treaty of September 1800. Napoleon was careful to keep the Louisiana retrocession a secret "by avoiding taking possession of it," because "the war with England was still ongoing." At the time of the signing of the preliminary peace treaty with England in October 1801, it was clear that the latter truly welcomed peace; but Napoleon's warlike nature precluded a long period without conflict.

11. The consequent restart of the war in 1803 "had an impact on the situation regarding Louisiana and on the respective interests of France and England in America." Negotiator Cornwallis at Amiens had failed to insert a standard clause confirming all prior treaties that did not contradict that of Amiens of March 1802. This let stand the French occupation of all of St. Domingue, which the Basle treaty had established and which the English feared would be used by France as a base from which to attack Jamaica. Moreover, the "reunion" of France and Belgium threatened England. Finally, Amiens's silence created doubt in England regarding its retention of Acadia, Canada and Ile Royale. On top of all this came a report of the retrocession of Louisiana, which could imply a threat to Canada, French domination of the U.S. and eventually a Franco-American alliance against England. In fact, England knew of the retrocession prior to Amiens, which Hawkesbury openly derided as merely "an experimental peace."

12. Napoleon's plan was first to reconquer St. Domingue and then send "part of the army to Louisiana. The events of which St. Domingue was the bloody setting are closely tied to the history of the cession of treaty." Leclerc's troops left France on February 3, 1802, "about 18,000 in total." He died on 2 November with Rochambeau succeeding him. But within a year he was cornered at the Cap, where an English fleet blocked his exit, forcing him to capitulate on November 18, 1803, first to Dessaline's St. Domingue forces and then to English forces. Dessaline on January 1, 1804, declared his country's independence and then ordered the massacre of all the remaining whites. The St. Domingue "disaster" reduced the value of Louisiana to Napoleon, who had seen it as a supplier to France's American colonies of "food, beef and wood."

13. Meanwhile, General Victor in September 1802 replaced the overdemanding Bernadotte as commander of the planned expedition to Louisiana. Bernadotte in early 1803 was then appointed as minister plenipotentiary to the U.S. "So as to soften the blow of a form of exile, Napoleon informed him the post's work would include being the negotiator for ceding to the U.S. a part of Louisiana, success for which would lead

to personal gains for himself." He accepted, but in La Rochelle he learned that the French-English war was "about to break out and so on his own returned to Paris," and it would be "some time before the two friends would be reconciled."

14. Laussat, the designated prefect, left for Louisiana on January 12, 1803, and there "said by proclamation that his two colleagues would be coming." But only Victor had the rank and authority "to receive the colony from Spanish officers." Still, Laussat issued French laws, especially on 20 May when he reestablished the slave trade. "At the same time, a serious difference arose between the U.S. and the administrators of Louisiana," where governmental authority had remained with Spain's Salcedo and Casa Calvo, who were given "the title of commissioners by order of the King for the cession of the province to the French Republic." They "announced this change."

15. As regards the Spanish attendant's action of October 1802 canceling U.S. privileges at New Orleans, many saw the retrocession to France as the source of it (for example, p. 7 in Monroe's memoir). Since the Spanish king's decree of July 30, 1802, required Louisiana to be ceded "in its present state, Americans saw the intendant's action as excluding the U.S. from French Louisiana due to a "concertation," according to Monroe's memoir, between France and Spain.[4] The U.S. population was 800,000 in its western lands and American produce now lost half its value, whether at Natchez or New Orleans, where "the shipment offices" were located. Daniel Clark, visiting Paris from that region, urged that Natchez, 120 miles above New Orleans, be developed to replace that port, but this was never acted upon. The Americans now began to "recall the activities of the French governors on the Canadian frontiers" and feared Napoleon's expedition that was "being prepared [at Helvoet-Sluys in the Netherlands] was designed to reestablish old boundaries of Louisiana." "In vain" did the French seek to ease American concerns by their publishing a letter to Robert Livingston assuring that the treaties with the U.S. would be fully honored.

"Part Two: France's Cession of Louisiana to the U.S."

16. Livingston's effort in December 1802 to convince France to cede Louisiana west of the Mississippi and north of the Arkansas failed. He then urged the U.S. to use force on grounds that it would never achieve its goal by treaty. His correspondence and other communications with the French government confirmed him in this opinion. "But the wise Thomas Jefferson

did not share that hostile attitude and persisted in his hopes for a negotiated settlement," as is made clear in his January 1803 letter to Monroe [excerpts from which then follow].

17. Livingston's notes were so firm as to astonish a Napoleon who was not used to receiving such language and who, had it come from any other power would have resulted in an immediate occupation of that country. But in this instance Napoleon kept still lest he reveal his "impotence" versus the distant U.S. All this gave fodder for Americans seeking an "alliance with England." One such American was Gouverneur Morris, a member of Congress who was pushing for military action in answer to the New Orleans attendant's pronouncement. Morris was "of easy and elegant speech, very bright, and even more so vain and insolent." These qualities were appealing to the American voting public from the start of the American revolution and gave to those who have them "a kind of importance in time of agitation; but these men are rarely right for the management of affairs, and Morris, who at that time enjoyed some prestige, soon saw it disappear. He fell into a kind of obscurity as soon as the clouds disappeared." It is "probable that the opinions of Mr. Ross [a Federalist senator] and Mr. Morris had their origin in their correspondence" with Livingston.

18. Prior to Monroe's 8 March departure from the U.S., news had arrived there that the departure of the French division for Louisiana had been suspended for some period, and this was agreeable to pro-peace officials like Jefferson. Monroe's mission was kept "secret" [sic] in the U.S. and therefore had no effect on the crisis atmosphere there until his results were known five to six months after his having left for France. In the meanwhile, it was the work of Pichon and Yrujo in Washington that calmed the New Orleans crisis. Meanwhile, Napoleon foresaw a war against England and was taking appropriate measures to meet it. Pitt "hated France in line with the heritage transmitted to him by his father," and he implicitly backed Grenville's pro-prerogative party in contrast to Fox's anti–Pitt policy so devoted to the good of his country, although only his private life prevented his deflating Pitt. Napoleon only wanted the post–Amiens peace to be a long period if he could become "universal dictator." In 1802–03, however, he was seen as wanting peace in order "to do beautifying public works and to give the people enjoyment of a tranquil peace." Therefore, he gathered "able counselors" and focused his time on better civil laws and reform codes, and on reestablishing the financial situation and reactivating commerce and industry. If only he had stayed on this course, "the present century would be labeled with his name."

19. Napoleon saw England's strategy as including the goal of stripping

France of all but "a few colonies, so as to wear us out by vain expenditures in an effort to retain them and to render us peaceful for fear of losing them.... One could only glimpse then what is so clear now, i.e., that having colonies is a dangerous burden for a state to whom the ocean is closed once a maritime war begins." News had arrived at Paris in mid–January [actually, 2–3 weeks earlier] of Leclerc's death, and Napoleon regretfully delayed dispatching "new forces" to "America" and specifically to St. Domingue and Louisiana. Therefore, it was "even before" English moves of early March threatening the cancellation of Amiens that Napoleon had decided on no further troop expeditions to America.

20. At a *Council meeting* [emphasis added; no date given, but very likely 9 April], Napoleon, after reading out a British member of Parliament's statement demanding revenge for France's alliance with the U.S. of 1778, said that France should be the first to attack. He then gave "the first indication of his policy towards the U.S.... We need a maritime counterweight to England which one day would become England's rival; that counterweight is the U.S. Therefore, by creating it, I would be helpful to the entire world in blocking English domination of America as they now are dominating Asia."

21. By following the correspondence between Livingston and Talleyrand in the period of October 1802–January 1803 "after a long silence," one can see how Napoleon's policy only gradually changed in practice. Napoleon's navy was greatly reduced by this period, and he feared Victor's expedition would be captured at sea. "Louisiana had been the only acquisition he made without sword in hand," and he now wanted to be the manager of the negotiations for its sale. He sought out the two ministers who knew that land and also one of whom had experience in colonial administration.[5]

22. "The meetings began that very day [sic]."[6] But Livingston lacked the necessary powers; after about two years here, he was, as a "proud Republican ... irritated ... mistrustful, fearful that the overtures regarding Louisiana were only a device to gain time. Therefore, he received without real confidence the overture for the cession of the entire province." These "preliminaries" were "barely begun" when Monroe arrived at Le Havre.[7] Livingston, "always inclined toward mistrust, which so frequent a French failure to act on its words justified," wrote Monroe that the way to succeed would be "to be able to declare that New Orleans was already in U.S. hands." Monroe arrived in Paris on 12 April and was immediately discouraged by Livingston from "expecting a successful mission" [source: Monroe's "Journal"].

23. The conferences that then followed were, unusually, conducted

by plenipotentiaries who all knew each other for a long time and were "disposed in advance to a reciprocal confidence.... The three negotiators had seen the birth of the American nation" and had long exchanged intimate views of the situation. This was "unusual for ministerial envoys and those of the host power. But that didn't prevent each from regarding as a duty negotiating a deal having maximum value for his country.... Still struck by Livingston's mistrust, Monroe heard with surprise the opening offers of Marbois." It was too late to change the Americans' powers, which were only "to regulate what concerned the left bank of the Mississippi, including New Orleans," but a delay in the cession would mean Louisiana would become an *English* colony [emphasis added]. "From the start," the Americans concurred in negotiating over the entire Louisiana and for an amount beyond their authorization. The resultant cession later helped the U.S. to blunt English demands at Gand for an independent buffer zone, for the free navigation of the Mississippi, and even for the return of Louisiana to Spain [source: Monroe's letters to his 1814 negotiators].

24. Given the French treaty of October 1800 at St. Ildefonso with Spain, Spanish "prior consent without doubt was necessary; on the other hand, the slightest delay was accompanied by great danger."[8] Therefore, Spain was told of it only after the cession treaty's signature, and it was so unhappy that it took "nearly a year," February 10, 1804, before Madrid wrote U.S. minister Pinckney that Spain's "opposition ... was lifted."

25. The original draft by the Americans would have required France to obtain Spain's agreement to cede the Floridas to the U.S., but Marbois convinced them to drop that demand on the assurance that Napoleon, "the occasion arising, would help the U.S." to the extent of his ability. Marbois also obtained agreement that it would have been "awkward" to have expressed in the treaty itself that, at one and the same time, Louisiana, "a sovereign territory" of France, was being "abandoned," and also that it was being "sold at a price pegged at the territory's utility." Therefore, we developed three separate instruments.

26. At the signing, Livingston stated that it was "the most beautiful work of our lives.... England no longer can maintain exclusive influence over the affairs of America. Thus, America no longer will be a major cause of European rivalries and hatreds, and the U.S., henceforth, is placed among the first powers of the world. One day, France will have in the New World a natural friend.... The U.S. will be the instrument by which all peoples will reestablish their maritime rights which today are usurped by one nation alone."

27. The ambassadors of France and England left their respective posts

on 17 May and "hostilities began on 22 May by the seizure of French merchant ships.... That same day," Napoleon ratified the cession treaty without awaiting U.S. ratification, because it was important to show all that "Louisiana was no longer French."[9]

Chapter Notes

Preface

1. David H. Miller, *Treaties and Other International Acts of the United States of America*, vol. 2 (Washington, D.C.: U.S. Government Printing Office, 1931). For technical reasons explained by Miller, the agreement between the U.S. and France was labeled by the parties as a "convention" instead of "provisional treaty," the original intention (485). Arthur P. Whitaker, *The Mississippi Question* (New York: D. Appleton-Century, 1934). The treaty between France and Spain was signed at San Ildefonso, a summer Bourbon court north of Madrid.

2. For ease of identification, the present study will generally use "Napoleon" rather than his full name or only his family name, although it should be understood that it was not until he became emperor in 1804 that he adopted the title of "Napoleon I."

3. Whitaker, *The Mississippi Question*, P. 185.

4. Livingston Papers at New-York Historical Society. Also, as King pointed out in his letter of March 10, 1802, to Livingston: "The boundary between Canada and Louisiana is alike unsettled."

5. Leclerc had left from Brest 22 November and would put Toussaint on a ship for France on June 10, 1802.

6. Robert Livingston Papers at New-York Historical Society. Lawrence S. Kaplan's *Thomas Jefferson*, considers that the threat to have "recourse" to Britain was "not a serious prospect; rather it was a gambit," in part because Britain was seen as the "greater danger" to U.S. interests and security (131). That writer makes the additional observations that: (a) "It was clear in the 1790s that an unintended consequence of the Federalist quasi-war with France could be the latter's occupation of Louisiana" (131); and (b) "Nothing in Livingston's dispatches indicates that the President's threat of making common cause with Britain was clearly communicated to the First Consul" or "ever reached" him (136). But see Appendix B for indications that that threat indeed was known to that French leader. United States Department of State, *State Papers and Correspondence Bearing Upon the Purchase of the Territory of Louisiana* (Washington, D.C.: U.S. Government Printing Office, 1903): Livingston wrote Madison on May 12, 1803 that Napoleon "paid me some compliments on ... my *Notes on the relative naval force and commerce of France and England and the United States*" (187–96). George Dangerfield, *Chancellor Robert R. Livingston of New York, 1746–1813* (New York: Harcourt, Brace, 1960): Joseph was an "efficacious channel" to Napoleon, while Talleyrand was not (338).

7. United States Department of State, *State Papers and Public Documents of the United States* 3rd ed. (Washington, D.C.: U.S. Government Printing Office, 1819), 15–18.

8. Dumas Malone, ed., *Correspondence Between Thomas Jefferson and Pierre Samuel Du Pont de Nemours, 1798–1817* (New York: Da CapoPress, 1970), 16–49.

9. Pichon to Talleyrand, July 20, 1801, in James Madison, *The Papers of James Madison: Secretary of State Series*, vol. 1, ed. Robert J. Brugger, et al (Charlottesville, VA: University of Virginia Press, 1986), 403. Alexander DeConde, *This Affair of*

Louisiana (New York: Charles Scribner's Sons, 1976): By its 1778 treaty with the U.S., the French gave up Canada; "they did not, however, extend this renunciation to Louisiana" (75).

10. United States *State Papers and Correspondence*, 247–49.

11. Robert Livingston Papers at New-York Historical Society.

12. Whitaker *The Mississippi Question*. Whitaker points out that the Spanish-language version of the treaty might have given Spain the right to "suppress the deposit altogether"; and, that the treaty provided for no U.S. role in choosing an alternative site to New Orleans (89–90).

Chapter 1

1. Albert Sorel, *L'Europe et la Revolution Française*, vol. 1, 4th ed. (Paris: Plon, 1897): "The war between France and England lasted 23 years" (that is, 1792–1815) (355). A. M. B. Hauterive, *De L'État de la France a la Fin de l'année VIII* (Paris: Chez Henries, 1800): there were 82 years of war in the 152 years between Westphalia (1638) and 1790; Russia, Prussia and England were absent as decision-making powers at Westphalia; and, there never was a naval war, properly speaking, in those years. Hauterive goes on to say: "All the wars which have desolated the world for a century [he was writing around 1800] have been the work of [English] diplomacy or the result of its alliances," and that England's "standard twin policy pillars" will upset the European balance of power and increase its maritime and commercial powers. Therefore, he concludes, it now is seeking to seize Malta as a permanent possession that commands the commerce of Sicily, Italy, Barbary States and Turkey, and only France is able to counter England in the name of public law at sea, and it accordingly is about to sign a treaty with the United States in support of that law, although France also needs similar actions by the other maritime powers (5–6, 164–65, and 186).

2. Robert Livingston Papers at New-York Historical Society U.S. minister plenipotentiary to Britain Rufus King to Livingston, March 23, 1802: "We cannot doubt that the acquisition of Louisiana has for a long time been an object with France." According to Whitaker's *Mississippi Question*, Spain would have been willing to let Britain retain East Florida "in the peace settlement of 1783" so as "to share with so powerful a nation as the British the burden of frontier defense against the U.S" (165).

It was precisely this security concern that motivated foreign secretary Jay to seek an accommodation with Spain in 1786 — an effort that cost him dearly in the south and west, whose inhabitants understandably were upset at his willingness to pay the price of having the U.S. even temporarily forsake its claims to access to the Mississippi River. See note number 9 in this chapter for what the present writer sees as an overly harsh assessment (in Jon Kukla, *A Wilderness So Immense* [New York: Alfred A. Knopf, 2003]) of Jay's performance and goals: while Jay could well be faulted for having overestimated the Spanish military threat to U.S. territorial integrity, and for having certainly misjudged the economic and political importance to the U.S. *even in the short term* of having access to the Mississippi down to the Gulf of Mexico, it surely is overkill for Kukla to charge that strong nationalist with having the goal of breaking up the Union. As Professor John Kaminski, an expert on this aspect of Jay's career, remarked in a communication to the present author, "Kukla's intimations that Jay supported a separate and independent Northern confederacy are exaggerated and not justifiable."

It is Whitaker's opinion in *Mississippi Question* that Spain, "as early as 1795," was "not reluctant to part with Louisiana"— but excluding Florida — for the right price and/or Italian territory (vi–viii, 176–77, 184, and 308).

3. Robert Livingston Papers at New-York Historical Society. This and all subsequent translations from the French, unless specified otherwise, are by the present writer. The joint effort to press Spain regarding West Florida had been agreed to by France at the request of the American negotiators of the 30 April agreement. This is apparently the first time that French memorandum has been made available in English. An authoritative, but retrospective, explanation for France's strong effort to so assist the U.S. in 1803 is contained in the Talleyrand to Napoleon memorandum of May 6, 1806 (see Appendix B).

4. The point being made here was that the Italian territory to be transferred by France to the Spanish Bourbons generated

much more annual revenue than did Louisiana.

5. France in 1763 had agreed to meet English demands even for that part of French-owned Louisiana east of the Mississippi River up to the Perdido River, just short of Pensacola, and northward to the juncture of the Mississippi and Iberville Rivers, but excluding New Orleans, which the English agreed to let remain in Bourbon hands. It was only after 1763 that this eastern part of Louisiana began formally to be referred to as "West Florida," an administrative division established by the English.

6. United States Department of State, *State Papers and Correspondence*. Madison wrote to Livingston on March 31, 1804: The 1783 treaty giving Spain the Floridas was "in consequence of a war to which Spain had contributed but little compared with France" (275–85).

7. By November 1804, the French government, or at least foreign minister Talleyrand, would become so annoyed with the pressure tactics the U.S. was applying to Spain regarding the Florida issue that it remarkably would argue against the point of view contained in this 1803 memoir (see Talleyrand's memorandum to Napoleon dated November 19, 1804). An obvious motive for Talleyrand's position was his priority concern at this time to lead Spain to declare war on Britain, already at war with France (Spain did so in December 1804). On May 6, 1806, Talleyrand would return to this issue in a memorandum to Napoleon. The texts of both memoranda are in Appendix B.

8. The key steps in the negotiations and agreements were in 1795–96, 1800, 1801 and 1802. Per Whitaker's article on the retrocession, the 1795 Basle Treaty preceded the Pinckney Treaty later that same year, and it was important to Godoy to hold back Louisiana from France in order to use it in his upcoming negotiation with Pinckney.

9. For an elaboration on these matters, see Frank Brecher *Securing American Independence: John Jay and the French Alliance* (Westport, CT: Praeger Publishing, 2003), passim. Kukla's *Wilderness* is to be read with great caution regarding his treatment of this preliminary period to the Louisiana Purchase and regarding his strongly felt case that "many East Coast Americans" were in favor of keeping the U.S. away from the Mississippi River. Instructive examples of basic factual errors and wildly inaccurate charges include:

- "The American army and the French navy engineered the siege and surrender of Cornwallis at Yorktown" (11— which leaves out a separate French army of about 6,000 men fighting alongside Washington's own of 8,845).
- "France had been forced to surrender ... Louisiana to Spain" in "1761" (17 and 140 — it actually was in November 1762, as is discussed in Chapter 7)
- Quebec is located "at the mouth of the St. Lawrence River" (30)
- John Jay: (a) as foreign secretary was a leader in 1786 of a group seeking to establish "a separate New England Confederation," "to push the southern states out of the confederation," and to "surrender" the U.S. claim to the Mississippi (a scheme, according to Kukla, brilliantly foiled by an alert Monroe); (b) was as fluent in Spanish as was Ambassador Gardoqui in English but was played by that Spaniard "like a fiddle" and ended up like a squeezed orange, "an empty rind"; (c) as minister to Spain, too readily followed congressional instructions to give up the American claim to the Mississippi boundary (he in fact risked his career by watering down that offer to Spain); (d) was influenced, as was a George Washington "indifferent to the Mississippi River," by Gardoqui's gift-giving; and (e) had as his house guest in Paris his personal and legal nemesis, Lewis Littlepage (15, 52–53, 60–61, 68–69, 91, 98–100, and 124)
- In 1759, Spain's "Carlos III still resented his humiliation by a British [naval] commander, who had threatened to shell his palace in Naples in 1744" (32 — actually, the year was 1742)
- Floridablanca became "chief minister" in 1780 (52–53 — actually, it was in 1777, two years prior to Spain's entrance into the war against England)
- Talleyrand "was forced from office by critics of his greed for bribes in what Americans called the XYZ Affair" of 1798 (213 — actually, he briefly left office in mid-1799 in order to participate in Napoleon's November coup)
- And, in his most concrete error, Gibraltar is a "two-three acre rock" (213 — of course, its harbor alone covers 450 acres,

while the Rock overall is two and three-quarters miles long and three-quarters of a mile wide, according to the *Columbia Encyclopedia*).

For a balanced view of the Jay-Gardoqui negotiations of 1786–87, see John P. Kaminski, "Honor and Interest: John Jay's Diplomacy During the Confederation," *New York History* (Summer 2002).

10. Robert Livingston Papers at New-York Historical Society. Since the exact boundaries of the sold territory remained undefined, there have been various estimates of its size. An authoritative, official U.S. government figure is 885,697 square miles (Franklin K. Van Zandt, *Boundaries of the United States and the Several States*. [Washington, D.C.: U.S. Government Printing Office, 1966], where the following additional figures may be found: pre–1783 U.S. territory — 869,735 square miles; 1819 Florida treaty with Spain — 58,666 square miles; Texas annexation — 388,687 square miles; Alaska purchase — 586,400 square miles; total U.S. in 1962 — 3,615,211 square miles [262–63]). Andro Linklater observed in an article in the *New York Times*, April 28, 2003, that, "without their knowledge of the booming land market, the American negotiators would have found it hard to accept the French price. It exceeded Congress's appropriation by $13 million. But Monroe and Livingston were aware that federal land was selling for $2 an acre," as compared to the three cents per acre their agreement would cost the U.S. (A major theme in Andro Linklater's book *Measuring America* (2002) is that the policy of selling off or otherwise disposing of western land to the broadest possible range of inhabitants was instrumental in the establishment of American democracy as we now know it.)

11. Favier, et al, *Politique de Tous les Cabinets de l'Europe Pendant les Rignes de Louis XV et Louis XVI*, editor Anonymous (Paris, chez Buisson, 1794). For example, foreign minister Vergennes wrote Louis XVI on March 1784: At the opening of the negotiations leading to the treaties with the U.S. of February 6, 1778, France didn't want to break with Austria over Bavaria, especially given the situation regarding England, "against whom Your Majesty was about to go to war" (216ff.).

12. Sorel, *Revolution*, vol. 1, 303.

13. *Ibid*.: The abolition of the Convention at the end of 1795 marked the end of "the essential period of the French Revolution" (6); and: "War concentrates the mind and forces a resort to empirical acts based on precedents and a comfort zone — vice chimerical, idealistic ideas. During the Revolution, one saw being insinuated, on grounds of expediency, all the behavior patterns of the Old Regime.... There was an assembly which represented the people.... It was concentrated into a committee of twelve members, then into a directory of five, then into a consulate of three, then into an emperor" (225). In this manner, we see Montesquieu's constitutional monarchy change into Voltaire's "Constitutionelle," which moved to Rousseau's Gironde ("Heloise" and "Emile"), then to the "Encyclopedia's" Condorcet and Danton, and finally to Rousseau's Robespierre ("Social Contract").

14. Robert Livingston Papers at New-York Historical Society.

15. Robert Livingston Papers at New-York Historical Society. As put in Elie Barnavie and Saul Friedlander, eds., *La Politique étrangère du General de Gaulle* (Paris: Presses Universitaires de France, 1985), "One could write of de Gaulle that, if he had wished to retain certain characteristics of Napoleon, they would have been those of the First Consul, because de Gaulle had loved the restorer of order and institutions, the pacifier more than the conqueror in endless wars; and he would have felt himself justly proud of having given to France ... that peace which the First Consul had barely touched upon by virtue of the Amiens treaty of 1802, but which he very quickly lost" (26).

16. F. P. Renaut, *La Question de la Louisiane, 1796–1806* (Paris: Edouard Champion, 1918). Amiens was signed by France, Holland, Spain and Great Britain, ending the "maritime war." It was ratified by France on 18 April, opening up the sea lanes allowing France to take possession of Louisiana in accordance with the St. Ildefonso and March 1801 conventions. France in effect regained control of its empire: the mouth of the Senegal River and island of Gorce, the islands of France/ Bourbon, St. Pierre/Miquelon, Tobago, Guadaloupe, Martinique and St. Lucie, and the colony of Guyana — plus two new possessions, the "eastern part of St. Domingue and Louis-

iana" (St. Domingue, despite the 1795 treaty with Spain, having been "more theoretical than practical under the Directory") (81–83).

17. Lawrence S. Kaplan, "Jefferson's Foreign Policy and Napoleon's Ideologues," *William and Mary Quarterly*, third series, 19, no. 3 (July 1762). In contrast, Napoleon's motives for wanting the treaty with the U.S. was two-fold: enlist the U.S as a partner in his "League of Armed Neutrality" seeking to curb British maritime power; and, lull the U.S. into passivity while he prepares and dispatches a military expedition to Louisiana in implementation of the Spanish retrocession of that territory to France.

18. Robert Livingston Papers at New-York Historical Society. The ƒ600,000 was payable in dollars at $4.44.

19. Albert H. Bowman, *The Struggle for Neutrality: Franco-American Diplomacy During the Federalist Era* (Knoxville: University of Tennessee Press, 1974). Under the 1778 commercial treaty between the U.S. and France, the two had "obligated themselves to deny other rights to the enemies of one party in time of war" (5). William Stinchcombe, *The XYZ Affair* (Westport, CT: Greenwood Press, 1980). The Jay treaty's "redefinition" of the principle "free ships make free goods" was a "reversing" of the "policy ... that had been the basis of the commercial treaty with France in 1778" (8).

20. *Ibid*.: President Washington had recalled Monroe "in disgrace" (10).

21. Samuel F. Bemis, "Washington's Farewell Address": James Monroe was assigned to France to "mask" Jay's mission to England, and he never saw Jay's instructions and "possibly was not aware of their real scope" in deferring to England. In Paris, Monroe was "importuning" and totally undercut by the Jay Treaty. He and Paine were convinced that the treaty would be rejected. Monroe failed to report to the U.S. government that on February 1, 1796, he had hinted to the French foreign minister that there would be a change in the American administration "in the course of the present year." Jules Michelet, *Histoire de la Revolution Française*, vol. 9 (Angers: Gallimard, 1952): Monroe told Carnot of the Directory (and minister of war in 1800) that, "France, far from giving up any of its conquests, should everywhere plant its flag. It's that of liberty" (86).

22. Whitaker, *Mississippi*: The affair began in 1798 with "publication" of the "XYZ," diplomatic correspondence (116ff and 179). Stinchcombe, *XYZ*, has pointed out that there was a fourth obscure but rarely mentioned Frenchman — a "W" — in that American diplomatic correspondence from France, and, therefore, the episode should be more accurately called the "WXYZ affair" (4). Per United States Department of State, *State Papers and Public Documents*. vol. 4: The first time a demand was made for a specific amount was by Y on December 17, 1797. Talleyrand on 28 October had "told the envoys that the Directory were wounded by the President's speech [of 16 May]"; therefore, Talleyrand said to Gerry that he thought the Directory would have to have U.S. money to get over that speech (246 — see *Ibid*., vol. 3, 84ff for the text of Adams' speech). Irving Brant, *James Madison: Secretary of State, 1800–1809* (New York: Bobbs-Merrill, 1953): Talleyrand was demanding payment personally in the XYZ affair (111). Renaut, *Louisiane*: "Talleyrand had tried to corrupt these [American] diplomatic agents; from that came a scandal known under the name of the XYZ affair, which once again deeply offended America's pride (1797–98)" (55–58).

23. United States Department of State, *State Papers and Public Documents....*, vol. 4. The one Republican and pro–French member of Adams's original negotiating team, Gerry of Massachusetts, who had served in the Continental Congress and would be Madison's vice presidential running mate in 1812, alone of the three remained in France with the encouragement of the Directory. This earned him a reprimand from the strongly Federalist Secretary of State Thomas Pickering, whose dispatch of June 25, 1798 (*Ibid*.) included his "recall" and an expression of "regret" that he "did not concur with your colleagues in demanding passports to quit the territories of the French Republic" and that, instead, he had allowed the French to pick and choose among the three as to which one they wished to negotiate with. Gerry was back in the U.S. by that October. This episode is reminiscent of the Directory's similarly showing favor to the departing U.S. minister to France, the Francophile Monroe, over his designated successor in 1796, Charles C. Pinckney, who was refused accreditation (153–54).

24. Bowman, *Neutrality*. Bowman gives July 7, 1798, as the date of the abrogation (331, 419, and 426).

25. Brant, *Madison* 11–12.

26. United States Department of State, *Calendar of the Correspondence of Thomas Jefferson*, vol. 2 (New York: Burt Franklin, 1970; Jefferson to Madison, January 30, 1799 (that is, even after it was quite clear that there *was* a bribe request via Talleyrand).

27. Whitaker, *Mississippi*: John Adams "administered the *coup d'état* to the war party" with the implementation of the Pinckney Treaty and rejection of a planned American-supported rebellion in Spanish America under Miranda. Both France and Spain were "pacifically inclined," the western population distrusted the Federalists, and France "had not meant a request for a bribe as a challenge to mortal combat. President Adams accepted Talleyrand's peace overtures, nominating three commissioners to treat with France" in February 1799, and he sent them in October, 1799. From then until October 1802, "relations" with Spain "were undisturbed by any serious controversy" (128–29).

28. Frédéric Masson, *Le Départment des Affaires Étrangeres Pendant la Révolution: 1787–1804* (Paris: E. Plon, 1877): Talleyrand very probably was "always venal.... If the [1798] negotiation with the U.S. failed, perhaps his venality was the cause" (430). Stinchcombe, *XYZ*: Both Talleyrand and John Adams "made the necessary decisions" to "achieve peace" by dismissing the "ideological commitments" of others opposing it (11).

29. Talleyrand's 1799 correspondence was through the channel of his representative in Holland, Louis-André Pichon (the future French minister to the U.S. during the negotiations over Louisiana), who passed it on to Murray, the U.S. resident minister at The Hague. Brant *Madison*: Bowman's doctoral dissertation reports that it was Pichon who got Murray to change his mind and then got him to get Adams to authorize the renewal of U.S.-French negotiations post–XYZ, thereby ending the quasi-war (59–60). Livingston Papers at the New-York Historical Society: With further regard to Murray: (1) A disillusioned Livingston would write Madison as early as December 30, 1801, that his own past "character" as a supporter of rebellion was "so well known" in now-conservative France that Murray would have been "very agreeable" in his stead, and that, "You may act as exigencies require with the smallest personal attention to me"; and, (2) in a similar vein, Livingston would write Morris on May 24, 1802, that, on arrival, he saw that "a respected royalist would have been more acceptable" as U.S. minister.

30. Robert Livingston Papers at New-York Historical Society.

31. As Miller's *Treaties*, vol. 2 explains it in his helpful notes to the texts of the 30 April agreement, the three components "formed ... one transaction"; each depended for its validity on the execution of the other two (523–27). The text of those agreements and of the 1795 Pinckney Treaty are perhaps most readily available to the reader in an appendix to Kukla's *Wilderness*.

32. Carl L. Lokke, "Secret Negotiations to Maintain the Peace of Amiens," *American Historical Review* 49, no. 1 (October 1943): The British bribe effort was conducted by Whitworth, the ambassador to France, and was initiated right after the 13 March episode when Napoleon publicly "vented his wrath upon [that] hapless British ambassador." Napoleon was personally uninvolved in the bribery scheme, but his family and Talleyrand were.

33. As is discussed elsewhere, apparently Marbois made no mention of such a debate in his historic meeting with Livingston the night of 13–14 April, 1803, a meeting reported on in great detail by Livingston in his dispatch to Madison dated 13 April but, as discussed elsewhere, most likely was the 14th. (See Appendix C for a more detailed analysis of this "debate" matter.) Also note that, per Renaut, *Louisiane*: (1) Napoleon "on 10 April called in some men who had competence regarding American matters; he had already decided to give up Louisiana entirely but needed to know how best to do it. Present were Marbois, Decrès, and even Berthier, the negotiator of the Aranjuez Treaty" of March 1801; Napoleon "purposefully" kept Talleyrand out of it, "either because he thought him hostile to the Americans and would therefore decline to participate, or because he feared the venal and corrupt side of him would get the better of this famous statesman, or finally because he believed Marbois was better qualified to negotiate these matters." (2); In fact, this "debate" was pro-forma, Napoleon, "in secret, having already firmly made

his decision once it was clear that hostilities at sea were about to restart and at a level more violent than ever." (3); "No report regarding the negotiations with the Americans exists in the French archives, and the Americans in Paris didn't report until the "one dispatch" of 13 May, which arrived in Washington only on 14 July — and that dispatch was only in "summary form"; and (4) "Marbois only published a narration of these events under the Restoration" (117–18). Also note Daniel C. Gilman, *James Monroe* (Boston: Houghton, Mifflin, 1898): Talleyrand was the one who debated Marbois on 10 April and, having lost out, maliciously delayed a Monroe-Napoleon meeting until 1 May (82–84).

34. Renaut, *Louisiane,* 98. But note also Deconde, *Louisiana*: at least in 1799 under the Directory, Talleyrand's purpose in his correspondence with Murray was to limit the scope of the quasi-war with the U.S., fearing that, "if it expanded, [it] ... would endanger his efforts to regain Louisiana" (89). The present writer's summary conclusion on Talleyrand's various pronouncements and policies on the colonial question might well be that he adjusted those to fit his circumstance of the moment, such as whether he was speaking as a private individual or whether his official positions were taken as a servant of the Directory or of Napoleon. But this conclusion does not negate Bowman's belief that Talleyrand "was mainly responsible for bringing peace in 1800" *Struggle,* x). James E. Lewis, *The Louisiana Purchase: Jefferson's Noble Bargain?* (Charlottesville: Thomas Jefferson Foundation, 2003) As for Murray, (who interestingly would anticipate a Livingston rationale of early 1800 in a letter to Mark Leavenworth, below) when he wrote Madison from the Hague on May 20, 1801, that a retrocession to France of Louisiana "might [prove] rather favorable to us," by creating "a new temporary interest ["in France"] to be well with the U.S." (27).

35. Madison, *Papers,* vol. 1, 281–82: Murray to Madison, June 9, 1801. Bowman, *Neutrality*: "The advent of the Republicans into power consummated the French-American reconciliation which John Adams's courageous initiative had begun" (425).

36. *Ibid.*: Congress' action amounted to a "unilateral abrogation of the American treaties with France.... The U.S. did not deny it was a *casus belli,* if not tantamount to a declaration of war" (426–28).

37. Joseph J. Ellis, *Founding Brothers: The Revolutionary Generation* (New York: Knopf, 2000), 136–38.

38. United States Department of State, *Calendar*, vol. 1: Jefferson to Livingston, November 4, 1803. Also note that youngest brother Jerome was in the U.S. during this period and, in 1803, would marry "Miss Patterson of Baltimore"— an act that would greatly displease Napoleon, who forced its annulment. Madison, *Papers*, vol. 1: Murray to Madison, June 1, 1801. Joseph was the "head of" a three-man "commission for treating with the U.S.," handling the treaty and its ratification, 1800–01, 253–54.

39. Madison, *Papers,* vol. 4, 343–44. Robert Livingston Papers at New-York Historical Society, Madison to Livingston, February 23, 1803. United States Department of State, *State Papers and Correspondence*, 88.

40. Madison, *Papers*, vol. 1, 281–82.

41. Dangerfield, *Chancellor*: The Chancellorship was, "in precedence ... second only to the governor and it placed him at the head of the bar.... The chancellor was chancellor ... during good behavior, and until the age of retirement." He was a member of the "chancery court," which was a "court of equity" (186).

42. For the text of Jefferson's inaugural address, see United States, Department of State, *State Papers and Public Documents*, vol. 4, 321ff.

43. Robert Livingston Papers at New-York Historical Society. Miller, *Treaties*, vol. 2: President Adams, although "opposed to the Senate proviso," had signed off on it on 18 February, but he "left the whole matter to the new administration." Therefore, it was not until Jefferson assumed office that it was sent to France on 18 March with "instructions regarding the exchange of ratifications" (483). Miller there also points out that those instructions were "silent" on the substance of the conditions that the French predictably raised with Murray once they learned of the two changes by the U.S. As is shown in the text, Livingston would be authorized to depart for France on the basis only of advance word from Paris that the French had concurred in the Senate-amended treaty — that is, before the instrument and its conditions were actually received and acted upon in Washington. Dangerfield's *Chancellor* reports that word of the formal French ratification was heard

by Livingston while at sea on or about 27 October. Jefferson's message to Congress of 11 December (see below) states that he received the document in early November.

44. Miller, *Treaties*, vol. 2, 457–87 (the 1800 Convention plus notes).

45. Bowman, *Neutrality*, 331, 419, and 426.

46. Robert Livingston Papers at New-York Historical Society. Actually, as just shown, the U.S. had implicitly rejected both treaties of February 6, 1778 (alliance and friendship/commerce).

47. Miller, *Treaties,* vol. 2, 483.

48. Bowman, *Neutrality*: Jefferson had resubmitted the treaty to the Senate on 11 December and the Senate "resolved" to consider it "as fully ratified" on 19 December (426–28).

49. Robert Livingston Papers at New-York Historical Society.

50. Robert Livingston Papers at New-York Historical Society.

51. Madison, *Papers*, vol. 1, 281–82.

52. United States Department of State, *Calendar*, vol. 1.

53. Robert Livingston Papers at New-York Historical Society. A rather carelessly drafted presidential commission read, "Minister Plenipotentiary ... to the French Republic of France." Livingston's Instructions accompanying the commission even then envisaged the possibility of an alliance with England, but only if New Orleans in the first instance would go to the U.S. and not to England. Further note that Madison here observed that, if France, in fact, was planning to take back New Orleans, that would represent a change from its policy of 1778.

54. Robert Livingston Papers at New-York Historical Society. Madison, *Papers*, vol. 1: "Virginia-born Thomas Sumter [sr.] settled in South Carolina. During the Revolution, Sumter was noted for his guerrilla forays against the British under Cornwallis. James Madison's colleague in the first and second congresses, Sumter returned to the House in 1797. In December 1801, he was elected to the Senate" (379).

55. Ulane Bonnel, *La France, les États-Unis et la guerre de course (1797–1815)* (Paris: Nouvelles Editions Latines, 1961) in Bowman, *Neutrality*: Morris was "an American Genet" and as "clumsy as he was" (98); and: Secretary Jefferson's instruction to Morris read as follows: He was to show "sincere friendship and attachment.... No call to express opinions which might please or offend any party" (100–02); but, Bowman continues, Morris's reports led to a change in President Washington's attitude toward the French Revolution, a change which Jefferson justifiably "blamed" on Morris. (Note that Livingston from the start of his mission in France, and also Monroe in 1803, followed this old Jefferson guideline to such a literal extent that their French friends told them they were overdoing it by their snubbing of even the most harmless of Frenchmen for fear of offending Napoleon and his conservative establishment. Livingston was most severe against Thomas Paine, who finally returned to the U.S. in 1802.)

As described in Stinchombe, *XYZ*, when Monroe wrote to ask Livingston, his "colleague from revolutionary days," why he rejected President Washington's job offer, Livingston answered on May 16, 1794, that "he could not accept the position because he was out of sympathy with the policies of the Washington administration"; and, when the President then turned to Monroe, the latter accepted the post with "alacrity" (7).

56. Robert Livingston Papers at New-York Historical Society.

57. Dangerfield, *Chancellor*, 78.

58. Robert Livingston Papers at New-York Historical Society: Jefferson to Livingston, May 31, 1801.

59. *Ibid.*, Livingston to Jefferson, March 16, 1801. *Ibid.*, Livingston to Burr, December 16, 1801: Mlle. Delarge was Burr's "adopted daughter" who was returning to her native France When Livingston finally did get ready to leave, in October, he prepared a will that included the following points of possible interest: "Being about to depart this country.... My slaves above the age of 26 years I leave free 6 months after my death and the rest when they shall severally attain that age." Dangerfield, *Chancellor*: Livingston brought with him "personal servants," as house slaves were typically called in that milieu (309). Robert Livingston Papers at New-York Historical Society includes a certificate signed by Minister of War Murat on April 17, 1803, authorizing his "domestic," William Harrison, "to reside with him [*rester chez son maitre*]." Dangerfield, *Chancellor*, "Any study of the various Livingston Papers would convince any reader that the Liv-

ingstons regarded slavery as, at best, an unpleasant necessity wished upon them by fate" (452). For a vivid description of how Livingston's racially mixed and uniquely dressed entourage (including the live animals brought by him aboard ship and now trudging alongside the caravan) struck the amazed inhabitants of the French countryside as it made its way from L'Orient to Paris during the harvest season, see Jean Devoisse, *L' Homme qui vendit la Louisiane* (Paris: Olivier Urban, 1989), 252–53.

60. Robert Livingston Papers at New-York Historical Society.

61. *Ibid.*, Livingston to his sister, Janet Montgomery, from L'Orient, November 13, 1801. *Ibid.*: As regards future relations between Livingston and Burr, the two would have a falling out by 1803, as reflected in the former's letter of 5 February to De Witt Clinton: "I too have been so unfortunate as to fall under the vice president's displeasure"; he "very coolly" received my son-in-law [the husband of daughter Maria, who, unlike Margaret and her husband, had not remained long in France] and "did not do me the honor to make any inquiries about me ... though I am ignorant of the why or wherefore" of his displeasure. Another incidental fact relevant to Livingston's tenure at Paris is that the captain of the ship that brought him to France behaved badly once in European waters: From L'Orient, Captain McNeill stopped at Gibraltar, where he stranded some of his officers ashore by precipitately putting back to sea; he then lied to the authorities at his next port of call, Toulon, claiming a direct voyage from L'Orient, whereas, had he acknowledged having stopped *en route* at Gibraltar, his ship would have had to undergo a quarantine, which he wished to avoid; and, after that, he embroiled his ship in an unauthorized battle with Tunisian "cruisers" in the Mediterranean Sea, creating an international incident unwelcome in Washington, D.C.—in part because it also involved Morocco, which had come to the aid of Tripoli in the face of the U.S. "expedition against Tripoli." Livingston, who had to apologize to the French authorities for the captain's behavior at Toulon, would advise Madison on March 27, 1802, that, although that officer had treated "me and my family" in a "perfectly proper way ... the violence of his passions unfits him for the command of a ship of war." The captain eventually was relieved of his command and left the service. On August 27, 1802, Secretary Smith advised Jefferson that he was sending McNeill "home" and appointing "a certain lieutenant" to replace him. Evidently, even prior to McNeill's taking Livingston to France, there were doubts about him: Smith to Madison, July 17, 1801: "The appointment of Captain McNeill to the *Boston* is unfortunate." (Robert Livingston Papers at New-York Historical Society; United States Department of State, *Calendar*, vol. 3: Madison to Jefferson, August 25, 1802: and Madison, *Papers,* vol. 1, 369.)

62. Robert Livingston Papers at New-York Historical Society. The full conversation, which was conducted through an interpreter, went along following lines, as recorded by Sumter and sent to Madison on 10 December: Napoleon at first asked Livingston "if he had been in Europe before; he answered in the negative; then Napoleon said, *Vous etes venu a un monde bien corrompu*—you have come to a very corrupt world." This last point by Napoleon is reminiscent of a "Report" Talleyrand had prepared in support of Napoleon's order of early 1800 for France to mourn the recent death of George Washington and to build a statue in his honor. Talleyrand there wrote: "A people that one day will be a great people, that today is the wisest and happiest on Earth, mourns the death [of Washington].... France ... from the dawn of the American Revolution watched with hope as a nation until then unknown prospered far from the vices of Europe.... [Washington] broke the mold" ("Talleyrand's *Memoires,* vol. 1" 333). Michelet, *Revolution,* vol. 10: Upon taking power in 1799, "many thought that Bonaparte would seek his glory by following in the footsteps of the great American who had just died, Washington, and for whom Bonaparte ordered a funereal celebration" (5); and: "While he was Consul, many hoped to see in him another Washington who would reveal himself one morning" (158). In further testimony of the sincerity of French regret at Washington's death, Marbois, according to Devoisse, *L'Homme,* while returning from his two-year cavalry as a prisoner of the Directory at Guyana, learned from a passing U.S. ship of Washington's death, sending him "paradoxically, at the very moment when his own misery was coming to an end, into a deep sadness"

(242). (Regarding this relatively recent French biographer of Marbois, note that, while he does include in his bibliography Lyon's 1934 work on the Louisiana Purchase, he omits any reference to Lyon's 1942 biography of Marbois under the same title as his own work. Lyon's closely tracks the same personal story as the Frenchman's, although in much less detail. The reasons for this neglect of Lyon by Devoisse may easily be guessed at, none of them attractive ones.)

63. Samuel F. Bemis, *The Rayneval Memoranda*. American Antiquarian Society Proceedings, New Series, 47, 1937, 85. One must be cautious about some of Bemis's judgments, because, as the present writer has had occasion to document in *Securing*, even that great historian was prone to err factually and with unfortunate consequences for some of his judgments regarding the diplomacy of the American Revolution. For example, in *Jay's Treaty: A Study in Commerce and Diplomacy* (New York: MacMillan, 1923), Jefferson was "at Paris in 1783" (89) and the British evacuated New York in April 1803 (actually, November 1803) (100).

64. Dangerfield, *Chancellor*, 10–11, 138–41, and 179–80.

65. For an articulation of that view, see Livingston's "unsent memorandum" to the Congress of December 1781 (Brecher *Securing*, Appendix B); that memorandum gives evidence that Livingston well understood the limitations of French support for the U.S. regarding the negotiation of possible peace terms. Also see the summary of Madison's notes on the congressional debates of that period regarding U.S. policy toward France (223).

66. Lee came to France directly from Britain and maintained relationships in that now-enemy land; this, along with his fractiousness, aroused the suspicions and dislike of the French government. While the suspicions of disloyalty to the U.S. cause were baseless, Lee being an unquestionable patriot, there is no doubt that he was out of sympathy with the congressional policy of placing American diplomatic interests almost entirely into French hands. Once back in the U.S., Lee at Philadelphia joined the so-called anti–Gallican party, which was being led in congress by New Englanders and members of his own Virginia family. Furthermore, Lee was a leading protagonist in the controversy that had wracked the congress in 1778–79 over whether his two colleagues at Paris — Franklin and Silas Deane — both of whom were strong favorites at Versailles, were financially corrupt and/or unduly under French control, as Lee was charging.

67. Robert Livingston Papers at New-York Historical Society. It is one of the dramatic stories of early American history that each of these three men took a turn as U.S. minister at Paris — both that their service had an important bearing on the shape of the times, and that each would end up politically and socially wounded from the experience (although Morris, unlike his other two friends, lacked the compensation of also being associated with a major diplomatic triumph for the U.S.).

68. Livingston had engaged in a similar sentimental exchange of lost friendships when he wrote John Jay a note of good wishes as the latter embarked on his mission to England in 1794. Jay's response, while equally brief and even more tightly controlled, also betrayed a sense of deep regret. There would be no further personal correspondence between the two men.

69. Livingston owned some 130,000 acres in upstate New York.

70. Dangerfield, *Chancellor*: In Livingston's "mind ... a healthy America was an agrarian America" (208–09).

71. Livingston Papers at the New-York Historical Society: For example, Robert Livingston to Morris, June 13, 1778, describes the American people as unworthy of liberty and lacking in civic virtue. Dangerfield, *Chancellor* observes that Livingston had "the aristocrat's moral contempt for any despotism but his own," and that he had a "private aversion to popular politics, which made him politically both an unpopular and an unreliable figure." (vii and 58).

72. United States Department of State, *State Papers and Correspondence*, 209–14.

73. Robert Livingston Papers at New-York Historical Society. In the same, Livingston to Jefferson, March 12, 1803, makes reference to "my difficulty of hearing." As early as his tenure as foreign secretary, Livingston was undergoing painful electric shock treatments to curb his worsening hearing problem. Livingston did easily read in French. Deconde, *Louisiana*, overstates Livingston's disabilities by writing that he was "deaf and could not speak French."

74. Robert Livingston Papers at New-York Historical Society.
75. Alexis de Tocqueville, L'Ancien Régime, ed. G.W. Headlam (Oxford: Clarendon press, 1933) "This revolution was prepared by the most civilized classes of the nation, and carried out by the most uncultured and crudest" (221).
76. Per G. W. Headlam, the editor of L' Ancien Régime: Not liberty but equality was the "real desire" of the French people, who "hated nobles—and this was the lasting passion" of France throughout the nineteenth century (xii).
77. Livingston Papers at the New-York Historical Society. Livingston's correspondence of 1802 with now–Virginia governor Monroe was initiated by the latter's request of December 15, 1801, that the minister purchase two swords his state wished to bestow upon two Virginia war heroes. Livingston carried out the request, per Monroe's November 4, 1802, report that the swords were received after having been nearly lost in a ship-wreck "near our coast" (Robert Livingston Papers at New-York Historical Society).
78. De Tocqueville, L'Ancien Régime: "Who seeks in liberty anything other than liberty itself is made to serve" (174).
79. Michelet, Revolution, vol. 10: Contrary to Napoleon's public announcement, Kosciusko refused to budge from France to join the Polish troops in St. Domingue. Those troops were volunteers who had served in Egypt. "Then, what was left of them, Napoleon had the barbarity to send to St. Domingue, which devoured them." Napoleon was unfriendly to Poland, "a democracy," because "he sensed that liberty resided there" (219).
80. Robert Livingston Papers at New-York Historical Society. Further to the discussion, regarding Livingston's keeping his distance from revolutionary types, he wrote Madison on March 22, 1802: "I at present stand well with the court" by having carefully avoided "the smallest interference in the politics of the country or any assertions that might give umbrage."
81. Ibid.
82. Masson's Départment: Napoleon quickly cleared the foreign ministry of all the Sans-Culottes types and brought back a number of career diplomats who adhered to the ministry's pre–Revolutionary traditions, including Vergennes's senior assistants, Rayneval and Henin (445–47).

83. In August 1802, a light referendum made Napoleon consul for life. As noted previously, when he became emperor some two years later, he had himself called by his first name in line with those who held such august titles. Deconde, Louisiana, incorrectly dates this change to the 1802 referendum (105).
84. Robert Livingston Papers at New-York Historical Society for both this and the following two letters.
85. Ibid. Monroe's 4 November response was that "an American observer [elsewhere, of "the French revolution," which "has been a great object from the commencement for the philosophic spectator"] has the advantage of the European, however impartial or abstracted from the scene he may be. I shall at all times be happy to hear from you.... Such hints shall not transpire so as to do injury to any person anywhere." (Of course, in the end, Livingston would indeed suffer "injury" to his reputation from having two such pairs of eyes observing his work as those of his Francophile predecessors at Paris, Monroe and Jefferson.)
86. Being governor was Livingston's major political ambition. He had been an unsuccessful candidate against Jay for that post in 1796. (Dangerfield, Chancellor, concludes that, since Livingston had been totally inactive in support of that 1796 candidacy, he had no presidential ambitions for 1800 [275].) In the event, conditions in New York would turn unfavorable for his chances at the governorship in 1803, including a falling out with the Burr faction and, as described later, certain legal problems encountered by Edward Livingston as mayor of New York City. Livingston never again would be a candidate for any political post once he returned to the U.S. Dangerfield also contradicts Brant's claim in Madison, that Livingston had a desire to return to the U.S. as soon as possible in order to run for vice president (349–50).
The fate of Edward Livingston is of possible interest:

• United States Department of State, Calendar, vol. 2: Gallatin to Jefferson, July 24, 1802, New York: "The offices of district attorney and mayor, both held by Edward Livingston, considered incompatible." Same to same, June 16, 1803: "E. Liv's defalcation said to be an open secret in N.Y. A removal or resignation will

follow. Thinks a successor should be provided for immediate appointment." Same to same, July 3, 1803: "Should Mr. Gilston be right in supposing that the list of June 18 had been paid to the district attorney, there is a defalcation of $30,000 or even more."
• As summarized by Peter J. Kastor, *The Nation's Crucible: The Louisiana Purchase and the Creation of America* (New Haven, CT: Yale University press, 2004), Edward was an "upstanding" man who had "found himself liable for public funds that a clerk had legally borrowed but failed to reimburse" (72–74).
• Edward would soon move on to New Orleans and create a new political base, which aided in his achieving the position of secretary of state under Jackson; Livingston was the only longtime western friend of Jackson who maintained political influence with the latter as president.

Moreover, Edward's legal and business activities in his new location would bring him into indirect contact with now ex–president Jefferson. Per United States Department of State, *Calendar*, supplemental vol. regarding the "Batture Case" of 1812, N.Y.: Jefferson's "written notes" for use by the U.S. government's counsel were incorporated in "a pamphlet" opposing Edward Livingston's "intrusion" on the "public beach of the Mississippi adjacent to New Orleans" (25). And, per the same, vol. 2, further regarding the "Batture Case": "A pamphlet with written notes by Jefferson" regarding the U.S. government's "maintaining the public right to the beach of the Mississippi adjacent to New Orleans against the intrusion of Edward Livingston ... prepared for the use of counsel by TJ, July 31, 1810." Brant in *Madison* untenably accuses Edward, as Jackson's secretary of state, of sanitizing State Department publications of Robert Livingston–era documents so as to excise certain phrases that prove, according to Brant, that Robert was financially corrupt and in a conspiracy with privileged American claimants to gain undue payments from French debts for spoliations that also involved a scheme of bribery of Talleyrand and other French officials. The present writer sees no basis for these charges against Robert and believes Brant erred because, as will be discussed in detail later, he failed to see that Robert's scheme for influencing the French was with regard not to Florida land in cahoots with private U.S. citizens, but to sale of land — in a joint venture between the *Bonaparte family* and the U.S. *government*—in territory that would be placed under American "jurisdiction" and that lay to the west of the Mississippi and north of the Arkansas. The alleged excisions that Brant attributed to Edward's machinations were much more likely due to problems of deciphering Livingston's coded sections of his dispatches—problems that, as Channing has pointed out, typically marred 19th-century publications of U.S. government documents of that earlier period.

87. De Tocqueville, *L'Ancien Régime*: Per its editor De Tocqueville proved that the French Revolution failed in achieving one of its central goals of weakening "the central power" (vii–xi).

88. Robert Livingston Papers at New-York Historical Society.

Chapter 2

1. *Ibid.* for this and the immediately following letters from Livingston. Marbois regularly signed his letters to Livingston "your old and most devoted friend" or "most affectionately."

2. Brant, *Madison*, regarding Washington's decision not to interfere in American suppliers' trade with the rebellious forces in St. Domingue: "In yielding to the self-interest of New England traders, the administration served its own object of delaying and discouraging the occupation by France" (93).

3. Channing, *History*, vol 4: Livingston's instructions regularly had him press France on this and that regarding New Orleans and the Floridas and the French debt to American claimants, but, "at the same time, he was not to arouse anybody's anger or to make any pecuniary offer that was likely to be effective." His were to be "educational efforts" similar to those Franklin had to make, but he "lacked the light touch and literary effectiveness that had stood Franklin in good stead." Livingston's "deafness and lack of training would seem to have unfitted him" for the Paris post (308–10).

4. Brant, *Madison*: Madison's own instructions of September 1801 to Livingston connected the sale of the Floridas with a

"fund" to compensate American claimants (71–72).

5. Robert Livingston Papers at New-York Historical Society, Pinckney to Livingston, April 3, 1803: Foreign Minister Pedro Cevallo's enclosed letter "is the first acknowledgment in writing I have been able to get since I arrived of the cession of Louisiana agreeably to its ancient limits, and that it was ceded subject to the subsequent treaties of Spain with other powers." (Charles Pinckney is not to be confused with his namesake, Thomas, negotiator of the 1795 treaty of San Lorenzo with Spain, nor with Thomas' brother, Charles C. Pinckney, the unfortunate 1796 appointee as Monroe's successor, who was then rejected by the Directory.)

6. Ibid. This quotation is included later in the present text in a more detailed description of the 2 March instructions to Livingston and Monroe.

7. Ibid., Graham to Livingston, July 12, 1802. It is worth noting, as regards Graham, that he was held in high repute by his colleagues and particularly by Jefferson and Madison. He was back in the U.S. as a senior State Department officer when President Jefferson sent him to the West in 1805 to investigate Burr's activities—it was largely on the basis of Graham's findings that Jefferson had Burr arrested and charged with treason (see Chapter 7, below, for more details on this Burr episode).

8. Ibid.
9. Ibid.
10. Ibid. For example, Livingston to Gilson, August 1, 1802: "Some of the most inveterate enemies of the administration have been here, and still hold important places in Europe." They were sending false reports on him to U.S. newspapers. "Let not what I say be considered as extending to our minister in Britain [elsewhere, to whom I write "almost daily"].... It is some in inferior appointments I have reason to suspect as the fabricators of falsehoods."

11. Ibid.
12. Ibid.
13. Ibid.
14. Ibid. Livingston to Jefferson, October 28, 1802.
15. Ibid. for this and previous two citations.
16. Also see Livingston to Madison, May 12, 1803, later in the text.
17. Miller, Treaties, vol. 2: The three American commissioners were John Mercer, Isaac Cox Barnet, and William McClure. Miller reports on a pair of letters to Talleyrand from Livingston (February 24, 1804) and Marbois (8 March) regarding certain procedural issues arising out of reviews of the individual claimants. (There was an obvious conflict of interest between the two parties given the provision in the 30 April agreement that the "rejection of any claim shall have no other effect than to exempt the United States from the payment of it, the French Government reserving to itself the right to decide definitively on such claim as far as it concerns itself.") Marbois' letter assured Talleyrand that he and Livingston had agreed on how to treat the debts so as to avoid the problem of the U.S. wrongly rejecting valid claims.

18. Robert Livingston Papers at New-York Historical Society, including the following letter from John Livingston (whose bold efforts to forward his private commercial interests through the influence of his brother had precedents during the Revolutionary War when Robert was foreign secretary). Dangerfield regrets that Livingston worked so closely in Paris with the American businessman and claimant James Swan. Swan, especially by summer 1803, would be doing his best to bolster Livingston's political standing in the U.S. by feeding to newspapers there the actual texts of Livingston's major memoranda to the French government regarding the debt-cum-Louisiana issue. For an interesting, rather favorable account of Swan's life, character and career, see Howard C. Rice, "James Swan: Agent of the French Republic 1794–96," *The New England Quarterly*, vol. 10, no. 3 (September 1937). (Among that writer's points: Swan's wife was a protégé of General Knox during the period Swan was in France, and Swan sat for a Gilbert Stuart portrait while in Philadelphia in the 1790s.) A key Swan-specific issue was with regard to his past role as a purchasing agent of the French government in the U.S.: Under the terms of the 30 April agreement, Americans serving as agents of the French government were barred from submitting claims related to that service. The complication in Swan's case was that he submitted claims characterized, with Livingston's endorsement, as being unrelated to his services for the French government but rather as stemming from his private commercial activities.

Some were skeptical as to the validity of Swan's claims and feared that they would be honored at the expense of other claimants less directly associated with Livingston. The present writer shares Dangerfield's assessment that charges of personal corruption against Livingston, such as those leveled by Brant and Kennedy (see Chapter 7), are without basis in fact. Moreover, as Rice points out: "Swan's claims against France were included in the Conjectural Note of claims attached to the Louisiana Purchase conventions by Livingston *and Monroe*" (emphasis added); some had opposed including him or any other "ex-agents" of France, but the two Americans obviously believed these were not part of Swan's work for France.

19. One cannot dismiss the likelihood that the disappointing role of Spain during the American War of Independence contributed to the harshness of American policy toward Spain and its possessions in North America during the first decades of the nineteenth century. If there was one diplomatic issue on which John Jay, the Continental Congress (of which Madison was a member) and Robert Livingston were all agreed upon in 1782–83, it was that Spain should not benefit from American goodwill in the postwar period.

20. Robert Livingston Papers at New-York Historical Society. Pinckney's 3 April letter to Livingston has been previously described.

21. *Ibid.* Per Whitaker, *The Mississippi Question*, Graham's advice to Livingston is particularly insightful given it was precisely in this period that Madrid was secretly ordering its intendant at New Orleans to end the U.S. right of deposit at that port city.

22. Robert Livingston Papers at New-York Historical Society. André Fugier, *Napoléon et L'Espagne*. (Paris: Felix Alcan), 1930, vol. 1: "The United States in March 1803 offered Spain, in exchange for purchasing from it some territories of the Mississippi region, a guarantee of the integrity of Spanish America" (194–95). Lewis, *Noble Bargain*: The Pinckney offer was on condition that Spain not retrocede Louisiana to France (the initial Madison authorization to Pinckney to make this offer having been contained in a dispatch as early as May 11, 1802 (37–39). Livingston believed Pinckney had not understood its implications once it became clear to all that the retrocession to France was no longer a conjecture but a fact.

23. Robert Livingston Papers at New-York Historical Society, Livingston to Madison, August 12 and 16, 1802: "I find all the old French maps mark the River Perdigo [now "Perdido"—just west of Pensacola] as the boundary between Florida and Louisiana."

24. *Ibid.*: Three thousand troops were to go under General Victor vice General Bernadotte.

25. *Ibid.*, for this and the immediately following quotations. In his dispatch to Madison of 10 August, Livingston reports that he had "struck off" 20 copies of his memoir, and that he planned to follow it up "with some proposition" to the French authorities. The memoir ran to over 30 pages and, according to the original draft, it contained "two points of view: first, as it affects the commerce and manufactures of France; second, as it affects her positive or relative strength."

26. *Ibid.*

27. In fact, of course, as we have seen, Spain did so subordinate its 1800 treaty with France to its 1795 treaty with the U.S.

28. *Ibid.*

29. This was a far-fetched claim by a leverage-seeking Livingston given that Britain never did show any such interest following her 1783 treaty with Spain.

30. Robertson, *Louisiana*, vol. 1, Merry to Hawkesbury, December 6, 1803: Now that it had Louisiana, the U.S. did not want to accept the provisions in the 12 May agreement giving us a link to the Mississippi. But, said Merry, there was no need for concern, because Spain had no territory in Louisiana east of "the line stipulated to be drawn" under the 12 May agreement (22).

31. *American State Papers, Foreign Relations*, vol. 2: The "convention" with Great Britain of May 12, 1803, was signed by Rufus King but "not consummated" (584).

32. Madison, *Papers*, vol. 4, xxxv–xxxviv; vol. 1, 220 and 233–34. United States Department of State, *Calendar*, vol. 2.

33. Robert Livingston Papers at New-York Historical Society for this letter and the two succeeding ones. Renaut, *Louisiane*: Parma and Plaisance were French-controlled territories in Italy being offered to the Spanish Bourbons in partial exchange for including the Floridas as part of the retrocession of Louisiana. The Duke of

Notes—Chapter 2

Parma had died on October 9, 1802, and France at this time was negotiating for the cession of the two Floridas in exchange for the Parmesan states, which were to be ceded by France to the Spanish Bourbon king of Etruria, who was the son of the defunct Duke. However, Spain was upset in November by Napoleon sending French troops and administrative teams to Parma/Plaisance in accordance with his interpretation of the French-Spanish treaty of Aranjuez (March 1801). Moreover, the British ambassador to Spain informed Godoy in January 1803 that his country would block any Spanish cession of the Floridas to France; still other obstacles to that cession included U.S. opposition to it and Russia's demand that Parma/Pleasance be given to the King of Sardinia and not to the Bourbons; for all these reasons, "the negotiation failed and was never renewed" (94–97).

34. Robert Livingston Papers at New-York Historical Society.

35. One reason given by Spain, per Renaut's *Louisiane*, was that Napoleon's ambassador in Madrid in 1802 had given Spain "a formal declaration ... by which he, in the name of France, committed never to alienate Louisiana" to a third power without first offering it back to Spain (69–70).

36. Michelet, *Revolution*, vol 9: Napoleon ruined his fine army by way of "two celebrated follies: Egypt, where he deserted it, and St. Domingue, where he exposed it to a certain death, in a devouring climate, condemned in the service of a crime, the futile effort to reestablish slavery" (81). *Ibid.*, vol. 8: Napoleon, "in geography, remained astonishingly ignorant, believing at thirty years of age that Egypt was quite close to India" (307).

37. Robert Livingston Papers at New-York Historical Society for Livingston's correspondence; *Napoleon Bonaparte, Napoleon on Napoleon: An Autobiography of the Emperor*, ed. by Somerset de Chair, (London: Cassell, 1992), 177.

38. Robert Livingston Papers at New-York Historical Society.

39. It would only be in July that the U.S. government learned of the April breakthrough, per Madison's 29 July letter to Livingston and Monroe expressing pleasure at the contents of their letters dated April 11, 13 and 17 and May 12 — the last reporting the signature of the 30 April purchase.

40. *Ibid.*

41. *Ibid.*

42. United States Department of State, *State Papers and Correspondence...*, 155–57.

43. Robert Livingston Papers at New-York Historical Society, Livingston to Madison, April 13, 1803.

44. *Ibid.*

45. Livingston here was assuming — quite wrongly — that the French expedition was already underway and therefore would arrive at New Orleans ahead of the arrival there of Madrid's countermanding orders. Livingston only belatedly would learn from King that the French expedition had been canceled while still in port and, in a letter to Talleyrand of 22 March, would express his irritation at having only learned that fact from a non-French source.

46. King, having warned him not to do so, would not appreciate Livingston's here having so obviously used him as his source of this privileged information.

47. Robert Livingston Papers at New-York Historical Society: Livingston to Madison, September 1, 1802: I will now "make an excursion" of a few days to the Netherlands; and November 2, 1802: "Nothing very important relative to our affairs having intervened for some time past, I have not thought it necessary to trouble you." (United States Department of State, *Calendar*, vol. 1. Incidentally, Jefferson in that November would write to ask Livingston to "superintend a purchase of books in Paris.")

48. Robert Livingston Papers at New-York Historical Society.

49. Whitaker, *Mississippi*: "The commerce of the Mississippi Valley was completely revolutionized in the two decades between the American Revolution and the Louisiana Purchase. The changes that came with the steamboat age were hardly more profound than those which occurred in this period"; and "[The] embargo of 1808 and steamboat competition brought about [the] decline" of the building of sea-going ships on the Monongahela River and then its total "disappearance" (79, 148–49). Also, Kukla, *Wilderness*: "Fulton's *Clermont* led to a new age of navigation on the Mississippi River"(237). And Lewis, *Noble Bargain*: "Upriver transportation was so difficult before the age of steam that places like Pittsburgh, Mariella, Lexington, and Nashville received most of their supplies through the difficult, and expensive, overland route from Philadelphia"(42).

50. Regarding: "scientist" and "millstones," see Dangerfield, *Chancellor*, 214 and 283. Kukla's *Wilderness*, reproduces the cover sheet of a technical paper written and published by Livingston on the merino sheep (237).

Chapter 3

1. Robert Livingston Papers at New-York Historical Society.
2. The "debate" may well have been fictitious, as will be discussed later.
3. Subsequent French history demonstrates that an imbalanced political situation such as existed during the Consulate need not be restricted to undemocratic governments. For example, per Barnavie and Friedlander, *La Politique*, a former De Gaulle minister, Jacques Soustelle, would write: "We were not allowed to offer a view on a range of problems, let alone offer one on a subject outside our immediate jurisdiction. In short, there was no government, but rather ... a bunch of clerks stuck to some tasks" (op. cit.).
4. Van Zandt, *Boundaries*: "The total payments made by the United States on account of this purchase, including interest, amount to $23,213,567.73" (36).
5. Napoleon Bonaparte, *Correspondance de Napoléon*, vol. 8 (Paris, Henri Plon, 1861): That it was only a ploy is suggested by the fact that Napoleon, following his quick ratification of the agreements with the U.S., wrote Marbois on 21 May of his "satisfaction" with the results of his "important effort," which added "many millions" to the republic's treasury; the first consul then granted him (192,000 livres "to supplement the meagerness of your regular salary" (320–21). (The standard historical judgment is that the funds Napoleon received from the sale to the U.S. were key to the financing of the cost of his subsequent victorious campaign in Europe.) Robert Livingston Papers at New-York Historical Society, Livingston to Madison, May 5, 1804: While Marbois in fact would remain in office for a few more years, Livingston here reported to Madison that "some circumstances make me fear that my friend Marbois is declining in favor. Talleyrand is all powerful and does not love him and has taken advantage of the bad bargain that he allegedly made with us to hurt him." Note that, by this time, tension had arisen between Livingston and Marbois due to conflicts of interest in implementing the agreement on payment of American claims, as discussed in an earlier note and as reflected in Marbois' 1829 book on the Louisiana Purchase. Also note that Monroe would later write with some exaggeration that, in fact, Marbois never felt a real friendship with, or a deep professional regard for, Livingston and largely ignored him prior to the negotiation of the Louisiana Purchase.
6. *Ibid.*, Livingston to Madison, April 17, 1803.
7. *Ibid.*, Livingston-Marbois, April 23, 1803.
8. United States Department of State, *Calendar*, vol. 2; United States Department of State, *State Papers and Public Documents*, vol. 4, 496–97; and, Malone, *Du Pont* 62.
9. Robert Livingston Papers at New-York Historical Society, Edward Livingston to Livingston, February 23, 1803: Monroe had been in New York since 19 February and would leave for Havre "in about 8 days" and was due to arrive "by the first of April." As will be discussed in further detail, Monroe arrived at Havre on 8 April: (a) Monroe to Livingston, 8 April: "I have this moment arrived.... I shall proceed to Paris either tomorrow or next day at farthest"; (b) Livingston to Monroe, 10 April, congratulates him on his "safe arrival." (Livingston had learned of Monroe's arrival by a note Monroe had sent hand-carried to Paris by a fellow passenger.) Monroe would later write in his autobiography that news of his arrival was immediately "telegraphed" (by semaphore) to Paris, although he admitted that this was only a conjecture on his part (155).
10. Robert Livingston Papers at New-York Historical Society, King to Livingston, March 18, 1803: "War is inevitable.... You doubtless know that the expedition to Louisiana [under General Victor from Holland] has been countermanded [as] announced by the French government to that of this country." (Livingston, in fact, hadn't known of the French action and, to King's likely discomfort, he went to complain to Talleyrand about having had to learn of it from a source at another court. King to Livingston, March 29, 1803: "Observe the greatest caution, in respect to these communications, as my situation would be very delicate in which it were supposed these

communications were derived from me.") Per the editors of Madison, *Papers*, vol. 4: "Even before Monroe arrived at Paris on 12 April, Napoleon had decided to divest himself of Louisiana lest it be lost as France's other American colonies had been lost during earlier Anglo-French conflicts" (xxiv-xxxv).

11. Robert Livingston Papers at New-York Historical Society, Livingston to Joseph Bonaparte, January 7, 1803: "I take this opportunity [to express my "deepest sympathy" regarding] "the loss that you have just suffered, along with all of France, in the person of General Leclerc."

12. Malone, *Du Pont*, goes so far as to describe the decision to cede all of Louisiana to the U.S. as due "largely" to "Napoleonic caprice" (xxi). One might with a certain gingerliness add to the various factors conditioning Napoleon's decision to cede Louisiana the following consideration: Napoleon, after all, did not initiate the project of getting Louisiana back from Spain but rather inherited it from the disrespected Directory, which had made it "a prominent feature" of its diplomacy (per Arthur Aiton in *Annals of the American Academy of Political and Social Science*, vol. 173, May 1934); this might well, if marginally, have eased his way to cutting his losses regarding a territory he apparently had never given much thought or study to prior to 1799.

13. Lewis, *Noble Bargain*, perhaps was unaware of this Du Pont memorandum, because he wrote that "there is no evidence" that "Du Pont actually disclosed ... to Napoleon or someone else high in the French government" the contents of Jefferson's 1802 private letters to him and Livingston with their "barely concealed threat to his native country."

14. This jibes with Livingston's letter to Joseph Bonaparte, January 7, 1803, where, as already quoted, he suggested that, if Napoleon "should consider it as an important object to retain a part of Louisiana with such parts as will give him a command of the Gulf of Mexico ... let him cede to the U.S. New Orleans and West Florida as far as the River Perdigo [Perdido], retaining Florida, which will give him the only good harbors in the Gulf, to wit, Pensacola and the Bay of St. Esprit." Monroe, *Autobiography*, regarding the agreement of 30 April: "It was understood" that the "province" extended on its "left" to "the River Perdido" (168–67).

15. Livingston Papers at New-York Historical Society. An abbreviated version is in United States Department of State, *State Papers and Correspondence*, 143–44, which gives no date. No other English translation seems to have been published.

16. Binger Hermann, *The Louisiana Purchase and Our Title West of the Rocky Mountains* (Washington, D.C.: U.S. Government Printing Office, 1898): This official U.S. government summary of those instructions may be accepted as the standard interpretation of what Jefferson and Madison had in mind. It states: "The instructions to our envoys were 'to procure ... a cession to the United States of New Orleans and of West Florida, or as much thereof as the actual proprietor can be prevailed to part with.'" Per Madison, *Papers*, vol. 4, Jefferson to Madison February 22, 1803: "I return you Monroe's instructions which are entirely right. One circumstance only might perhaps as well be left out. I mean the mention of my letter to Du Pont. As that correspondence will make no part of the public record, perhaps it is as well it should not be spoken of in them." This is in line with Jefferson's February 1, 1803, to Du Pont in United States Department of State, *State Papers and Correspondence*: "Whatever power, other than ourselves, holds the country east of the Mississippi becomes our natural enemy"; the U.S. could then ally with Britain; regarding his letters to him of 25 April and 5 May, Du Pont should burn them and the present one immediately to avoid, "like the hornet which attracts poison from the same flower that yields honey to the bee," having them create "the ground of blowing up a flame between our two countries," rather than "the reverse of what we are aiming at" at a time when each of them was "now at the time of life when our call to another state of being cannot be distant and may be near" (94–96). Per the editors of Madison, *Papers*, vol. 4: As host of a dinner, Madison told Pichon on 3 January 1803 that the French government's "silence might be regarded as a kind of declaration of war"; one week later, Jefferson named Monroe (xxv–xxxiv).

17. This policy not to appear oversolicitous of British military cooperation may help explain why the Jefferson government allowed the Federalist King to leave

his post and return to the U.S. in the midst of this crisis over Louisiana and a budding renewal of the war between France and Britain. Livingston shared King's wonder at that decision and appreciated King's delaying his departure as long into May 1803 as feasible, despite personal demurrage costs, so as to do all possible both to prevent a British attack on New Orleans (whose title was being transferred to the Americans) and to protect American maritime interests in the event of that war. Note that King lacked a senior-level deputy who could serve as chargé d'affaires and that Monroe would arrive only in July as his successor. Also note that Jefferson's having kept King on this long at his post, where he was so highly considered by the British, is seen with much plausibility by some historians (such as Lawrence S. Kaplan) as evidence of the president's policy of playing off France and Britain in an effort to extract maximum advantage — and also of Jefferson's having by 1800 become less enamored and trusting of the French than many, such as Livingston, were prone to believe. (In February, Edward Livingston had written his brother that Monroe likely was slated to be his successor in Paris — a report Edward rightly thought would be greeted as good news by Livingston.) As examples of Renaut's all-too-many errors regarding the subject of Britain and the U.S., see *Louisiane*: "King stayed in London until 1804"; and, Renaut, with one exception, always and wrongly referred to the U.S. as a "confederation" (78).

18. This position was in keeping with the treaties the U.S. signed with Britain in 1782, 1783 and 1794, all of which included a provision that both nations would have the right of navigation on the Mississippi. Towards that end, they attempted to draw a boundary line that would give Britain a foothold on that river at its source. But, as alluded to earlier, the state of geographical knowledge of that region was inadequate to the task. For example, Madison, *Papers*, vol. 4, King to Madison, February 28, 1803: "I am unable to give you any information concerning the line ... between the Lake of the Woods and the Mississippi" (359–60). It was learned during Washington's administration that the one drawn at the close of the American War of Independence did not extend to the Mississippi; subsequent efforts to reach agreement failed, and the region remained with an undefined boundary until 1842, when the Webster-Ashburton treaty settled on the present line. Thus, Britain never did win a Canadian border on the Mississippi itself; nor did it ever seek to take commercial advantage of the U.S. treaty commitment of 1782 onward to share with it the navigation of that river.

19. Robert Livingston Papers at New-York Historical Society. The crucial distinction Madison here draws between American "navigation" rights on the Mississippi and the right of "deposit" at New Orleans or other suitable port underlines the significance of a common error in the writing of the history of the Louisiana Purchase: that the U.S. was being threatened by cancellation of its right of navigation down the Mississippi to the Gulf of Mexico. Thus, Whitaker, *Mississippi*, usefully points out Henry Adams' mistake in heading one of the chapters in his *History* as "The Closure of the Mississippi" (195). United States Department of State, *State Papers and Correspondence*: That many at the time equated an ending of American privileges at New Orleans with a threat to close the Mississippi River itself to U.S. navigation is suggested by Livingston's letter to Pickney of October 21, 1802, arguing that the U.S. should establish ports on that river as alternates to New Orleans: "Any attempt to obstruct the navigation ... we shall know how to oppose them" (175–80). That Madison and Jefferson did not always synchronize their words on the same issue is illustrated by Jefferson's February 1, 1803, to Du Pont, where, unlike Madison's distinction between navigation and deposit rights, the president failed to so clearly distinguish: The U.S. is prepared "to hazard our existence" for the "maintenance" of "the use of the Mississippi," including "our rights of navigation and deposit" (94–96). Madison, *Papers*, vol. 4, Intendant Morales to Minister Yrujo, January 15, 1803: "Although the port remained closed, the navigation of the river was not impeded" (405).

20. For the full text of the 2 March instructions to Livingston and Monroe see: United States Department of State, *State Papers*, 122–36. (Note that these instructions bore the original date of "January 31," and apparently a copy was sent around that time directly to Livingston, who already was complaining about them in accurate detail in his 18 March correspondence with fellow

minister Pinckney (see following note). Hermann, *Louisiana Purchase* usefully summarizes those instructions as follows:

> It was Napoleon's belief that Monroe was clothed with instructions more extensive than the assumed authorization of Congress would warrant, both as to territory and as to price. In this he was mistaken.... It was ... required that "the navigation of the river Mississippi, in its whole breadth from its source to the ocean and in all its passages to and from the same, shall be equally free and common to citizens of the United States and of the French Republic." It was suggested that if France declined to cede to us the whole of the island of Orleans then a part should be sought for, if no more than space enough upon which to establish a large commercial town on the bank of the river; or, if unable to procure a complete jurisdiction over any convenient spot whatever, the envoys were instructed to secure a right of deposit with the privilege of holding real estate for commercial purposes. If the Floridas could not be secured the envoys were to seek for suitable deposits at the mouths of the rivers passing from the United States through the Floridas, as well as their free navigation.

21. It would seem that Du Pont went too far in his ideas of Franco-American commercial arrangements were the U.S. to purchase New Orleans—both Livingston and Jefferson expressed a dislike of the extent to which the U.S. was to offer the two Bourbon powers commercial privileges in its western territory under Du Pont's scheme. For example, in United States Department of State, *State Papers and Correspondence*, Jefferson in a letter to Du Pont dated February 1, 1803, states that the U.S. cannot endorse all the terms in his memorandum of 4 October (94–96).

22. Emphasis added.

23. This seems to contradict the fact, which Livingston regularly taunted to the French in pressing for American rights at New Orleans, that ocean-going vessels could reach as far as Natchez—which therefore could, if developed, serve as a replacement of New Orleans.

24. Robert Livingston Papers at New-York Historical Society. Livingston's unhappiness with this amount and the related formula is clear from his letter of 18 March to Pinckney: "Upon looking over the instructions to Mr. Monroe and me ... I almost despair of your success unless you are charged with any different ones or greatly exceed the limits assigned to us. By our instructions, we are empowered to give 50 million for New Orleans and both Floridas. The two latter were valued at one-fourth of the former, and east Florida at only one-half of West Florida, which reduces its value or the price we were empowered to give to less than $700,000." See also page 61.

25. As noted above, the final boundary between the U.S. and Canada would fail to bring the latter to the Mississippi.

26. A Du Pont letter to Jefferson was the clear source of the assumed specific financial expectations of the French authorities.

27. In keeping with this cautious approach of Madison, Livingston wrote Marbois on 22 April: "Some provision should be made in case it should so happen that France should not be able to put us in possession of the country, either from its being withheld by Spain or conquered by Britain before the treaty is carried into effect. In either of these cases, the Government of France must secure us the repayment of the money we have advanced."

28. Recall the exchange between Livingston and King regarding a possible guarantee of French or Spanish territory by the U.S.—the former's view seems to have prevailed, but only in a situation of duress. Also recall Livingston's later chastisement of Pinckney (April 20, 1803) for having wrongly applied the U.S. policy on guarantees.

29. As will be shown below, Madison's assumption was wrong—in fact, the Spanish intendant had acted on secret orders from Madrid.

30. United States Department of State, *State Papers and Correspondence*, 114.

31. Compare this with Du Pont's similar point in his memorandum to Lebrun.

32. United States Department of State, *State Papers and Correspondence*, 15–18. By 28 October, Livingston would advise the president, who long considered Du Pont as the best mind in France, that that Frenchman "has no personal interest" with Napoleon directly and, therefore, was of "limited aid" to the U.S. Like Jefferson, as noted above, Livingston had problems with the extent of commercial concessions Du Pont envisaged the U.S. was to make to France for New Orleans and West Florida. Monroe, following the purchase of Louisiana, would rather unenthusiastically opine that

Du Pont may on balance have been a positive factor in the negotiation. One reason for these doubts about Du Pont, as will be discussed later, is that his major memoir to the French authorities offered too many economic concessions to France (and Spain) for American tastes. Of course, there is also the point that ambassadors naturally bristle when their governments supplement them with outside agents to forward a negotiation. Shortly before this presidential message to Livingston, Jefferson, according to a King letter to Livingston of April 25, 1802, had told the British minister to the U.S., Thornton, that the retrocession to France "will unavoidably produce jealousies, irritation and hostilities, and, with regard to the [elsewhere, "the settlement of our northwestern boundary"], the president suggested the expediency of a diplomatic settlement, by its being agreed to run a line from the western bay of Lake Superior to such part of the Mississippi as is nearest to Lake Superior." (As noted, no such line to the Mississippi would ever be agreed upon between Britain and the U.S. Livingston, as has been discussed, would use this Anglo-American boundary negotiation as leverage with the French.) King went on to observe that the Jefferson administration "possesses in a higher degree than the former one did the confidence of the southern and western states and people," and that Livingston should "strenuously recommend" that every effort be made by it to assure harmony between "the western and Atlantic states."

33. The contrast is remarkable between this instruction and the argument Livingston had picked precisely at this time with Talleyrand over a matter of protocol, as will be discussed later in the text. Also remarkable is the contrast between Livingston's earlier charge that Jefferson was still being taken in by the French, as cited above, and the explicit denial of such a view by the president himself.

34. United States Department of State, *State Papers and Correspondence.* 182.

35. Madison, *Papers*, vol. 4: The president here clearly is in doubt as to what Livingston's recent references to creating a "personal interest" on the part of the Bonaparte family actually meant (434).

36. United States Department of State, *State Papers and Correspondence*, June 8, 1803: "It is proper to inform you that the treaty and conventions bear date from the period when [every]thing was agreed on, the 30th of April, but as it [was necessary] to reduce them to writing, the treaty was signed on the 2nd of May and the convention concerning the claims of our citizens the 9th or 10th" (216).

37. As we have seen, Livingston also made that case officially to Talleyrand, although minus the proposal of sharing the profits from the sale of land in "that country" between the U.S. government and the Bonaparte family. For Livingston's offer to Joseph, see later reference.

38. Interestingly, each of the first three major treaties signed by the U.S. in Paris (the French military alliance of 1778, the provisional peace treaty with Great Britain of 1782, and the Louisiana Purchase of 1803) was negotiated by commissioners with some trepidation, because they were acting in some important way outside the bounds of their formal instructions or even authority. In the present case, not the least of the assets Monroe brought with him was a presidential assurance that he needn't seek further instructions from Washington in order to close an agreement with the French that did not conform in its details with the ones he was carrying with him at the start. Nevertheless, neither man foresaw the geographical scope or the financial cost of the deal Napoleon would offer the U.S.

39. As Renaut and other historians have noted, there are no records in the French archives detailing the progress of the negotiations between Marbois and the two Americans. Moreover, per Deconde, *Louisiana*: "Sometime in these days of March [1803, Napoleon] apparently decided to give up Louisiana. Napoleon never directly revealed the timing for this decision or his reasons for it, and so his precise motives were a source of conjecture among his contemporaries and have remained so among scholars ever since"(154). Dangerfield, *Chancellor*: "There was a tragic laxity in one of the conventions"— the preamble to the claims convention stated "that its purpose was to secure payment ... under the second and fifth articles" of the Franco-American treaty of September 1800, whereas that second article had been "abandoned" in the ratification process (374–75).

40. United States Department of State, *State Papers and Correspondence*: However, there was a constitutional issue for Jeffer-

son, who wrote Breckenridge on August 12, 1803: Both Houses of Congress have a role in "ratifying and paying for" the purchase. "But I suppose they must then appeal to the nation for an additional article to the Constitution, approving and confirming an act which the nation had not previously authorized. The Constitution has made no provision for our holding foreign territory, still less for incorporating foreign nations into our union. The executive, in seizing the fugitive occurrence ... have done an act beyond the Constitution; if the nation rejects our and congress's act, we must get out of the scrape as [we] can.... But we shall not be disavowed by the nation" (233–34). (Of course, in any event, as further discussed in the final chapter, the president ultimately decided not to risk the purchase by going through a lengthy constitutional amendment process.)

41. France indeed immediately sold the stock to a firm that eventually made a handsome profit from the transaction.

42. United States Department of State, *State Papers and Correspondence*, 191–06.

Chapter 4

1. Daniel C. Gilman, *James Monroe* (Boston: Houghton, Mifflin, 1898), Monroe to Marbois, February 14, 1804: "In society with my respectable colleague [Livingston], to have met an old friend on the other side, who had experienced, as well as myself, some vicissitudes in the extraordinary movements of the epoch in which we live, is an incident which adds not a little to the gratification which I derive from the event [the Louisiana Purchase]" (89–90).

2. Robert Livingston Papers at New-York Historical Society.

3. For example, Livingston to Madison, December 20, 1802: Talleyrand "has changed his conduct very much for the better."

4. *Ibid.*

5. For example, Monroe, *Autobiography*: Marbois's book "furnishes useful light on the subject." It shows only on 10 April did Napoleon tip his hand; on that day, he discussed it "with two of his ministers." On 11 April, in the morning, he told Marbois of his decision. Napoleon on 10 April knew Monroe was already in France. The pomp on Monroe's arrival seems to confirm the report that his arrival had been "announced by the telegraph to the French government"; therefore, "it must have been known to the First Consul on the 8th." Napoleon's delay in announcing his decision was due to the need to await Monroe's bringing an American sale figure with him and his realization "that "nothing could be done until he did arrive" (155–60). (See the final chapter for an analysis of these assumptions by Monroe and the pro-Monroe supporting views of Kukla.)

6. Robert Livingston Papers at New-York Historical Society: as noted earlier, (a) Livingston wrote King on August 2, 1802, that he was sending him a copy of his "Louisiana" memorandum, copies of which he had "struck off" in French "with a view to place them in such hands as have influence to serve us;" (b) in his third-person cover letter to Consul Lebrun of August 10, 1802, Livingston advised that, although "printed," he has no intention of "publication ... several reasons inducing Mr. Livingston to wish that it may not pass into many hands;" (c) a day later, Livingston would send a copy of it to his brother, Edward: "You may share this [copy] where you think it will be of use to me, but not suffer for it to be printed" (Livingston went on to explain that he was running "a personal risk, since ... I am left without any precise information as to the wishes of the government as would serve to justify anything I may do or leave undone." As to be discussed below, it was, of course, published in newspapers with attendant diplomatic and personal complications for an apologetic Livingston.); (d) Livingston to Madison, March 11, 1803: Consul Lebrun was in charge of financial affairs, and he was on "a very friendly footing" with him, "and between whom my friend Marbois there is a family connection strengthened by the marriage of their children." Therefore, he "overrode Talleyrand's advice" to drop the part regarding debt in his letter to the first consul and won Lebrun's agreement to give it his support with Napoleon. (The "marriage" had taken place in November 1802 with Livingston part of the attending crowd.)

7. While many in the U.S. administration adopted a bellicose posture, Livingston went beyond that by actually and sincerely urging, officially and privately, that the U.S. immediately seize New Orleans and West Florida by force.

8. Livingston's Papers at the New-York Historical Society, March 28, 1802: As will

be shown below, Napoleon planned to send 25,000 black troops to Louisiana after having subdued the rebellion in St. Domingue.

9. *Ibid.*, Livingston to Tillotson, November 12, 1802.

10. Dangerfield, *Chancellor*: Livingston tried to make the case to the U.S. government to take West Florida by force. That historian goes on to say: "This solution, achieved in a more subtle way during the administration of James Madison, is among the less creditable events of that great man's [Madison's] career" (374–75).

11. Robert Livingston Papers at New-York Historical Society for this and the following three dispatches to Madison.

12. *Ibid.*, Even right in the middle of his and Monroe's negotiations with Marbois for the purchase of Louisiana, Livingston was criticizing Madison for a lack of instructions, this time regarding his "request as to the Italian Republic"—Livingston wanted to be accredited as U.S. minister to that new state, whose sovereign was Napoleon. On 17 April, he wrote the secretary: "I am sorry you have not thought it proper to attend to my request [and would appreciate your not passing in] silence [my] project, [because that would leave me in the dark regarding your] sentiments." Unsurprisingly, Madison regularly made caustic private comments to Jefferson, Monroe, and others of his friends regarding Livingston's constant push to expand his authority and to make policy suggestions that went far beyond his role as minister to France.

13. Marc de Villiers de Terrage, *Les Dernières Années de la Louisiane Française* (Paris: E. Guilmoto, 1904). Victor had planned to have twelve warships and 3,397 men. His instructions of December 9, 1802, called for him to establish "an *exclusive* commercial regime" for Louisiana (emphasis added). This gives added credence to Whitaker's view that France's *economic* goals in Louisiana were of fundamental importance. By May 3, 1803, the French government would announce the cancellation of his expedition, and by June 6, 1803, he would be serving as commander of Napoleon's Batavian army. Villiers de Terrage also observed that the "few words" announcing the cancellation of Victor's expedition were "written in haste" and in effect "contained the announcement of the definitive abandonment of Louisiana by France" (377–90).

14. Mary P. Adams' article draws almost entirely on Secretary of War Dearborn's correspondence to make a rather overstated case that Jefferson, indeed, was making preparations for early military action in this period, whether against France or Great Britain, and that the Lewis and Clark expedition from the start had such a military purpose. (For a totally contradictory, more persuasive view regarding this last point, see Ralph Guinnes, "The Purpose of the Lewis and Clark Expedition," *The Mississippi Valley Historical Review*, vol. 20, no. 1 [June 1933] where the case is made that Jefferson's goal from start to finish was commercial, political and scientific, but not at all military, in nature.)

15. Remarkably, as we have seen, France would do just that—but without success and only in the immediate aftermath of its sale of Louisiana to the U.S., having itself failed to obtain that territory from Spain.

16. Recall that chargé Pichon in July tried, apparently unsuccessfully, to disabuse him of this clear overstatement of what the French intention had been in negotiating the 1778 treaty, and of what restriction that treaty had actually imposed upon France regarding its possession of territory in North America.

17. Robert Livingston Papers at New-York Historical Society, Livingston to Lewis, December 7, 1802. The following letter was to Mark Leavenworth on 11 December; it contains a view of the alleged advantages to the U.S of a French-owned Louisiana that was quite close to that expressed by Murray to Madison in 1801 (described previously).

18. *Ibid.*, for this and the immediately following Livingston messages. Livingston was wrong on two counts in this letter: it was the intendant (acting on secret orders only to him from Madrid) and not the governor who first announced the end of port privileges at New Orleans for the Americans; and, as explained in detail by Richard B. Morris, *Peacemakers*, 213–17, the congressional instructions of June 1781 guiding the American negotiators at Paris in 1782–83 in fact left flexible how far they must go in insisting upon the Mississippi River as the country's western boundary. Thus, the instructions stated that, "[W]e think it unsafe at this distance to tie you up by absolute and peremptory directions upon disputed boundaries and other particulars."

The only irreducible demands made on the negotiators were "to accede to no treaty of peace which shall not be such as may, first, effectually secure the independence and sovereignty of the thirteen States according to the form and effect of the treaties subsisting between the said States and his most Christian majesty [Louis XVI]; and, second, in which the said treaties shall not be left in their full force and validity." The instructions made clear that "independence and sovereignty" meant "that Great Britain be not left in possession of any part of the thirteen United States"—the Congress was explicit that this requirement did not necessarily extend the boundary to the Mississippi River. (The present writer would add that, as Livingston of all people surely realized, those instructions reflected no such distrust of the French as he now intimated in this letter to Joseph. Livingston, with the passage of time, may honestly have believed what he wrote in 1803; also recall that he was not actively involved in the preparation or issuance of those instructions, having at the time been serving in New York as chancellor and arriving in Philadelphia only much later in that year to serve as foreign secretary.)

19. Robert Livingston Papers at New-York Historical Society, Spanish Foreign Minister Cevallos to Pinckney, February 28, 1803: The minister of finance had informed the intendant at New Orleans "that he should suspend the effects of whatsoever edict he might have issued as to the said deposit," and "that in this affair, he should regulate himself by the provisions of the treaty of 1795." *Ibid.*, Pinckney to Livingston, March 2, 1803: "This government also declares they knew nothing of the order" issued by the intendant; and, as regards the offers Pinckney was making for the purchase of New Orleans and the Floridas, the Spanish were giving "no answer ... except that the French have pretensions." *Ibid.*, Livingston to King, March 23, 1803: Pinckney had informed him that the Spanish intendant had been disavowed. As documented in Whitaker, *Mississippi*, the intendant's move had been secretly ordered on 11 July by Madrid. The real and continuing problem is to understand why Spain acted in this way; Whitaker rejected fiscal motives as the sole explanation (190–92, 230–32, 234). *Ibid.*: Godoy in late 1797 "ordered the evacuation of the southwest posts ... because he feared that the Americans would invade Louisiana," and he'd "learned the French would not cooperate in the defense of Spanish America." Spain evacuated Natchez on March 30, 1798. "There is no evidence" the deposit issue ever arose between France and Spain, which in fact concealed its Morales order from France. In early 1803, the was a war threat and Spain now saw France as unlikely to back it in Louisiana; therefore, Madrid rescinded its closure order. This left the 1803 situation much like that of 1795 as regards Spanish policy toward the U.S. The change in Spain's New Orleans policy was "a brilliant diplomatic and political victory" for Jefferson (65–66).

20. Livingston Papers at the New-York Historical Society. That Jefferson and Madison fully recognized the international as well as domestic import of Spain's move is clear from Madison's dispatch to Livingston of 23 February stating that Spain was in "violation of our right of deposit at New Orleans." Per Whitaker, *Mississippi*: The demand by Congress on January 4, 1803, for "information relating to the cession of Louisiana to France" forced Jefferson to drop his policy of "procrastination" and send Monroe to Europe. Monroe "owned extensive tracts of land in the west." The Monroe Mission would have been "a success even if he never reached Paris," because Jefferson's goal was not regarding France and Spain but that of calming "the western people" pending Madrid's response to the deposit issue one way or another (202–10).

21. Livingston Papers at New-York Historical Society. That Livingston was far from being alone in attributing the Spanish action at New Orleans to the French is clear from Madison's dispatch to him of January 18, 1803: Congressional debates showed that "the cession of Louisiana to France has been associated as a ground of much solicitude with the affair at New Orleans." Moreover, as pointed out by Bonnel, *France*, evidence that France may well have been involved in the Spanish move against U.S. interests at New Orleans is present in Talleyrand's instructions to Bernadotte, the then-minister-designate to the U.S. There, the foreign minister wrote that France did not plan to continue the Spanish "concessions" to the U.S. in Louisiana (This also ties in with the previously-cited instruction to Victor of a few weeks earlier, but apparently

prepared only after France had learned of the intendant's October action, that he should establish an "exclusive" economic zone for Louisiana.) (160–62). Per Brant, *Madison*: "General Victor had referred to the Spanish-American treaty as waste paper, as far as the American right of entrepot was concerned. An attack on Natchez was probable" (97). Perhaps the most convincing analysis of the French role in the intendant's action is in Arthur P. Whitaker, "France and the American Deposit," *The Hispanic American Historical Review*, vol. 11, no. 4 (November 1931), which holds that, while France indeed had not been consulted in advance of the Spanish action, nor did it ever request such action, once it took place France favored its continuance.

22. Robert Livingston Papers at New-York Historical Society.

23. *Ibid*., As put by Pinckney in his letter to Livingston of March 14, 1803: He told the Spanish government that, given the "uneasiness and discontent" in the U.S., the president "had thought proper to adopt the mode frequently used by our government of sending a special minister." Pinckney added that if what he heard from a U.S. official based at Bordeaux was true, Monroe was appointed as that minister. (Two prominent examples of precedents are, of course, John Jay to London in 1794, and London minister Thomas Pinckney's own subsequent appointment as envoy "extraordinary" to Madrid in 1795.)

24. *Ibid.*, including Madison's February 23, 1803, reaffirmation to Livingston that Spain was in "violation of our right of deposit at New Orleans."

25. *Ibid*. The answer to Madison's question regarding why Spain in 1803 seemed still to be planning a future agreement with the U.S. over its treaty rights for an alternative port to New Orleans is that he misunderstood the Spanish ambassador's letter to him announcing the revocation of the intendant's decree. That letter referred to a previous year's policy, not to Spain's current policy regarding the deposit issue. By 4 May, Cevallos would rather shamelessly give Pinckney the following untenable reasons for Spain's rejecting the American claim for compensation for damages caused by the intendant's action: (a) under the Pinckney treaty, the U.S. rights at New Orleans were only valid for three years—until 1798—and therefore after that year any such rights depended solely on the "King's generosity"; and (b), Madrid cannot be held responsible for the actions of the local intendant—indeed, "the revocation of that official's edict was precisely the King's way of putting his seal of authentication on his generous policy of friendship" toward the U.S.

26. *Ibid*. By erroneously putting the date of Monroe's arrival back a day and a half to the night of the 13th, and by denigrating that minister's official status (he had been received by Talleyrand on the 14th and was assured that he could participate in the negotiations even prior to being received by the first consul, not to mention Napoleon had publicly announced his welcome of the Monroe mission), we see an early indication of the paper trail Livingston was trying to create designed to magnify his own role and minimize that of Monroe in what he already knew would be a major diplomatic coup.

27. United States Department of State, *State Papers and Correspondence*, 247–49, and, United States Department of State, *Calendar*, vol. 3. Madison's analysis of Spanish behavior seems close to the historical truth as established by Whitaker's research.

28. United States Department of State, *State Papers and Correspondence*, 209–14. That Jefferson shared this field opinion is clear from his note to Madison of August 25, 1803: "By the help of my books here ... I am satisfied our right to the Perdido is substantial.... P.S. Louisiana, as ceded by France to the U.S., is made a part of the U.S. Its white inhabitants shall be citizens" (235–36).

Chapter 5

1. Robert Livingston Papers at New-York Historical Society, Livingston to Madison, February 18, 1803.

2. *Ibid*., for this and the following letter.

3. *Ibid*., for all documents.

4. Brant, *Madison*: Livingston's seeking Arkansas territory went beyond "his reasoning," while Madison's "sustaining logic" went beyond his goals; this "put Madison's reasoning behind the combined projects, with the force of it coming from the temper of the American people" (110).

5. Whitaker, *Mississippi*: Only with the

closing of the deposit did sea-going vessels move past New Orleans to Natchez, which had been established as a port only in 1791, by the Spanish. "The 179-ton Mary of Boston, which arrived at Natchez in January 1803, was said to have been the first ship of American registration that ever performed the feat." Therefore, Jefferson "seems to have had some ground for believing that the U.S. could, in case of necessity, make itself independent of New Orleans by developing the rival port of Natchez." "Outright [Spanish] exclusion of American commerce from New Orleans would have been suicidal" (146–47).

6. The justified ridicule that Choiseul heaped on the idea of some of his colleagues, who were anxious to promote the importance to France of Canada — that there was a "boulevard" down which military units could easily travel from Canada to New Orleans — would seem to be valid and applicable to Livingston's similar claim to Talleyrand. Of course, this may only have been a negotiating tactic in Livingston's mind.

7. Robert Livingston Papers at New-York Historical Society. The draft letter in French was seven dense pages long, the first five treating the debt issue and only the last two to three containing his proposal for the cession of lands by France to the U.S.

8. *Ibid.*

9. As also quoted earlier in this study.

10. Livingston here has in mind ways in which to protect the U.S. Treasury bonds from losing their value at the hands of speculators to the cost of both the French and American governments as well as the legitimate, original claimants to those funds. This concern was openly reflected in the detailed arrangements contained in the 30 April conventions as regards how to manage the disposition of the U.S. Treasury bonds. One example of Livingston's concerns was that there should not be too much of that stock brought to market in any one period for fear that would lessen its value. Some overly partisan historians, such as Brant and Kennedy, misread Livingston's efforts in this direction as a scheme for the bribery of Napoleon personally and for satisfying get-rich ambitions of American insiders, such as John Livingston and James Swan.

11. Livingston was a bit ahead of himself on this point, because only in early March would he be informed by Pinckney of the disavowal by the Spanish government. Livingston clearly was putting too much stock in the influence on the intendant of the latter's colleagues in America.

12. *Ibid.*

13. *Ibid.*

14. *Ibid.*

15. *Ibid.*, Livingston to King, March 8, 1803. Livingston without basis boasted that he had "worked hard, and happily the Floridas were not in the cession," and that he had "labored" to assure they wouldn't be "unless we can previously arrange for them."

16. United States Department of State, *State Papers and Correspondence*, 226.

17. It is hard to fathom Madison's criticism given that the instructions of 2 March also would have left France in "the possession and jurisdiction of one bank of the Mississippi."

18. Apparently Madison, along with the Congress, as noted above, conceived West Florida as including Pensacola and extending further eastward to the Apalachicola River. This was the administrative boundary established by the British after 1763. However, Livingston, along with Jefferson, was necessarily working on the basis of the Bourbon view of the boundaries of pre-1763 Louisiana, whose Florida component only went to the "Perdigo" just west of Pensacola, which port had been part of Spanish Florida and not French Louisiana. United States Department of State, *State Papers and Correspondence*: Also note the congressional commission's report of January 12, 1803, recommending an "additional appropriation of $2 million for the purpose of intercourse with foreign nations," where West Florida is said to extend to the Apalachicola (84–88).

19. Livingston's letter to Madison of May 12, 1803, clearly did not include among its enclosures a copy of his 7 January to Joseph that contained the proposed sharing with the Bonaparte family of land sales in territory under U.S. "jurisdiction" west of the Mississippi and north of the Arkansas; the present writer was unable to locate such an enclosure in the archives of the U.S. government. The dispatch's text itself lacks any specificities. See the previous text and the final chapter for a detailed discussion of Livingston's 12 May letter to Madison.

20. Robert Livingston Papers at New-

York Historical Society, Madison to Livingston, October 15, 1802.

21. See Livingston to Jefferson, October 28, 1802, for evidence that Livingston had indeed "anticipated" Madison's wishes to find a direct channel to Napoleon.

22. United States Department of State, *State Papers and Correspondence*: Thus, Jefferson, upon learning that the U.S. unexpectedly was now the sovereign of all of Louisiana, wrote on August 12, 1803, to John Breckenridge that his policy would be to move the "eastern Indians" to the newly acquired territory west of the Mississippi "in exchange for their present country" (232–33). Malone, *Du Pont*: Jefferson to Du Pont: "Our policy will be to form New Orleans, and the country on both sides of it on the Gulf of Mexico, into a State and, as to all above that, to transplant our Indians to it ... until we shall have filled all the vacant country on this side" (78–79).

23. See the earlier discussion of the New Orleans problem for Livingston's analysis, in this message to Joseph, of that Spanish circular.

24. In fact, the Jefferson Administration was not interfering with American trade with the anti-French forces on Hispaniola, implicitly as part of its effort to obstruct French plans to take possession of Louisiana once that island's rebellion was suppressed. See, for example, Adams' article. (Note that, prior to hearing of rumors of a retrocession by Spain to France of Louisiana, newly elected President Jefferson had been assuring Pichon in 1801 that the U.S. government certainly would support French military efforts to put down the Toussaint-led rebellion; but, once it became clear in 1802 that, were the French to succeed on that island, they would then move on to Louisiana, Jefferson changed his tune and declined to block American trade with the rebels. Some historians, such as Brant, seek to attribute this presidential change of policy to the influence of the allegedly more insightful Secretary Madison, but the evidence is that Jefferson altered his policy only upon receiving reports of the retrocession to France of Louisiana.)

25. Livingston Papers at the New-York Historical Society: In a separate note to Joseph that same day, Livingston, referring to Du Ponceau, his longtime French friend from his days as foreign secretary, who actually served as a congressionally paid deputy secretary to Livingston, wrote: "Further to my memoranda regarding Louisiana, I recommend my private secretary as an English-fluent aid to the French negotiator" so as to keep all "perfectly secret."

26. Joseph, as noted, would end up spending the rest of his life after 1815 living in New Jersey.

27. Livingston Papers at the New-York Historical Society, Livingston to Joseph Bonaparte, January 7, 1803. While Dangerfield, *Chancellor*, does refer briefly to Livingston's proposal of a land deal in "Louisiana" between the U.S. and the Bonaparte family "that required no money at all," he apparently missed the significance of the phrase underlined in the previous text, which he does not quote in his otherwise accurate treatment of this Livingston postscript (341–43). That biographer's normally fine grasp of detail at times falls short in his treatment of Franco-American relations, as when he wrote that it was "George Washington's peace commissioners" who were the recipients of a bribe demand in the XYZ affair (313). To appreciate how substantively significant this distinction is between Washington and Adams, see Stinchcombe, *XYZ*, 13–31. A more serious problem this writer has with Dangerfield is his strong criticism of Talleyrand as a confirmed opponent of French concessions to the U.S. and as having overnight, from 11 to 12 April, changed his tune with Livingston regarding France's ceding Louisiana to the U.S. because of the influence of a British bribe. As the previous text explains, a much more tenable analysis is that Talleyrand only in that period of April 11 to 12 learned that it was to be Marbois who would alone negotiate that cession. Also note that the bribery scheme had been afoot for several weeks prior to those April days.

28. Livingston elsewhere made clear that his goal was to create a "personal interest" among the French, but to do so in a way that did not involve any direct financial cost to the U.S. government; he felt the scheme described in this 7 January letter to Joseph fully met that goal. As shown by his use elsewhere of the term "jurisdiction" to describe the prospective post-retrocession status of Louisiana under French *sovereignty* (his letter to Napoleon of February 28, 1803), Livingston here, too, means by that term that the U.S. would have "sovereignty" over the territory north of the Arkansas.

29. Robert Livingston Papers at New-York Historical Society.

30. Ibid.

31. Ibid. In his 12 March letter to Jefferson, Livingston uses "Louisiana" vice this last reference to "New Orleans." Regarding Bernadotte, he of course never went to the U.S., although he was sent out of Paris to the coast to leave for America just as Monroe was arriving in the capital. Monroe, in his *Autobiography*, untenably argues that Napoleon's "motive" in ordering Bernadotte "to leave Paris on the day in which it was expected that Mr. Monroe would arrive there was no longer involved in mystery"—his popularity led to jealousy by Napoleon, who therefore wanted to get personal credit for the understanding with the U.S. Had Bernadotte stayed in Paris "a few days only," he would "have seen that his mission [to the U.S.] ... would have proved as to fame an empty phantom.... By mere accident," the frigate that was to take him there went on another mission and so he returned to Paris, but only after our agreement had been signed (180–81). (In point of fact, as shown by Napoleon's having in 1802 tried to get Bernadotte out of France as the commander of the force later given to Victor to go to Louisiana, it is wrong to try to connect Bernadotte's assignment to the U.S. to Monroe's arrival in France and the decision to cede Louisiana.)

32. This note has already been more fully described earlier in the text.

33. For example, see later for Monroe's letter of May 25, 1803, to the two Virginia senators and his autobiography. Thiers, *History of the French Revolution*, p. 387: "On 10 April," Napoleon met with Marbois and Decres, although the issue was already decided."

34. The following letters are from Robert Livingston Papers at New-York Historical Society.

35. Ibid. Also see United States Department of State *State Papers and Correspondence*, 157 ff.

36. This shows Livingston by now not only knew of Monroe's presence in France but also of Napoleon's decision even before Marbois came to tell him of it two days later—evidently, Talleyrand knew of it, contrary to Marbois's later account, and shared it with Livingston at least as early as 11 April. Also note that, in his previously-cited 10 April note of welcome to Monroe, Livingston, as shown in the next paragraph, rather ingenuously says: "*I have paved the way for you....* I have apprised the minister of your arrival, and told him you would be here on Tuesday or Wednesday" (emphasis added).

37. If Livingston was correct (and he probably was despite his contradictory report to Madison of 13 April that Napoleon had made his decision "on Sunday ... as I told you [sic]"), this would help explain (a) Talleyrand's *informed* interventions in the *two to three* days prior to Marbois's pronouncement to Livingston on the night of 13–14 April that he alone would be the negotiator for the sale of the *whole* of Louisiana; (b) Talleyrand's quick withdrawal from the negotiation (after a final April 12, conversation with Livingston and a non-substantive meeting with him and Monroe on the 14th, Marbois also being present), presumably because only late on the 11th or on the 12th did he learn of Napoleon's choice of Marbois as the sole negotiator; and (c) the gap between what Marbois told Livingston on the night of 13–14 April regarding the circumstances of Napoleon's decision and what Marbois self-promotionally wrote in his book 26 years later of a previously undisclosed debate he took part in with the anti-sale navy minister in front of Napoleon—we know that Marbois had a talent for fabricating historical documents (e.g., his famous book of the 1770s, republished in France as a serious work of history in 1985, containing alleged correspondence by Mme. Pompadour). A final point: If in fact Napoleon took his decision on Saturday, 9 April, Monroe might well have been right, that his arrival at Havre that previous day had been telegraphed to Paris and passed directly and immediately to Napoleon, provoking a need for a decision by France on the Louisiana question. (See later for a further discussion of this issue.)

38. For reasons discussed later, the date Livingston used, "April 13," has been changed to that shown. The text is a summary.

39. Monroe on 15 April drafted a private letter to Madison, but, as explained in a following note, it was not sent directly by Monroe—who, however, had his friend John Mercer make a copy, which of course made its way to interested parties in the U.S. See later for a more detailed description of it, including confirmation that the

famous dinner when Marbois unexpectedly showed up was on the 13th of April despite Livingston's dating his reporting letter to Madison as post-midnight on the 13th (he presumably honestly erred and meant to write the 14th). Monroe's letter reported that Livingston had told him at that dinner that he was going to Marbois's office "to confer relative to the purchase of Louisiana." A reader is struck by the combination of Livingston's openness of purpose with Monroe and the latter's apparent passivity in allowing such an obviously important meeting on the subject of his mission to occur without his presence. Possible explanations are that the Americans still were unaware that it would be with Marbois that they would be negotiating with, and that it was Monroe's sense he needed to remain behind the scenes at least until he met with Talleyrand, the still-presumed lead negotiator of the upcoming negotiation. Another consideration arising from this incident is that it surely contributed to Monroe's conviction that the reports he had been hearing from third parties regarding Livingston's unfriendly reaction to his mission were accurate, as reflected in Monroe's severe comments regarding Livingston in that private — and so early — draft letter of 15 April to the secretary. (The text of Monroe's draft letter duly appears in United States Department of State, *State Papers*, 164–65.) To confuse the date situation even further, Marbois' very undependable book (see Appendix C) gives 11 April as the day both when Napoleon told him he alone was to negotiate over Louisiana and when he had his first meeting with Livingston (301). On top of that, Dangerfield, *Chancellor*, accepts Livingston's dates given in his "midnight April 13" letter to Madison — that is, the Marbois meeting was on the 12th following the dinner with Monroe. Brant in *Madison*, like Dangerfield, accepts as valid the dates given in Livingston's "official dispatches" (137–38). The present writer, as reflected in the previous text, fully shares Kukla's view, which he derived from Harry Ammon's biography of Monroe, that the famous dinner was on the 13th and not the 12th. This correction of Dangerfield and Brant renders Livingston's own dispatch of "April 13" more consistent with the facts, as, for one of many possible examples, when he says he and Monroe will meet with Talleyrand "tomorrow," that meeting indeed took place on the afternoon of the *14th,* whereas, had his letter actually been written in the "wee hours" of the *13th,* he more likely would have meant that the Talleyrand meeting was to be on the 13th itself, the very next day.

40. Actually, as we have just seen, Livingston had also left open the threat of a direct *American* seizure of New Orleans, but this was before he had the benefit of his instructions and Mr. Monroe's more prudent papers and views.

41. Napoleon's reference was to a British bribe offer to Talleyrand, Joseph Bonaparte, et al, whose purpose was to have them convince Napoleon to keep the peace and allow the British to remain in Malta. The alleged connection of this British effort with the issue of Louisiana was that Talleyrand and Joseph, to accomplish their goal, would presumably dangle before Napoleon's eyes the prospect of France's being able to go ahead with the taking of Louisiana were he to keep the peace with Britain. Brant's analysis of why Talleyrand on 12 April suddenly dropped the idea of ceding Louisiana to the U.S. unconvincingly rests on this alleged connection with the British bribe. A more likely explanation, as mentioned earlier, is simply that only on 11 or 12 April did Talleyrand learn that Napoleon had cut him out of the negotiation over Louisiana in favor of Marbois.

42. Note this next meeting with Napoleon occurred on 10 April, not — as Kukla's *Wilderness* would have it (269), based on Marbois's book — the next day, 11 April.

43. Presumably, Livingston had obtained Monroe's agreement on this point at their meeting that afternoon.

44. It is remarkable that this opening salvo was also the precise amount finally agreed upon — perhaps a compliment to the insight Marbois brought to the table regarding the political perspective and financial capabilities of the country with which he was to negotiate.

45. See the resultant French memoir described in Chapter 1.

46. Livingston here obviously was underlining to Madison — as part of his paper trail — that the U.S. was getting much of what it wants even without Monroe's involvement.

47. A further illustration of Livingston's conviction that it was not in the U.S. interest, even in the long term, to possess the

territory west of the Mississippi below or above the Arkansas, and of his surprising naivety regarding the solution: finding a suitable European buyer. Also note that this seems to be a variation on Livingston's earlier idea of the U.S. and the Bonaparte family sharing in the profits of the sale of land west of the Mississippi — only now it would be with a European power that the U.S., having given up its "jurisdiction" there to that power, would share in those profits.

48. This is a patent effort by Livingston to cut Monroe out of the action and to rationalize his unilateral moves, including this very dispatch, whose actual departure for the U.S. presumably did not have the benefit of an awaiting ship; it also is part and parcel of his above-mentioned effort to create a paper trail establishing his personal role in these events.

49. United States Department of State, *State Papers and Correspondence*, 164–65. Madison, *Papers*, vol. 4: where a separate, official letter from Monroe of 15 April is given, it is reported that Monroe drafted a "private" one on that same date, "of which John Mercer made a copy, complaining of Livingston's conduct in continuing to press for the sale of New Orleans and the Floridas after being informed of Monroe's mission.... On the verso of the draft is Monroe's notation: 'not sent — communicating incidents relating to Mr. Livingston — with a copy to Col: Mercer. This is very full, as to Mr. Livingston's conduct, on my arrival.'" In Monroe's official letter of 15 April, he wrote: "On the 12th, I arrived here.... It is said that this government has resolved to offer us by sale the whole of Louisiana. This was intimated by Mr. Marbois to Mr. Livingston *the day after my arrival*" (emphasis supplied). Monroe adds that he only learned of this through "another channel" and not Livingston.

50. Skipworth was a Virginian who had been serving in Paris as U.S. Consul even during Monroe's tenure there as minister plenipotentiary. The parallels between this situation of April 1803 and that of 1796 are uncanny, and Monroe might well have sympathized with Livingston's feelings. As noted, on December 20, 1796, C. C. Pinckney, as Monroe's designated successor, wrote Secretary Pickering from Paris that he arrived there on 5 December and gave Monroe his recall papers: "I have seen Mr. Monroe very often since my arrival; his conduct has been open and candid, and I believe he has made me every communication which he thought would be of service to our country. He undoubtedly felt himself hurt at his being superseded, but I am convinced he has not on that account left anything undone which he thought would promote the objects of my mission. The Directory and Ministers had, for some time before they were informed of his removal, treated him with great coolness. But as soon as they heard of his recall, their attentions to him were renewed."

51. Monroe here is being unfair, given that Livingston's previously-quoted note to Talleyrand of 10 April reports his arrival at Nantes and implicitly his impending presence in Paris.

52. Again, Monroe is overstating the case, as Livingston's 11 April report to Madison advises that the "terms" he offered Talleyrand (20 million livres) were clearly derisory, and that he did tell the minister he'd have to first consult with Monroe before offering other terms. It is worth observing that Livingston evidently refrained from sharing with Monroe at least his April 11 and 13 letters to Madison, and probably also that of the 17th.

53. Monroe clearly means the 13th. That, as discussed earlier, would make the night of the 13th the time of the famous Marbois meeting with Livingston.

54. Here is another reference to the future French document excerpted in the first chapter of the present study.

55. Recall that, in his 28 February letter to Napoleon pleading for an immediate appointment of a French official to negotiate with him, Livingston went so far as to assure the first consul that he would never propose anything that would be upsetting to France.

56. United States Department of State, *State Papers and Correspondence*, 165–72.

57. *Ibid.*: For Madison's claim of "an error of the clerk," see his message of July 29, 1803 to Livingston (221–22). Per Bemis, *Jay's Treaty*: Thomas Pinckney, in his letter of June 23, 1794, "confessed to Randolph an unpleasantness in his situation" regarding Jay's going to England as "extraordinary envoy" (196–98).

58. Robert Livingston Papers at New-York Historical Society. As if to bear out Morris's last point, Monroe on June 24, 1803, would make a pre-departure call on

Napoleon in a rare private audience without Livingston in attendance. In the absence of a more innocent explanation, this would appear to be a slight by a visiting U.S. minister of the resident minister, one reminiscent of John Adams' similar meetings with Vergennes in 1781 without Franklin's attendance and without Franklin even being briefed by Adams on those meetings or on his letters to Vergennes, whose reaction to Adams' démarches and style was to inform the U.S. government and Franklin that he no longer would work with Adams.

59. Surely, Livingston was only writing, even at this late date, because he needed Morris' political aid in countering the perceived negative effects on his reputation of the Monroe Mission.

60. As noted previously, a phrase frequently used cryptically by Livingston. Although here and elsewhere it referred to the sale of Arkansas land with the proceeds to be shared by the U.S. government and the Bonaparte family, and not to insider sales of Florida lands by a Livingston-organized conspiracy aimed at corrupting Talleyrand, it would be misinterpreted by many historians, and not only the overly partisan ones, in their coming across the phrase elsewhere in Livingston's correspondence.

61. Livingston Papers at the New-York Historical Society: (a) Livingston to William Cutting, December 1, 1802: Britain's "ambassador extraordinary" had been in Paris near three weeks and wouldn't be received until 15 December, which is "the usual day on which Bonaparte receives all the foreign ministers — make your own comments." And, (b) Livingston to Spencer, January 13, 1803: Napoleon only saw the diplomatic corps once a month without individual private appointments. United States Department of State, *State Papers and Correspondence* Monroe's journal for May 1, 1803: "Presented to the First Consul," who asked, "You speak French?" Reply: "A little." (How typical of *all* the major U.S. diplomats in France during the first few decades of independence — even Franklin, the most proficient of them, spoke French poorly and got by mainly on his personality.) Then Napoleon to "both of us" (the other was not Livingston, also present along with Marbois, but rather Monroe's "friend," Colonel Mercer): "Our affairs should be settled." Later, at dinner, Napoleon: "You the Americans did brilliant things in your war with England, you will do the same again" (an accurate forecast).

62. This is in line with Monroe's previously-mentioned belief that his arrival had been telegraphed by semaphore to Paris.

63. As noted, a possible initial announcement by Napoleon of his decision to cede all of Louisiana to the U.S. came on the 9th, when the first consul met with his Council.

64. That now-famous message to Monroe, which so undercut Livingston's claims that Monroe arrived after he had already been assured of an agreement, included, as previously mentioned: "War may do something for us — nothing else would. I have paved the way for you, and if you could add to my means an assurance that we were now in possession of New Orleans, we should do well."

65. A comment is in order regarding Monroe's claim of Paris's near-immediate knowledge of his arrival in France: In his *Autobiography*, Monroe states that the French most probably transmitted news of his arrival to Paris by "telegraph." While an earlier note in the present study regarding the date of Napoleon's decision to sell the whole of Louisiana to the U.S. credits the possibility that the first consul was already informed on April 9 by a telegraph system of Monroe's arrival, this must remain a matter of conjecture. It is based on Monroe's impression that, had it been otherwise, the local port authorities would not have put themselves out so formally and ceremoniously, because, according to Monroe, "no examples of a like attention had been shown to a minister from another power." In point of fact, Monroe is mistaken. As shown by the similar manner in which Livingston had been greeted by port officials on his totally unexpected arrival at L'Orient in November 1801, such formalities were not unprecedented and did not require specific authorization from Paris. (Livingston Papers at the New-York Historical Society, Livingston to Janet Montgomery, November 13, 1801, reports that he was going to Paris under "escort" at the insistence of the local "commandant," who saw it as "his duty to France.") Therefore, even though Napoleon may well have taken his decision as early as Saturday, 9 April, to cede all of Louisiana to the U.S., it is far from clear that he already knew Monroe

had landed in France. On the other hand, even if Marbois' late-life version of events is correct, and Napoleon made his decision only on 10 April after an alleged debate between himself and the navy minister, it is clear that by then, with or without a telegraph system, all the parties, including Livingston, knew of Monroe's arrival at Havre. Kukla, *Wilderness*, copying Monroe's claim, goes so far as to assure the reader that the telegraphed news of Monroe's arrival went directly and immediately within hours to Napoleon himself (259-63).

66. Robert Livingston Papers at New-York Historical Society, where the year is misdated as 1803.

67. Marbois would remain in office until early 1807; after a few months of being out of favor and residing away from Paris, he returned there thanks to Lebrun's influence, to assume a different position — head of the newly reestablished *Cours des Comptes*, an agency similar in function to the General Accountability Office of the U.S. government.

68. United States Department of State, *State Papers and Correspondence*, Livingston/Monroe to Madison, June 7, 1803: Augustus Jay was carrying the "ratification" to the U.S.; he had to wait for the Government of France to give him a passport and would leave for America the "day after tomorrow." The French "delay ... surprises us," and, per the enclosed Marbois letter, it was due to some dislike of their agreement. According to Talleyrand, even Napoleon disliked the clause linking the U.S.'s actually taking possession to activating the convention regarding the 60 million livres. Talleyrand also said that Napoleon would take a page from the U.S. book after the 1800 treaty and "annex a condition to the ratification explanatory of his sense of it." Their position to the French was that they reject any and all changes in the agreement. Marbois "accepted" the letter stating this, and this "will, we presume, remove every difficulty to the execution of the treaty." A P.S. stated: "Since writing the above, the government has, of its own accord, restored our letter and retaken its own." Pichon was instructed, "on exchanging the ratification ... to declare that [the agreements] are void if the funds ... are not created by our government in the term stipulated." (Augustus Jay, son of John Jay, was Livingston's godson and traveling in Europe as a private citizen. This honor for Augustus did not help Livingston heal his long-standing, initially unsought breach with John Jay.)(pp. 209-14)

69. Robert Livingston Papers at New-York Historical Society, Livingston to Jefferson, October 28, 1802, and, Livingston to Tillotson, November 10, 1802. United States Department of State, *Calendar*, vol. 3: Madison advised Jefferson on August 18, 1802, that Sumter "retains the good opinion of the Executive."

70. Sumter after that would end his diplomatic career with an assignment as U.S. minister to Portugal at Brazil.

71. Robert Livingston Papers at New-York Historical Society. The reader of Brecher, *Securing*, will be struck by the unfortunate parallel between Livingston's problem with Sumter and Jay's situation at Madrid, 1780-82, where the latter had to contend with a difficult relationship with *his* secretary of legation, William Carmichael. Their correspondence at times was as intense and lengthy as that between Jay and the government of Spain itself. As Livingston pointed out to Jefferson 20 years after the Revolutionary War, the practice of the U.S. government of recruiting and commissioning secretaries of legation without first consulting its chiefs of mission intrinsically created opportunities for conflict between those two levels of diplomats, because the junior officers believed they owed their appointment and loyalty to the political forces at home and not to their immediate superiors. An additional complication for Livingston was that Sumter's job description included duties as Livingston's private secretary — as Jay's case well demonstrated, a separation between the two secretarial functions was often in order both for official and for personal reasons on the part of the chiefs of mission as well as the secretaries involved (152-56).

72. *Ibid.*: Livingston to Burr, April 6, 1801: "The President informs me that he intends to send Mr. Sumpter [sic] (a son of General Sumpter) with me as secretary to the legation — to whom he gives a very exalted character — but he has no information yet whether he will accept. Do you know anything of him?"

73. The U.S. government only gradually worked out a more professional and career-oriented personnel system for its foreign service, most definitively in the Rogers Act of 1924.

74. That is, Sumter saw Livingston's correspondence with such private American claimants as his brother, John, and James Swan as not falling within the definition of official business. Later, from London, he would charge Livingston with being involved in corrupt Florida land sale schemes designed to bribe Talleyrand and other French officials as well as to line his own pocket and those of his confederates at the expense of claimants not in on the conspiracy — and at the expense of the American taxpayer.

75. Mountflorence was Skipworth's deputy, and like Skipworth was performing duties as a private agent of claimants. Dangerfield uses this comment as an illustration of Sumter's humorlessness. Apparently, knowing of the enmity between the two, Livingston was merely joking when he suggested to Sumter that Mountflorence would replace him. (Mountflorence actually had expected to replace Skipworth with the arrival of Livingston, but he did not get that appointment.)

76. This is with reference to Livingston's having just brought on the previously-mentioned Du Ponceau as private secretary.

77. United States Department of State, *State Papers and Correspondence*, 266–69.

Chapter 6

1. In sum, Livingston ended up as the junior partner in two of Jefferson's greatest historical achievements, the Declaration of Independence and the Louisiana Purchase; in contrast, Monroe gained more personal credit than he rightfully deserved regarding the Louisiana Purchase and the Monroe Doctrine (the brainchild of Secretary of State John Q. Adams). Whitaker, *Mississippi*, points out that Monroe, who "owned extensive tracts of land in the west," earlier had also received more credit than he deserved in western regions of the U.S. when, as minister to France, 1794–96, he was seen as successfully pressing France to support American claims against Spain for their rights down the Mississippi. The French did so, but not due to Monroe's efforts, "as he believed" (207). (Also recall that, as early as 1786, Monroe had earned the plaudits of the west by taking the lead as a member of Congress in 1786, in opposing Jay's efforts to reach an understanding with Spain's Gardoqui. Jay's willingness to close the Mississippi to Americans for 20–25 years had in the west earned him the epithet "evil genius.")

United States Department of State, *Calendar*, vol. 3: That Madison should later appoint Armstrong as his secretary of war is consistent with his comment of March 17, 1805, to the president, that he "is glad to find [that Armstrong] understands the language in which the honorable policy of this country should be expressed"— a clear slap at Livingston's "language." Armstrong arrived in France in October 1784, and Livingston left for the U.S. from France on May 26, 1805, arriving at New York in June.

2. Channing, *History*, vol 4: "James Monroe was one of those men of persistent mediocrity from whom useful and attractive Presidents have been made." Jefferson, "may be," got him out of the U.S. due to his having "poked into" his "personal affairs" with "a certain Mrs. Walker," just as Monroe earlier did with regard to Hamilton and Mrs. Reynolds (314–15).

3. United States Department of State, *Calendar*, vol. 2, Monroe to Jefferson, July 30, 1796, from Paris. To add to the irony, Monroe, as would be Livingston, was also charged with financial "speculation," which he vehemently denied.

4. For Jay's dispatch of November 17, 1782, to Secretary Livingston see Brecher, *Securing*, 203–04. Robert Livingston Papers at New-York Historical Society and United States Department of State, *State Papers and Correspondence*, 187–97: Interestingly, Jay there, like Livingston in his 12 May letter to Madison, offers a blatant falsehood to bolster his position — Jay claimed that he and Franklin never disagreed on their negotiating strategy, whereas Jay's 12 September letter to Livingston had reported in no uncertain terms, as Livingston's 4 January response explicitly noted, that Franklin did in fact disagree with his analysis of French policy toward the American negotiations with Britain.

5. For the complete text of this letter, see Madison, *Papers*, vol. 4, 590–95.

6. The editors of Madison, *Papers*, here note: "See Livingston to Jefferson, 12 March, 14 April, and 2 May 1803."

7. To recapitulate: Possibly included among the enclosures to this letter was Livingston's 7 January note to Joseph Bonaparte, which contained his previously unreported proposition that the U.S. and

Bonaparte family share in the profits from the sale of lands in the territory to be placed under U.S. jurisdiction west of the Mississippi and north of the Arkansas. Also as mentioned previously, the present writer was unable to locate that letter in the archives of the U.S. government. The editors of Madison, *Papers*, in their various notes on this 12 May letter, write:

(a) "Livingston no doubt referred to his undated letter to Joseph Bonaparte discussing the expense of maintaining a colony in Louisiana and *suggesting that Napoleon transfer New Orleans and the Floridas to the Bonaparte family and to the U.S.*, [sic] which would obtain jurisdiction over the territory in exchange for a payment of ten million livres. The land could serve as a safe refuge for the Bonapartes in the event of an unfortunate political change in Europe, while the cash could be immediately useful. Livingston added that if this was unacceptable, Napoleon might transfer New Orleans, West Florida, and all of Louisiana west of the Mississippi and above the Arkansas to the U.S., while retaining for France the southern portion of Louisiana, building a port across from New Orleans, and sharing navigation of the river with the U.S." (Comment: The editors on this point miss the purpose of Livingston's variation of his original cession proposal: it was not to add to it "all of Louisiana west of the Mississippi and above the Arkansas," which in fact was already part of his original proposal, but rather to state that the U.S. would accept that France may not wish to cede both Floridas to it, preferring to keep East Florida to itself. It was in outlining this variation that Livingston's postscript made explicitly clear that the "land" he was proposing for joint U.S.-Bonaparte family ownership was only that in the territory above the Arkansas.)

(b) "Enclosure no. 3 was *probably* Livingston to Joseph Bonaparte, 24 December 1802, pressing for an answer to his proposition of a treaty transferring northwestern Louisiana, New Orleans, and West Florida to the U.S."; and, "Enclosure no. 4 *may have been* Livingston to Joseph Bonaparte, 7 January 1803, stating that he had just learned of the closing of the port at New Orleans by the Spanish government and urging immediate negotiations for a treaty arranging the transfer of the territory. Livingston described the difficulties that would occur if negotiations were delayed until Bernadotte reached Washington and the welcome he would receive if he arrived bearing a signed treaty needing only ratification by the U.S." (Comment: The parts underlined by the present writer in both (a) and (b) demonstrate: (1) the continuing confusion of exactly what land Livingston was proposing be sold for the joint account of the U.S. and the Bonaparte family — it was only that land above the Arkansas River, as documented in the present study — and (2) the fact that, even if Livingston eventually did send to Washington as an enclosure to this 12 May letter his December and January letters, the full details of his proposal for "personal objects" of interest specifically to the Bonapartes never surfaced sufficiently for use by historians until now.)

8. The editors of Madison, *Papers,* here refer readers to Livingston's 13 April to Madison, but, for reasons explained before, the present writer shares the Ammon-Kukla view that Livingston should have more accurately dated his dispatch as the 14th. What Livingston meant with his reference in this 12 May letter — to his understanding only "the next day" the reasons for Talleyrand's change of line from 11 to 12 April — surely was that it was at his pre-midnight meeting with Marbois on the 13th that he understood that the latter, and not Talleyrand, was to be the negotiator of the cession and sale of Louisiana.

9. For example, as reported by Victor Arriaga Weiss, *La Compra de Louisiana* (1996), 126: Livingston's 1802 memorandum appeared in the following North American newspapers in mid-1803: *Palladium*, Boston; *Gazette of the United States*; *Evening Post*, N.Y.

10. Livingston did not restrict to Anglo-French relations the stark scenarios he included as contingencies in his diplomatic communications to the Europeans. For example, see the previously-excerpted Livingston to d'Azara, Spanish ambassador to France, May 28, 1802.

11. United States Department of State, *Calendar*, vol. 3.

12. Robertson, *Louisiana*, vol. 1. A dispatch by British minister Thornton in early 1804 demonstrated that he was upset by Jefferson's change in policy toward his country due to the Louisiana Purchase. Jefferson was claiming "sole" credit and was now pressing for "concessions and advan-

tages from us" as a way to repeat the Purchase now at British expense and as a ploy to win the 1804 elections (24). (This episode supports Lawrence Kaplan's thesis, described in further detail in a following note, that, after the Purchase, Jefferson felt he could personally influence the policies of the European powers.)

Whitaker, *Deposit*, points out that there is no record of Napoleon's having the "deposit in mind" in April 1803 given the "scanty" information on the negotiations of that month.

13. United States *State Papers and Correspondence*, 220–21. Madison, too, would adopt a magnanimous posture regarding the rivalry between Livingston and Monroe. For example, his letter to Dr. T. W. Francis, November 7, 1831, commended both men for their impressive "zeal" meriting them an equal share in the credit. But Madison also wrote that, as Marbois' book "sufficiently" showed, "the real cause of success is to be found in the sudden policy suggested to Napoleon by the foreseen rupture of the peace of Amiens," because war with England meant that the latter would seize "Louisiana," turning it "politically and commercially against [France], in relation to the United States or Spanish America" (291). Livingston and Monroe had no sooner signed the Louisiana Purchase agreement than they began to dispute who was entitled to the greater share of the credit, but John Quincy Adams, in his *Lives of James Madison and James Monroe* (1850), commented that "the acquisition of Louisiana, whether to be considered as a source of good or evil, is perhaps due to Robert Livingston more than to any other man." Adams supported this conclusion by noting that Livingston's public use of Napoleon's debt promise in Talleyand's letter to him of March 11, 1803, helped make the first consul feel his "honor surely would not allow him to renege on such a solemn commitment," and by the fact that the pressure Livingston in 1802 exerted on Napoleon by the channels of Talleyrand and Joseph Bonaparte showed that "he followed faithfully his instructions to discourage the French from taking possession of Louisiana."

Chapter 7

1. Cox's article stated that "the West Florida policy of Livingston, Jefferson, Madison, and Monroe is the most tortuous, mismanaged, and indefensible in our diplomatic history"; the "name of West Florida" suggested "the most disgraceful diplomatic transaction in our history"; and, the U.S. adopted a "specious interpretation of the treaty of St. Ildefonso" by claiming that it gave back West Florida to France.

2. Villiers du Terrage, *Louisiane*: Note that French Ambassador to Spain Berthier had reported to Paris on September 17, 1800, that "The Spanish King would give France [elsewhere, at the "general peace," and if Napoleon so wishes] Mobile and that which formed part of Louisiana prior to the peace treaty of 1763" (373–74).

3. Kastor's *The Nation's Crucible* is the most recent and exhaustive study of this aspect of the Louisiana Purchase; James E. Lewis's *Noble Bargain* also provides a brief but good overview of it. One interesting contrast in the views between these two writers is Kastor's belief that Jefferson finally concluded that a "constitutional revision was neither feasible nor necessary" (46), while Lewis maintains that Jefferson, although he overrode his qualms for practical reasons, never changed his mind on the legal necessity for such a revision (69–73). Lewis, in line with the views of Lawrence S. Kaplan, who provides an introduction to this volume, rather controversially sees the threat to the Union of "an independent American nation" *between the Appalachians and the Mississippi* as the "real fear" of American leaders of the period and not so much "a weak French colony beyond the Mississippi" (23–24). As for Kastor's book, its focus and value are with regard to events following the signature of the accords of April 30, 1803, and its brief account of the pre-signature situation is too marred by errors and misconceptions to be read with confidence. For example: (a) "In 1763, France ceded Louisiana ... to Spain, while Spain ceded West Florida ... to Great Britain"; (b) Madison's instructions to Livingston and Monroe were dated March 2, 1802; (c) the treaty between France and Spain of 1801 "retroceded Louisiana to France.... Napoleon had little interest in promoting French settlement in Louisiana.... As a result, the Treaty of San Ildefonso ... preserved Spanish administration of Louisiana.... Louisiana now belonged to one unreliable nation and was governed by another" from the U.S. point of view; (d)

"Repeated delays in Paris led Jefferson and Madison to dispatch James Monroe as minister plenipotentiary to bolster American diplomatic efforts" (26, 37, 39, and 245). Kastor's main thesis is valid and worth capsulating: Many historians err in "reading Manifest Destiny back to 1803.... Yet by collapsing expansion into a single rubric, scholars have ignored both the complexities of expansion in 1803 and the changes that came in the half-century that followed" (40 and 244.)

As suggested by the conflicting, equally incorrect dates given by Kukla and Kastor for France's cession of Louisiana to Spain, there is a widespread confusion in the literature regarding that key event. Accordingly, it would be useful here to recall Lyon's correction (in a review of *Our Rising Empire*, in *Journal of Modern History*, vol. 13, no. 2, [June 1941] of Darling's statement that the "cession of Louisiana to Spain was a part of the renewal of the family compact of 1761." Rather, as Lyon stated, that cession took place in November 1762 by separate agreement between those two nations during the negotiations leading to the signing of the Preliminary Peace Treaty ending the Seven Years' War.

4. Roger G. Kennedy, *Mr. Jefferson's Lost Cause: Land, Farmers, Slavery, and the Louisiana Purchase* (New York: Oxford University Press, 2003): The author states that the book's "theme" is that, between 1802 and 1820, the downward drift could have been reversed by different policies by Jefferson and his successors. That writer then indulges in psychology to bolster his case: a "significant portion of the gap" between what Jefferson asserted in the 1770s and 1780s was his goal and what actually "occurred in his beloved southland" was due to "his willingness to pay the price" of keeping his "popularity among his fellow planters"—he lacked the courage of his convictions in his need to have "sympathy and love" from "his brothers of the comforting and familiar class of upcountry planters" (28 and 34).

5. Per Deconde, *Louisiana*, Franklin in 1751 had praised "the Prince that acquires new territory if he finds it vacant, or removes the natives to give his own people room" (22).

6. As noted earlier, the most recent detailed case for this point of view is by Andro Linklater.

7. Kukla, *Wilderness*: In one of his many excursions into ideology over obvious facts, Kukla has Rufus King leaving England on April 21, 1803, a full month earlier than (as Kukla himself had previously noted) he actually did, so as to allow him to write of that returning official: "Ten weeks at sea gave King ample time for reflection upon the implications of the Louisiana Purchase"; just as in his 1785–86 "flirtation with separatism," he doubted the governability of the Louisiana territory on grounds that it was, in his words, "too extensive" (284–89). (As will be shown below in connection with a similar assertion regarding Hamilton, King was most definitely not a separatist.)

8. Kukla, *Wilderness*, dates the Trafalgar battle in 1803, two years earlier than it actually occurred (328–30).

9. Thomas Fleming. "Hamilton on the Louisiana Purchase," *William and Mary Quarterly*, vol. 12, no. 2 (April 1955): Fleming's view of Hamilton's goals are, to say the least, controversial: The standard view is that Hamilton, Rufus King and John Q. Adams "were the only prominent Federalists not in outright opposition to the Purchase in 1803." It is also pointed out there that Hamilton "never shared in the disunion plots of the sort that had damned the Federalist party past any hope of salvation after the Hartford Convention of 1815."

10. As pointed out in Bowman, *Neutrality*, Hamilton's admiration for the military side of international life is suggested by the fact that his "idol" was Wolfe, who had died "gloriously while securing a continental empire for Great Britain" (17). Similarly, Kukla, *Wilderness*, states that Hamilton saw Julius Caesar "as the greatest man who ever lived" and therefore, as "the American Caesar," favored a military solution to the intendant problem at New Orleans (259–60).

11. Channing, *History*, vol. 4: Napoleon's reasons for the Louisiana cession had "nothing to do with the United States"(319)—all the Americans had to do was catch and hold the provinces thrown at them by Napoleon.

12. Woe to any historian who seriously tries to prove that any of these three men *really* merited these accolades; one who did, James Q. Howard, was immediately and properly skewered by Edward S. Corwin in a review of *History of the Louisiana Purchase* in *Michigan Law Review*, vol. 1, no. 8 [May 1903], for claiming that Livingston deserves

essentially the entire credit for the Louisiana Purchase, and that Jefferson was but an insignificant actor in this matter.

13. Lewis, *Noble Bargain*: "Within hours of visiting Barbé-Marbois's office, Livingston had decided that the United States should buy Louisiana. He had not conferred with Monroe and apparently had not even read the instructions that Monroe had brought from Washington" (58). This last point is based on a misunderstanding found in the historiography beginning at least with Lyon *Louisiana* 219–20. Lyon there asserted that, because Livingston only on 14 April had noticed the disparity in titles between himself and Monroe as stated in their "powers" document, he therefore hadn't even read his instructions. In point of fact, the instructions, per standard procedures, were contained in an entirely separate document, one which Livingston surely *did* read on or before 12 April, when Monroe spent the afternoon with him going over their papers. The evidence goes even further that Livingston was quite familiar with the instructions even prior to Monroe's arrival, apparently having received at least the preliminary version of them (dated 30 January) directly by dispatch from Madison. Recall that on 18 March Livingston had written to Pinckney expressly citing the "instructions" to himself and Monroe and complaining about the slight amount allotted therein to purchase the Floridas out of the fifty million francs the U.S. was prepared to offer France and/or Spain for New Orleans and the Floridas.

14. One might also point out that the first official suggestion from the government of France for the sale of all of Louisiana was made solely to Livingston by Talleyrand on 11 April.

15. Dangerfield, *Chancellor*: The claims convention erred by its preamble's reference to the second article of 1800 as being covered by the present treaty. Actually, the U.S. had given up this category "in return for France's giving up the obligations due them under the treaties of 1778" (375). Also, in Madison, *Papers*, vol. 4: the editors observe that the claims convention has "remained unsettled in the middle of the twentieth century" (xxixff). And Bonnel, *France*, notes that, "The personal papers of Livingston ... are singularly revelatory of the atmosphere which reigned at the American Legation, where speculators in American credits had easy access" (17). (The reader will recall that Livingston worked hard, risking his diplomatic situation, in order to protect the original American claimants from selling out too cheaply to speculators—e.g., his publicizing Talleyrand's answer to his letter to Napoleon of February 27, 1803, assuring Livingston in the name of the first consul that France most definitely would live up to its 1800 commitment to the U.S. to pay off the American claims.)

16. Armstrong, as noted, would become President Madison's (ineffective) secretary of war, 1813–14. One source of friction with the French authorities was per Claude–François de Meneval's *Memories of Napoleon Bonaparte*, vol. 1, pp. 200–01 that Napoleon "at first would have been satisfied with 50 millions," but after the 30 April agreement was signed, he also wanted as much of the 20 millions as could be kept from the American claimants so that it too could go into the French treasury.

17. Kennedy's *Jefferson's Lost Cause*, as noted earlier, is the latest and most notorious of the criticisms of Livingston's personal ethics: "The greatest private beneficiaries of the Louisiana Purchase were the Livingston family.... A substantial part of the funds used for that purchase went to the Livingston clan to liquidate debts owed it by the French government." Kennedy bases his case mainly on what Sumter and Skipworth were reporting — and maliciously so, as we have seen. Moreover, Kennedy, whose book is as ideologically driven as is Kukla's, ignores the fact, as previously reported, that Livingston's instructions *from the start* envisaged the possibility of blending the acquisition by the U.S. of New Orleans and the Floridas with the liquidation of French debts to Americans; rather, he erroneously claims that this blending only evolved as a solution to the debt problem when it gradually became clear to Livingston that France lacked the funds and/or will to pay the Americans directly from its own funds (174, 257–58).

18. Kukla, *Wilderness*, 304–05. That writer does recognize that "Monroe's interest in gauging the warmth of his welcome was almost obsessive, and it did incline him to undervalue Livingston's accomplishments in the months prior to his arrival" (262–63). And Kukla does ridicule Monroe's stance with the following sarcasm:

"Surely the surprising turn of events that awaited them in Paris owed principally to the triumphant return of James Monroe, minister extraordinary and plenipotentiary" (268). Lewis, *Noble Bargain*, points out on page 27 that "The United States did not appoint 'ambassadors' until the end of the nineteenth century" (27). (This diplomatic practice was in keeping with America's 19th-century stance of being above the power struggles of the European powers.)

19. Madison, *Papers*, vol. 4: Congress "authorized" the $2 million on 26 February "for the purchase of New Orleans" (352).

20. Ibid., Jefferson to Madison, March 19, 1803, regarding Livingston's recent letters: "I hope the game Mr. Livingston says he is playing is a candid and honorable one. Besides an unwillingness to accept any advantage which should have been obtained by other means, no other means can probably succeed there. An American contending in stratagem against those exercised in it from their cradle would undoubtedly be outwitted by them. In such a field and for such an actor nothing but plain direct honesty can be either honorable or advantageous." Per Livingston to Madison, May 12, 1803, postscript: "I have thought it prudent not to enclose No. 1..." (434).

21. Kukla, *Wilderness*: In typical errors regarding international and diplomatic matters, Kukla claims that Livingston's proposal involved using the "two million dollars" appropriated by the Congress to "buy half the land from the Bonapartes," and that, as early as December 1801, "after arriving in Paris, Livingston suggested that France offer Louisiana [sic] in settlement of the nation's debts to American merchants" (239 and 242).

22. United States Department of State, *State Papers and Correspondence*: Livingston's previously-cited letter to Napoleon of 27 February, 1803, is an excellent example of his giving quite open and free range to his thinking as to how to resolve his diplomatic problems. He actually there suggested that France "hypothecate for a term of years" *East* Florida to the U.S. as a way to safeguard that land from British naval power in the growing period of tension between France and Britain; the French proceeds from that transaction, according to Livingston's proposal, would be used to pay off the American claimants (115–22).

23. Kaplan, "*Jefferson's Foreign Policy and Napoleon's Ideologues*," provocatively attaches an importance to the question of Du Pont's role that transcends the narrow issue of what credit historically is due to him for the Purchase. According to Kaplan, the "apparent importance" of Du Pont's role misled Jefferson into thinking that it was "his own diplomacy" that produced the cession, and this "illusion" led Jefferson to believe that his diplomacy "could bend the governments of Europe to his will." Masson, *Département*, Talleyrand was appointed by the Directory as foreign minister on July 18, 1797, with the backing of Du Pont, who was "the majority's orator" (405).

As regards the alleged role of Du Pont in 1782, see Malone, ed., *Correspondence Between Thomas Jefferson and Pierre Samuel Du Pont*, xiv. A few years before Malone's book appeared, a biography of Du Pont by Saricks traced this myth to his innocuous, long-distance correspondence, in 1781 and the early months of 1782, with a private British citizen, James Hutton, who had initiated it on the basis of an earlier relationship between the two. Saricks concludes that, while foreign minister Vergennes supervised Du Pont's end of the correspondence, "It is very doubtful that Hutton's letters were inspired by his Government and even more uncertain that the correspondence between Du Pont and Hutton had any influence whatever in the eventual preliminaries of peace conducted between England and the United States in November 1782" (76–78).

24. Cox's article states that Skipworth felt "resentment" at Monroe's and Jefferson's failure to back him "in his previous controversy with Armstrong [regarding claims to be awarded under the 30 April treaty], through which he lost his position as consul at Paris." Kastor, *Nation's Crucible*, notes that Skipworth had made himself a candidate for the governorship of Louisiana but was rejected by Jefferson, who wrote Madison on January 8, 1804, that Skipworth "lacked the habits and feelings, and the tact" for that post (109).

25. Kukla, *Wilderness* 328–30. Also note Masson, *Départment*: Talleyrand, who had resigned as foreign minister on July 13, 1799, in anticipation of the 9 November coup which brought him back to office, left Napoleon's service on June 17, 1807 (405); and "Bonaparte always had a weakness for

Talleyrand; he believed that, even when tricking him, Talleyrand respected the proprieties" (457).

26. Thiers, *History of the French Revolution*: Marbois was "fired for a maladroit financial operation," prompting the following exchange between the two: Marbois: "I dare hope that Your Majesty at least won't accuse me of being a thief." Napoleon: "I'd prefer that one hundred times, because thievery has its limits, while stupidity has none" (392). (As noted earlier, Marbois quickly received a different, quite satisfying government posting from Napoleon.)

27. Masson, *Département*: Marbois' experience is a good example of the Directory's bloodless way of getting rid of people. It was known as "the dry guillotine" and featured deportation. Thus, Marbois in 1797, "because his name was found in some papers of royalist conspirators," was sent off to Guyana (497). (According to Jean Devoisse, *L'Homme qui vendit la Louisiane* (Paris: Olivier Orban, 1989), the Directory, as part of its September coup against the legislature, had arrested and deported Marbois because he was a leading member of the opposition in the *Conseil d'Anciéns* obstructing laws the Directory wished to have passed (204–14). It is, in fact, remarkable how, during the revolutionary period, Marbois braved imprisonment and even death not only on this occasion but also previously, at the end of his tenure as intendant on St. Domingue and then as mayor of Metz.)

28. Bonnel, *France*: Talleyrand's instructions to Bernadotte in January 1803 included that France will not continue the Spanish "concessions" to the U.S. in Louisiana (160–62). Whitaker, "France and the American Deposit at New Orleans" states: "The explanation ["that Napoleon had dictated Morales's proclamation"] is still a seductive one, but careful research has failed either to confirm or to destroy it."

29. Roberston, *Louisiana*, vol. 1: Jefferson's July 12, 1790, "Considerations on Louisiana," stated that, if England tried to take Louisiana as part of a war versus Spain, the U.S. couldn't win it and block England unless it had both Spain and France as allies. Therefore, the best U.S. policy was delay: "[Let's] choose our own time. Delay gives us many chances to avoid it altogether." There was a possibility of the U.S. together with France and Spain guaranteeing Louisiana's and Florida's "independence" (265–67). (Livingston actually would float a variation of the latter idea at one stage in his proposals to France.)

For the case that historians too often err in failing to give "Jefferson credit for making military preparations" in the face of the closing of the American deposit at New Orleans, see Mary P. Adams, "Jefferson's Reaction to the Treaty of San Ildefonso," *The Journal of Southern History* (May 1955). In contrast, Kaplan's *Thomas Jefferson*, argues that the threat to have "recourse" to Great Britain was "not a serious prospect; rather it was a gambit"; Great Britain was a "greater danger" than France (131). (Also recall Adams' doubtful claim, described in an earlier chapter, that the Lewis and Clark expedition's purpose from its start was strongly military in nature.)

30. Talleyrand's flexibility regarding the fate of Louisiana is further suggested by what Whitaker's article on the retrocession called his "perfidy" of Spain when, as the Directory's foreign minister in 1797, he offered England Louisiana in exchange for its recognition of French gains in Europe.

31. Also according to Whitaker, "The Retrocession of Louisiana in Spanish Policy," *The American Historical Review*, vol. 39, no. 3 (April 1934), Talleyrand had promised Spain a French "wall of brass" as sovereign of Louisiana in opposition to the U.S. and England.

32. On the other hand, as Walter Borneman points out in *1812: The War that Forged a Nation*, p. 297, regarding British policy into the post–Ghent Treaty period: "Great Britain had never recognized Napoleon's coercive dealings with Spain and his subsequent sale of Louisiana to the United States" (297). (Of course, this non-recognition policy did not necessarily contradict British sincerity in having, as noted previously, assured Rufus King in 1801 that, were they to capture New Orleans in a renewed war versus France, they would hand over that place to the U.S. after such a war.)

Appendix A

1. Robert Livingston Papers at New-York Historical Society (also in United States Department of State, *State Papers*). Livingston around this period also distributed—but more selectively and without

having it "printed"—his essay entitled, *Notes on the relative naval force and commerce of France and England and the U.S.,* regarding which, according to his letter to Madison of May 12, 1803, Napoleon "paid me some compliments on it." United States Department of State, *State Papers and Correspondence,* Livingston-Madison, July 30, 1802: Enclosed was a copy of the "essay," which he had translated and had 20 copies made, but, only if Talleyrand liked it would he "come forward with some proposition." (Presumably, only receipt of Jefferson's 18 April letter to him can explain this bold move.)

2. This viewpoint was common to American opinion and would pose a constitutional dilemma for Jefferson upon learning of the Louisiana Purchase, which theoretically would require a constitutional amendment to effect.

Appendix B

1. This memorandum and the following one are from Renaut, *Luisianne,* 227–40. Monroe was in Paris en route to a boundary negotiation with Spain when he prepared and submitted to Talleyrand the above-cited memorandum. Monroe's lengthy stay in Madrid starting the following January proved unrewarding for the U.S. Lyon, *Louisiana,* 203–04, has a rare, brief reference to these post–Purchase memoranda by Talleyrand, but they apparently have not heretofore been translated into English.

2. Renaut's note: "An allusion to the Mobile Act."

3. Per the editors of Madison, *Papers,* vol. 4: Pinckney had negotiated and signed a convention with Spain (August 11, 1802) covering this point, but the Senate delayed its ratification and it had to be submitted to Spain for its re-ratification. Spain by then had become upset by the Mobile Act of 1804 threatening Spanish control of West Florida and so declined to take that step. Only in 1819 was the convention fully ratified (262). (This subject is also discussed in some detail in the second of Talleyrand's memoranda contained in this Appendix.)

4. By Pinckney's Treaty of 1795, the line was at 31°.

5. Renaut's comment: "In reality, the federal government only had some vague notions of expelling the Marquis de Casa-Yrujo, who, despite the tension in the diplomatic relations between Spain and the U.S., remained as ambassador in Washington until 1808."

6. Renaut note: "The Miranda expedition ended in disaster."

7. Renaut's note: "This is an allusion to the victory at Austerlitz on December 2, 1805, over the combined armies of Austria and Russia, and to the peace of Presbourg concluded with Austria on December 26, 1805.

Appendix C

1. This appendix is based on the original, French-language version of the book, per the listing in the Bibliography. An English translation with some omissions was published the following year.

2. Marbois, of course, generally referred to Napoleon in this pre–Empire period only as first consul or as Bonaparte.

3. Here is another example of Marbois' theme that it was England and not the U.S. that most undermined and threatened French interests in the Americas; in this example, Marbois studiously avoided noting that it also was American shipping that participated importantly in the supplying of anti–French forces in the West Indies.

4. For an astute analysis of this issue, see Whitaker "France and the American Deposit at New Orleans."

5. There next follows a detailed account of an alleged debate on Easter Sunday, 10 April. As discussed earlier in the present study, there are grounds for considering this event as the product of an imaginative mind by one who could not resist the temptation of once again fabricating an entertaining historical fiction. Note that in Devoisse, *L'Homme,* Marbois' biographer, in another context, concluded that he was nothing less than a "genius as a forger" (26–29). One might observe, in this connection, that Marbois even forged his own name by adding or eliminating, depending on the political times, the "de" to his originally fabricated "Marbois." It is a suitable irony that a century ago at least one historian, James Q. Howard, attributed the writing of Marbois's 1829 book to an American, William Beach Lawrence, who was working "in the political interest of Monroe." This information is found in a note by Edward A. Parsons in *The Original Letters of Robert*

R. Livingston, 1801–1803 (New Orleans: Louisiana Historical Society 1953), 15, which itself is a skimpy book with a pretentious title, given that all but one of the few letters therein are taken from Livingston's correspondence with Rufus King. That is a shame, because, as Channing observed in *History*, vol. 4: "It is regretted that no collection of the writings of Robert R, Livingston has even been printed" (315–16).

Marbois' book poses a dilemma for historians: As editor Headlam commented on de Tocqueville in *Ancien Régime*, that writer was "the first scientific historian [elsewhere, who "refused the aid of every work which lay between himself and the Revolution"]. He accepted nothing but the original authors" (vii–ix). Can we confidently accept Marbois' retrospective book as a document by an "original author"? Clearly not! A final point: James Monroe, in his often-quoted letter of May 2, 1829, to Lafayette regarding Marbois' just-released book, surely revealed himself as being nearly as big a self-inflating and self-protective fibber as was Marbois himself. For example, Monroe belatedly would have it that Marbois had not even seen Monroe when he unexpectedly came to Livingston's house on 13 April, and that he, Monroe, had in fact proposed to accompany Livingston to Marbois' office once Livingston explained the purpose of Marbois's visit, but that Livingston objected to his doing so.

6. According to Deviosse, *L'Homme,* Marbois did try to see Livingston on 11 April but was turned away at the door on the double grounds that Livingston was away meeting with Talleyrand, and that his home was being prepared for Monroe's visit (334). (If true, that still leaves open the question of why Marbois apparently then waited until two days later, early in the evening of 13 April, before once again calling at Livingston's home.)

7. The reader will have observed that this entire chronology is erroneous unless—and this is very doubtful—Marbois has in mind here Livingston's meeting not with him but with Talleyrand on 11 April. E. Wilson Lyon, *The Man Who Sold Louisiana: The Career of François Barbé-Marbois* (Norman: University of Oklahoma, 1942), wrongly has Marbois actually meeting with Livingston on that 11 April (119).

8. Marbois errs here, because it was not the St. Ildefonso treaty but a letter in 1802 to the Spanish government from the French ambassador in Madrid that put explicitly and in writing the "prior consent" commitment on the part of France.

9. De Méneval, *Memories*, vol. 1: Per de Méneval (his private secretary beginning in 1802), Napoleon feared that, without a quick ratification, he would lose the American funds, because the looming war with England risked that "he would only have had an empty title-deed to offer the Americans" (200–01).

Bibliography

Adams, Henry. *History of the United States of America During the Administration of Thomas Jefferson*. New York: Albert & Charles Boni, 1930.
Adams, John Quincy. *The Lives of James Madison and James Monroe, Fourth and Fifth Presidents of the United States*. Buffalo: G. H. Derby, 1850.
Adams, Mary P. "Jefferson's Reaction to the Treaty of San Ildefonso." *The Journal of Southern History* (May 1955).
Aiton, Arthur S. "The Diplomacy of the Louisiana Cession." *American Historical Review*, 36, no. 4 (July 1931).
_____. Review of *Louisiana in French Diplomacy, 1759–1809*, by E. Wilson Lyon. *Annals of the American Academy of Political and Social Science*, 173 (May 1934).
Arriaga Weiss, Victor Adolfo. *La Compra de Luisiana y las Ideas Sobre la Expansion Territorial en Estados Unidos*. Mexico: Miguel Angel Porrúa/CIDE, 1996
Barbé-Marbois, François. *Histoire de la Louisiane et de la cession de Cette colonie par la France aux Etats-Unis de l'Amerique Septentrionale*. Paris: Firmin Didot 1829. (Published the following year in English translation with some excisions.)
Barnavie, Elie, and Saul Friedlander. *La Politique étrangé du General de Gaulle*. Paris: Presses Univesitaires de France, 1985, 26.
Bemis, Samuel F. *Jay's Treaty: A Study in Commerce and Diplomacy*. New York: Macmillan, 1923.
_____. *Pinckney Treaty: A Study of America's Advantage from Europe's Distress, 1783–1800*. Baltimore: John Hopkins Press, 1926.
_____. "The Rayneval Memoranda." *American Antiquarian Society Proceedings*, New Series, 47, 1937.
_____. "Washington's Farewell Address: A Foreign Policy of Independence." *American Historical Review*, 39, Jan. 1934.
Bonaparte, Napoleon. *Correspondance de Napoléon*. Henri Plon, 1861.
Bonnel, Ulane. *La France, les États-Unis et la guerre de course, 1797–1815*. Paris: Nouvelles Editions Latines, 1961
Borneman, Walter. *1812: The War That Forged a Nation*. New York: Harper Collins, 2004.
Bowman, Albert H. *The Struggle for Neutrality; Franco-American Diplomacy During the Federalist Era*. Knoxville: University of Tennessee Press, 1974.
Brant, Irving. *James Madison; Secretary of State, 1800–1809*. New York: Bobbs-Merrill, 1953.

Brecher, Frank W. *Losing a Continent; France's North American Policy, 1753–1763*. Westport, CT: Greenwood Press, 1998.
_____. *Securing American Independence; John Jay and the French Alliance*. Westport, CT: Praeger, 2003.
De Chair, Somerset, ed. *Napoleon on Napoleon: An Autobiography of the Emperor*. London: Cassell, 1992.
Channing, Edward. *A History of the United States*. New York: Macmillan, 1917.
Cox, Isaac J. "The American Intervention in West Florida." *The American Historical Review*. 17, no. 2 (January 1912).
Dangerfield, George. *Chancellor Robert R. Livingston of New York, 1746–1813*. New York: Harcourt, Brace, 1960.
Darling, Arthur Burr. *Our Rising Empire, 1763–1803*. Hamden, CT: Archon Books, 1962.
DeConde, Alexander. *This Affair of Louisiana*. New York: Scribner's, 1976.
Devoisse, Jean. *L'Homme qui vendit la Louisiane*. Paris: Olivier Orban, 1989.
Ellis, Joseph J. *Founding Brothers: The Revolutionary Generation*. New York: Knopf, 2000.
Favier, et al. *Politique de Tous Les Cabinets de l'Europe Pendant les Règnes de Louis XV et Louis XVI*. Editor anonymous. Paris: Chez Buisson, 1794. (The first section was written in 1773 by Favier as a confidential, but widely circulated, government paper from Count de Broglie to Louis XVI as *Conjectures Raisonées*; other documents cover the early years of Louis XVI's reign and were written by his ministers).
Fleming, Thomas. "Hamilton on the Louisiana Purchase." *William and Many Quarterly*, 12, no. 2 (April 1955).
_____. *The Louisiana Purchase*. Hoboken, NJ: J. Wiley; Hoboken, 2003.
Fugier, André. *Napoléon et L'Espagne*. Paris: Félix Alcan, 1930.
Gilman, Daniel C. *James Monroe*. Boston: Houghton, Mifflin, 1898.
Guinnes, Ralph. "The Purpose of the Lewis and Clark Expedition." *The Mississippi Valley Historical Review*, 20, no. 1 (June 1933).
Hauterive, A. M. B. *De L'État de la France a la Fin de l'année VIII*. Paris: Chez Henries, 1800.
Hermann, Binger. *The Louisiana Purchase and Our Title West of the Rocky Mountains*. Washington, D.C.: U.S. Government Printing Office, 1898.
Kaplan, Lawrence S. *Thomas Jefferson: Westward the Course of Empire*. Wilmington, DE: Scholarly Resources, 1999.
_____. "Jefferson's Foreign Policy and Napoleon's Ideologues." *William and Mary Quarterly*, third series, 19, no. 3 (July 1962).
Kastor, Peter J. *The Nation's Crucible: The Louisiana Purchase and the Creation of America*. New Haven: Yale University Press, 2004.
Kennedy, Roger G. *Mr. Jefferson's Lost Cause: Land, Farmers, Slavery, and the Louisiana Purchase*. New York: Oxford University Press, 2003.
Kukla, Jon, *A Wilderness So Immense*. New York: Alfred A. Knopf, 2003.
Labouchere, G. "L'Annexion de la Louisiane Aux États-Unis et les Maisons Hope et Baring." Paris: *Revue d'Histoire Diplomatique*, 1916.
Lewis, James E. *The Louisiana Purchase; Jefferson's Noble Bargain?* Charlottesville, VA: Thomas Jefferson Foundation, 2003.
Linklater, Andro. *Measuring America: How an Untamed Wilderness Shaped the United States and Fulfilled the Promise of Democracy*. New York: St. Martin's, 2002.

Livingston, Robert R. *The Original Letters of Robert R. Livingston, 1801–1803, Written During His Negotiations of the Purchase of Louisiana. To Which Is Prefixed: A Brief History of the Louisiana Purchase from Original Documents* by Edward Alexander Parsons. New Orleans: Louisiana Historical Society, 1953.

Lokke, Carl L. "Secret Negotiations to Maintain the Peace of Amiens." *American Historical Review* 49, no. 1 (October 1943).

Lyon, E. Wilson. *Louisiana in French Diplomacy, 1759–1804*. Norman: University of Oklahoma Press, 1974.

_____. *The Man Who Sold Louisiana: The Career of François Barbé-Marbois*. Norman: University of Oklahoma Press, 1942.

Madison, James. *The Papers of James Madison; Secretary of State Series*. Edited by Brugger, Robert J., et al. Charlottesville: University Press of Virginia, 1986.

Malone, Dumas, ed. *Correspondence Between Thomas Jefferson and Pierre Samuel DuPont de Nemours, 1798–1817*. New York: Da Capo Press, 1970.

Marbois *see* Barbé-Marbois.

Masson, Frédéric. *Le Départment des Affaires Étrangeres Pendant la Révolution: 1787–1804*. Paris: E. Plon, 1877.

Matthewson, Timothy. "Jefferson and Haiti." *Journal of Southern History*. 61, no. 2 (May 1995).

Meneval, Baron C. F. *Memories of Napoleon Bonaparte*. New York: P. F. Collier, 1910.

Michelet, Jules. *Histoire de la Revolution Française*. Angers: Gallimard, 1952.

Miller, David H. *Treaties and Other International Acts of the United States of America*. Washington, D.C.: U.S. Government Printing Office, 1931–48.

Monroe, James. *The Autobiography of James Monroe*. Edited by Stuart G. Brown. Syracuse: Syracuse University Press, 1959.

Morris, Richard B. *Peacemakers: The Great Powers and American Independence*. New York: Harper & Row, 1965.

Napoleon Bonaparte. *Napoleon on Napoleon: An Autobiography of the Emperor*. Edited by Somerset de Chair. London: Cassell, 1992

Raynal, Guillame. *Histoire Philosophique et Politique des Deux Indes*. Edited by Yves Benet. Paris: Maspero, 1981.

Renaut, F. P. *La Question de la Louisiane, 1796–1806*. Paris: Édouard Champion, 1918.

Rice, Howard C. "James Swan: Agent of the French Republic 1794–96." *The New England Quarterly* 10, no. 3 (September 1937).

Robertson, James A. *Louisiana Under the Rule of Spain, France, and the United States, 1785–1807*. Freeport, NY: Books for Libraries Press, 1969.

Saricks, Ambrose. *Pierre Samuel Du Pont de Nemours*. Lawrence: University of Kansas Press, 1965.

Sorel, Albert. *L'Europe et la Revolution Française*, 4th ed. Paris: Plon, 1897.

Stinchcombe, William. *The XYZ Affair*. Westport, CT: Greenwood Press, 1980.

Talleyrand-Périgord, Charles Maurice de. *Memoires*. Eds. Paul-Louis Couchoud and Jean-Paul Couchoud. Paris: Plon, 1957.

Thiers, M. A. *The History of the French Revolution*. Philadelphia: Carey and Hart, 1847.

Tocqueville, Alexis de. *L'Ancien Régime*. Edited by G. W. Headlam. Oxford: Clarendon Press, 1933.

Turner, Frederick J. "The Policy of France Toward the Mississippi Valley in the

Period of Washington and Adams." *American Historical Review*. 10, no. 2 (January 1905).

United States. *American State Papers, Foreign Relations (Selected Under the Authority of Congress)*. Washington, D.C.: 1832.

_____. Department of State. *State Papers and Correspondence Bearing Upon the Purchase of the Territory of Louisiana*. Washington, D.C.: U.S. Government Printing Office, 1903.

_____. _____. *Calendar of the Correspondence of Thomas Jefferson*, vol. 2. (New York: Burt Franklin, 1970.)

_____. _____. *State Papers and Public Documents of the United States*, 3rd ed. Washington, D.C: U.S. Government Printing Office, 1819.

Van Zandt, Franklin K. *Boundaries of the United States and the Several States*. Washington, D.C.: U.S. Government Printing Office, 1966.

Villiers du Terrage, Marc de. *Les Dernières Années de la Louisiane Française*. Paris: E. Guilmoto, 1904.

Whitaker, Arthur P. *The Mississippi Question, 1795–1803*. New York: D. Appleton-Century, 1934.

_____. "The Retrocession of Louisiana in Spanish Policy." *The American Historical Review* 39, no. 3 (April 1934).

_____. "France and the American Deposit at New Orleans." *The Hispanic American Historical Review* 11, no. 4 (November 1931).

Index

Adams, John 9, 12–15, 17, 25, 28, 118
Adams, John Quincy 107
Addington, Henry 47
Adet, Pierre-Auguste 13
Arkansas River 44–45, 81, 107, 123
Armstrong, John 27–28, 69, 106, 122, 134
Azara y Perera, José Nicolas de 31–32, 38–40

Barbé-Marbois *see* Marbois
Barras, Paul, vicomte de 12–13
Bernadotte, Jean Baptiste 49–50, 70, 85, 92, 94, 99, 108
Bonaparte, Joseph 18, 36, 43–44, 65, 72, 74–75, 80, 82, 85–91, 101, 107–8, 123
Bowman, Albert 19
Brant, Irving 107
Breckenridge, John 44
British Proclamation of 1763 9
Burr, Aaron 22–23, 28, 119–20

Cambecérès, Jean Jacques 42
Canada 2–3, 8, 34, 43–44, 46, 81, 84, 113, 118–19, 129, 133
Cevallos y Guerra de la Vega, Pedro Felix de 39
Charles IV of Spain 39, 66, 124, 130–31
Clinton, De Witt 53
Clinton, George 23, 28, 116

Dallas, Alexander James vi, 70
Davie, William R. 15
Decrès, Denis 16, 53
Delarge, Nathalie 22
Duane, William 5, 26
Dupont de Nemours, Pierre S. 3, 26, 32, 55–56, 58, 62–63, 72, 92, 123–24

Ellsworth, Oliver 15, 18
Etruria *see* Italy

Federalist Party (U.S.) 5, 15, 17, 23, 25, 64, 111–12, 118–19
Fleming, Thomas 120
France: policy toward the Floridas 7, 79, 114–15; treaties of 1778 with the U.S. 4–5, 8–9, 14, 17, 19, 33–35, 113, 121; treaties with Great Britain 4, 11, 34, 46, 113, 132–33; treaties with Spain 1, 7–8, 41–42, 113, 130–39; treaty of 1800 with the U.S. 1, 11–12, 15–19, 30, 33, 36, 73, 107, 131, 135
Fulton, Robert 51

Gallatin, Albert 44, 54
Gates, Horatio 26, 111
Gerry, Elbridge 14
Gibraltar 8, 125
Graham, John 22, 39, 45, 82, 124
Great Britain: policy toward Louisiana/Floridas 1, 3, 34–35, 43, 47–48, 57, 60, 79, 81, 105, 109, 115, 125, 133; Seven Years' War 4, 35, 115; treaties with the U.S. 11, 35, 60, 121, 123–24; War of 1812 117–18; wars vs. France and Spain 7, 40, 46, 49, 55, 107, 110–11, 116, 119, 128

Haiti *see* St. Domingue
Hamilton, Alexander 119–20
Hawkesbury, Robert Banks Jenkinson 35
Hispaniola 3, 27, 46; *see also* St. Domingue

Indians (American) 3, 34, 39, 43, 81, 85, 93, 116–18
Italy: Etruria (Tuscany) 46, 54, 66, 132; Parma, 10, 45, 132

Jackson, Andrew 114
Jamaica 46
Jay, John 9, 23, 108
Jay Treaty of 1794 12, 14, 17, 60, 75, 106
Jefferson, Thomas 10, 15, 20, 27, 44, 54–56, 103, 118–21; attitude toward Livingston 100, 110–111; correspondence with Livingston 3, 20, 22, 46, 53, 62–64, 71–72, 85, 108, 111, 124; issue of Purchase's constitutionality 65, 115–16

Kaplan, Lawrence S. 107
Kennedy, Roger 117, 122

King, Rufus 1, 3, 12, 34, 40–41, 44, 46–48, 70, 116, 125
Kosciusko, Tadeusz 26

Lafayette, Marie Joseph du Motier, Marquis de 23, 26, 123
Leavenworth, Mark 107
Lebrun, Charles-Francois 42, 55–56, 92
Leclerc, Charles 46, 55
Lee, Arthur 23
Lewis, Morgan 26, 28
Lincoln, Levi 18–19
Livingston, Brockholst 36
Livingston, Edward 42, 75
Livingston, Elizabeth 22, 25
Livingston, John 37, 110, 122
Livingston, Margaret 22, 25
Livingston, Mary 22, 25
Livingston, Robert R., Jr.: acceptance of mission and departure for France 18, 20–23, 72, 99, 120–23; attitude toward France and relations with its leaders, 10–11, 23, 25–27, 29, 50, 53, 74; career and political ambitions, 21, 23, 28, 101, 110; major memoranda 41–42, 45, 69, 85, 105, 107, 109, 121, 127–29; personal reputation and qualifications 16, 20, 23, 37, 42, 45, 64, 76, 82, 93, 99, 101–2, 106ff, 120–23; technological activities 21–22, 51, 106
Louis XVI of France 9, 18, 124
Louisiana Purchase Treaty 4, 8–9, 64–66, 83, 107, 114–15, 122, 130–39

Madison, James vi, 1, 4, 9, 46, 78, 124, 138; issues with Livingston 18–19, 27, 31, 45, 48, 69–72, 75–76, 85–86, 99–100, 105, 110; negotiating instructions of 1803 33, 36, 47–48, 53ff, 76–77, 86, 124
Malone, Dumas 123–24
Malta 16, 46
Marbois, François Barbé 30, 67–69, 97, 107, 124; author 16, 69, 92, 140–48; negotiator of Purchase treaty 16–17, 25, 53ff, 95ff, 102–3, 121, 124–25
Marengo, battle of 10
Marshall, John 14, 120
Mercer, John 98
Mexico 41, 137
Miller, David H. 20
Miranda Conspiracy 138
Mobile River 59, 72, 81, 84, 132–33, 136
Monroe, James: competition with Livingston for credit of Purchase 67ff, 77, 80ff, 92, 98–99, 101–2, 105–6, 111, 122; co-nego-tiator of Purchase 9, 41, 49, 53ff, 77; resident minister to France 1794–96 12–13, 98, 106
Montgomery, Janet 27
Morris, Gouverneur 21, 23–24, 27, 36, 100, 121
Murray, William V. 15–18, 20

Napoleon Bonaparte 1, 4, 7, 10, 15, 17, 23, 26–27, 37, 45–46, 48, 50, 53–54, 75, 81, 83, 91, 103, 119, 124, 132; negotiations with U.S. over Louisiana 58ff, 78, 93–94, 96, 101, 108–11, 116, 137
Natchez 31, 35, 71, 81, 129
Netherlands 9
Northwest Ordinance 116

Ohio Valley 8
Otto, Louis-Guillaume 71

Paine, Thomas 26
Parma see Italy
Perdido (or Perdigo) River 81, 114–15, 125, 133, 136
Pichon, Louis André 4, 16, 25, 93, 121
Pickering, Timothy 13
Pinckney, Charles 2, 4, 31, 39, 41, 48, 75, 78, 131
Pinckney, Charles C. 12–14, 116
Pinckney Treaty of 1795 see United States
Ponceau, Peter Stephen du 35

"Quasi War" (U.S. vs. France) 5, 12, 15, 107, 137

Republican Party (U.S.) 5, 14, 17, 23–25, 29, 107, 116

St. Domingue 31, 46, 55, 69–70, 107, 110, 127, 138
Skipwith, Fulwar 98, 102, 104–5, 124
slavery issue in U.S. 2, 116–18
Spain: American War of Independence 78–79; Louisiana/Floridas policy 3, 36, 41, 45, 73, 75, 108, 125; protests Louisiana Purchase 46, 78–79, 114
Spencer, Ambrose 10, 37
Sumter, Thomas, Jr. 21–22, 102–4, 124
Sumter, Thomas, Sr. 124

Talleyrand, Charles Maurice de 10, 12, 36, 47, 50, 67–70, 80–82, 92, 107, 109; Louisiana Purchase Treaty 94–96, 108, 124–25, 130–39; policies and character 15–17, 79, 111, 114–15, 123–24
Thornton, William 44
Tillotson, Thomas 29, 51, 104
Toussaint Louverture, Francois D. 3, 46
United States: treaty with Great Britain of 1783 11, 23, 121; treaty with Spain of 1795 5, 33, 38–39, 49, 60, 74, 133
Urquijo y Muga, Mariano Luis de 132

Victor, Claude (Perrin) 71

Washington, George 21, 106
Wilkinson, James 114
Williamson, Hugh 64

"XYZ" Affair 14–15, 23, 125

Yorktown, battle of 9
Yrujo y Tacón, Carlos 83, 138

www.ingramcontent.com/pod-product-compliance
Ingram Content Group UK Ltd.
Pitfield, Milton Keynes, MK11 3LW, UK
UKHW042011140426
5217IPUK00015B/1097